THE ENCYCLOPEDIA OF GOLF TECHNIQUES

CHRIS MEADOWS

WITH
ALLEN F. RICHARDSON

This is a Parragon Book

This edition published in 2003

Copyright © Parragon 2001

Parragon
Queen Street House
4 Queen Street
Bath BA1 1HE, UK

Designed, produced and packaged by
Stonecastle Graphics Limited

Edited by Philip de Ste. Croix

ISBN 1-40541-752-8

Printed in Indonesia

Photography by Bill Johnston

Film kindly supplied by Fuji

I would like to thank The Wisley Golf Club,
Surrey, England and Le Prince de Provence,
Vidauban, France for allowing me the use of
their wonderful golfing facilities. They are
truly two of the finest golf courses to be
found anywhere in Europe.

Thanks also go to my professional colleague
Daniel Belcher, Nicola Bustin, my wife
Kayo, to the two men who worked so
closely with me in over a year of preparation,
Allen F. Richardson and Bill Johnston, but
most of all to my teacher Ian Connelly who
developed my love for golf and gave me the
passion to teach this great game.

CONTENTS

◆ ◆ ◆ ◆ ◆

A VOYAGE OF DISCOVERY

◆ ◆ ◆ ◆ ◆

CHRIS MEADOWS' love of the game began at the age of 12. While caddying at a golf club in North London, he was introduced to a Scottish professional, Ian Connelly. In the mid 1970s Connelly was coaching the cream of European talent including his star pupil Nick Faldo. Meadows, himself aspiring to become a successful tour player, found himself intrigued by the array of skills Connelly possessed and the way he developed players' minds and movements, turning them from nothing into scratch golfers. By the age of 16 Meadows knew that he had begun a voyage of discovery that would last a lifetime.

Over an eight-year period working with Connelly as both pupil and teacher, Meadows spent literally thousands of hours watching players of all standards being taught by Connelly on practice grounds around Europe. By now he'd begun using his own game as a testbed, seeking to understand the perfect motion. His golf was improving to a high standard, but he found that his own stable of players were demanding more and more of his time.

THE RIGHT ENVIRONMENT

Although commanding his own head pro position by the age of 21, increasingly Meadows became frustrated with the generally poor teaching conditions in the UK. He vowed to develop his own school of excellence where golfers of all standards could be stimulated by their environment, as well as by their teacher. In 1987 Meadows acquired The Regent's Park Golf & Tennis School in the heart of Central London. Driven by the belief that seeing is believing, he installed the most advanced video systems of the time so that students of the school could understand and see for themselves their own swing in action. The school soon became an outstanding success

Left: A stimulating environment is an essential part of learning. Meadows designs all his golf schools with a strong emphasis on visual learning. He says 'A picture is worth a thousand words and that's why video analysis and mirrors are so useful to both pupil and teacher'.

and Meadows was invited to write instructional columns for numerous golf publications. He developed the concept for *Improve your Golf* (a golf learning manual) that was published in the UK, Australasia, Canada and even translated into Japanese selling over 500,000 copies in total. He has written and contributed to five golf books, appeared on BBC, Channel 4, Channel 5 and many satellite channels and has made four instructional videos.

In 1997 Meadows opened the first Metro Golf Centre in London. These are centres of golfing excellence incorporating everything a golfer might ever need to advance their game. Based on a golf-for-all philosophy, the centre has become the industry standard for golf centres in Europe.

www.chrismeadowsgolf.com

Meadows has always used his entrepreneurial skills to take the game to the people and he has recently launched an interactive website 'www.chrismeadowsgolf.com'. The site is a very different experience in learning. Driven once again by visual aids, simplicity and structure (the trademark of Meadows teaching), it helps players plan their improvement and effectively guides them to their chosen objective.

Above: If it's fun, you'll keep at it – enjoy your voyage of discovery.

Left: If your children want to play the game, put them in a group class first – they'll have fun and meet friends with whom they can play.

INTRODUCTION

*Offering so many challenges in
so many different environments
in the company of so many
friends — the game of golf is
truly a game for life.*

INTRODUCTION

◆ ◆ ◆ ◆ ◆

Golfers are dreamers and seekers.
From the first time we pick up a club and hit that small, round object
known as a golf ball towards the sky, we are part of a tradition that
stretches back through generations of time, linking us to an ancient
shepherd who first struck a rock with a stick along the coastal grassland
of Scotland.

FROM THAT moment we often embark on a life-long quest to improve how we play the game – a game that for most of us eventually becomes both a love and an obsession. From tour pro to club champion to rank beginner, we constantly tinker with our swings, adjust our grips and stances, and try to plant an endless series of 'swing thoughts' in our brains.

The hope is that by tomorrow, next weekend – or at least the end of the year – we will finally play a miracle round.

GOLFING DREAMS

The form that round takes will vary. We might dream of breaking 100 or 70, sinking an eagle putt, winning the club championship, or standing on the 18th tee with a chance to seize the Open. But at the very least, we all yearn for the day when we'll win that side bet struck with our similarly devoted friends, while savouring a drink at the 19th hole. Then we'll enjoy the afterglow of a memorable day, with everyone mentally replaying their rounds, and generously

The hours spent working on my game have been some of the most enjoyable of my life. I hope this book also makes learning fun for you in your quest to improve your game.

reviewing each other's remembered highlights.

But even when we are not playing the game, we take lessons, analyze how more gifted players perform on television and read countless articles about the the latest technology in club design, swing theory and putting technique.

I know. I've spent a lifetime playing, teaching and trying to improve my own game – and this book is the product of my quest, while your purchase of it is undoubtedly proof that you share my passion.

But now it's time to simplify things.

The Encyclopedia of Golf Techniques is structured around a single, essential idea: instead of worrying about all the things you think you need to know, this book will allow you to focus on the essentials that you simply cannot do without.

ONE SMALL STEP

They say that the journey of a lifetime starts with one step. So try my path, at least for a time. No matter to what standard you play at the moment, I believe I can quickly take you to your current goal, and then beyond.

In order to do that, I have structured this book so that anyone – from a complete beginner to an advanced player – can either dip into it for specific advice, or simply enjoy reading it from cover to cover. I've started with the basics of what equipment you need to play the game, how to assume a proper grip, stance and posture, the mechanics of how to develop and perfect your own 'repeatable' swing – plus everything you need to know about the short game around the greens, which can account for some 50 per cent of your strokes in any given round.

SECRETS OF THE PROS

Beyond that, I have included several chapters on the more sophisticated techniques of golf. I'll reveal the pro's secrets about how to get out of trouble spots such as the rough, water and sand. I'll teach you how to hit a wide variety of speciality

shots – which are often dictated by the course and conditions.

I'll also help you to develop a course strategy that lets you play the game within your personal limits. And I'll offer some tips about the complex rules of golf that can ultimately save you strokes. But perhaps best of all, I'll show you how to cure the many problems that can (and do) creep into anyone's game – including my own.

Take on board this knowledge, and you'll be ready to meet the the challenges of this game at any time in the future, because golf really is a game for life.

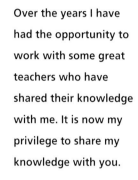

Over the years I have had the opportunity to work with some great teachers who have shared their knowledge with me. It is now my privilege to share my knowledge with you.

The great thing about golf is we are always learning. When man has mastered the wildest dreams of future technology, he will still be working on his golf swing!

Chapter 1

EQUIPMENT

Purchasing golf equipment is like choosing a pair of shoes for a child. If they do not fit correctly, they will be uncomfortable and have undesirable long-term consequences.

EQUIPMENT

◆ ◆ ◆ ◆ ◆

Having the 'proper' equipment is essential.
Even though the famous American champion of the 1920s Bobby Jones
could hit a sweet fade some 250 yards in his day, the old master would
have turned in his hickory-shafted driver in a heartbeat — and everything
else in his bag (including the bag itself!) — for the technically advanced
equipment available today.

FROM THE earliest origins of the game, the best players – including the meticulous Jones – either built their own clubs from scratch, or had others do it for them under strict supervision. Then they constantly improved on each model, in order better to suit their swing and changes in their game. In other words, at any given time, a golfer such as Jones had the best equipment available to him and his needs when he went into competition.

Today, that advantage is available to any golfer. I repeat – any golfer!

MILLIONS SPENT

With manufacturers devoting millions of pounds to research and development, and methods of mass production now common throughout the industry, new and better equipment is constantly being introduced, refined and sold at competitive prices. In addition, that equipment can easily be adjusted to suit the specific requirements and talents of each and every player, because no one swings a club exactly the same, be they the best tour players or the most humble hackers.

So why would anyone still use that old set of clubs which dad left sitting in the garage? Keep them for the sake of nostalgia, sentiment, or to use as a doorstop maybe, but go immediately down to your local pro shop or golf superstore and see what's available today.

After all, you wouldn't want to take a long journey in an aircraft designed in an earlier age, guided by a system employing yesterday's technology – now would you?

Make sure you have the same advantage that Jones did, and that such current superstars as Tiger Woods, David Duval and Colin Montgomerie continue to enjoy – the luxury of playing with golf clubs made specifically to suit them.

FIT FOR GOLF

But how does one select the right stuff? These days, golfers can choose from an extensive range at various stores devoted exclusively to golf, discount superstores, or even by placing an order on the Internet. But

Careful selection of equipment is essential for all golfers, from beginners to professionals. Your teacher is often the best person to advise you as he or she has a vested interest in your long-term improvement.

like everything else in life, you generally get what you pay for. Buying 'off the shelf' is definitely not the best option for improving your game, and will undoubtedly build some bad habits into your swing.

HEALTH WARNINGS

I think all golf clubs – even among the most popular and expensive – should be labelled with a 'health' warning:

CAUTION, THIS PRODUCT COULD BE HAZARDOUS TO YOUR GAME!

Remember that I began this chapter by saying that the proper equipment is vital, with the emphasis on 'proper'. I believe that every golfer – in order to develop his or her game to its full potential – should only purchase equipment that is precisely fitted to their physique and individual swing.

So do not necessarily think 'brand'; instead, think 'fit'.

A good fit for a glove is a tight fit that is still long enough for your hand.

A round of golf can take up to four hours so you need to be prepared for all weather conditions.

FROM HICKORY TO STEEL

The great Bobby Jones, and the golfers of his time, used clubs that were individually fashioned from wood and iron, then continually modified through use. This was done by the expert craftsmen of the day – many of them Scottish pros and clubmakers who had passed their knowledge and skill down through several generations in a tradition that dated back to the 18th Century. But in the late 1920s, with the introduction of steel shafts, the modern era of mass-production started. Now, golf clubs could be stamped out in matched sets, with numbers rather than names. The first steel shafts were made in Britain in 1912 – following experiments dating back to the 1890s – although steel did not officially replace hickory until 1929. Before that, the Royal & Ancient Golf Club of St. Andrews – the governing body of golf in this country – had frowned on the use of steel in club-making. But legend has it that when the then Prince of Wales (who would become Edward VIII) played with a full set of steel-shafted clubs at the Old Course at St. Andrews, the R & A was forced either to legalize steel or disqualify the Prince. The R & A chose the former, ushering in a revolution in future club design. Steel is still the choice of many golfers, whether amateur or pro, but it is increasingly being replaced by graphite and titanium, a 'Space Age' innovation.

SELECTING YOUR EQUIPMENT

◆ ◆ ◆ ◆ ◆

No two men or women are exactly the same, and none of us swings a golf club in an identical fashion. Our height, arm length, hand size, strength, tempo, swing speed and the shape of our average shot – whether relatively straight, a fade or a draw – inevitably differ to some extent.

A S A RESULT, when choosing clubs, you should consider at least four key factors: the swingweight, lie angle (the angle between the sole of the club and the shaft when the club is held with the clubhead flat on the ground), type of shaft, and the size – or thickness – of the grips. The length, weight and flex of club shafts can make a profound difference to your performance, as does grip thickness and the type of clubhead used. Stainless steel, mild steel, graphite and titanium heads are each better suited to some golfers than others.

In golf, like in love, one man's meat is another's poison.

RIGHT FOR YOUR GAME

The same holds true for golf balls. Selecting the right one for your game, and the weather conditions in your area, can make a big difference to your score. Even the right golf shoe can profoundly affect performance. Balance, the key to any good golf swing, starts from the spikes up.

Staying dry and comfortable over long rounds is also a contributing factor to performing well, so purchasing the correct clothing is essential to playing good golf.

Even the type of golf bag you pick can make a difference. If you have to carry your own bag, weight becomes a major consideration. And depending on the

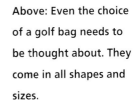

Above: Even the choice of a golf bag needs to be thought about. They come in all shapes and sizes.

Left: The pro shop is an Aladdin's Cave for most golfers. But if you're choosing golf clubs, make sure you can hit the ball with trial clubs on the range before making any decision.

weather conditions prevalent where you play, the number and depth of the pockets is important for storing wet-weather gear and/or warm clothing.

CUSTOMIZED GOLF CLUBS

Let's first consider clubs. Unless you know your own swing well, and have played the game in various situations and conditions, you may not feel comfortable enough – nor be knowledgeable enough – to select your own equipment from the vast amount available at retail.

Even if you do, I would suggest grilling the salesperson to see if they know enough about the clubs that they are touting and can assure you that they will fit your game – or *can* be fitted to your game.

But here's a better approach. If you are not already taking lessons from a qualified PGA (Professional Golfers Association) professional, find one. Now!

VESTED INTEREST

A pro can assess your swing and level of skill, then recommend a set of clubs that is right for you. Such a pro will also have a vested interest in your improvement – you may want to remain a team during the lifetime journey that golf can become. Consequently, the pro can generally be relied upon to give you good advice.

Ask for a variety of demonstration models – which most pros are happy to lend to prospective buyers – before buying any new club. The pro can watch you practise your swing and give you further advice on which particular club might suit your game, while you decide if you like the look and feel of the clubs.

Now you're finally ready to buy.

Again, you can pay good money for what's available off the shelf, or you can be smart. Increasingly, large manufacturers such as Ping, Titleist, Zevo and Dynacraft, to name only a few, build custom-made golf clubs at competitive prices. Ask your pro for a recommendation, and have some simple measurements taken so that a 'fitted' set can

be designed and made to suit your specific physique and swing.

Some manufacturers even offer components that can be temporarily assembled into demonstration clubs, building a variety of sample clubs you can test on a range until you feel comfortable and the pro is satisfied you have the proper fit – from driver to wedge.

Your new clubs will help you to develop the proper posture, grip and swing, the key to playing better golf and a lifetime of fun.

The conventional set of golf clubs is normally made up of nine irons, three woods, a putter and maybe a utility wedge or wood, totalling fourteen.

Even two-year-olds are well served these days.

THE STARTER SET

◆ ◆ ◆ ◆ ◆

You don't have to mortgage the house to buy that first set of golf clubs. Superstars such as Seve Ballesteros and Lee Trevino started out with only a few clubs, and in the case of the Spanish wizard Ballesteros, only a 3-iron, which he played with on the beach to refine his technique early in his career.

OFTEN, A pro will suggest that you purchase what's called a 'half-set', which can contain either 'even' or 'odd' numbered irons, a 3- and 5-wood, plus a putter. Most 'half sets' feature the odd numbered clubs, including a 3, 5, 7, 9, pitching wedge and sand wedge.

A GOOD OPTION

This is an especially good option for complete beginners and for youngsters who will soon have grown out of any set you buy them.

Using a half set will also help to increase your imagination and versatility around the course. You will have to think through your shots more carefully and concentrate on the course layout as much as the swing to achieve a good result. This can only help to develop your talent and skill as a player further.

SECOND-HAND CLUBS

Once a golfer is hooked on the game, he tends to become an equipment junkie. Digging deep into your pockets for the latest set of highly advertised clubs often seems to offer a quick solution to any swing fault or problems that develop with one's game.

But before splashing out a great deal of money, it might be wise to consider buying a second-hand set of clubs instead. Because most clubs are built to last, usage by someone else does not necessarily mean that

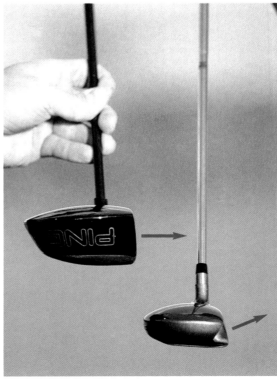

Far left: Irons come in a variety of shapes and this will affect the flight of the golf ball when struck.

Left: The same goes for the woods, as a rule the deeper the head (top to bottom) the lower the flight of the ball and vice versa.

In recent times most of the leading manufacturers have taken to supplying major golf centres with trial carts. These are full of every club in every lie, length, shaft flex, grip size, and so on. Just perfect when you come to choose your clubs.

you cannot acquire the right set for you from another owner. However, I would recommend carefully inspecting any set of second-hand clubs, and asking if you can hit with them at a range before making a decision. Also enquire as to whether they can be adjusted to suit your physique and game. If they can't, forget it.

INSPECTING USED CLUBS

When considering a purchase of second-hand clubs, the first thing to examine are the irons. Make sure that they are a matched set, identical in make and model. Mixing clubs can lead to an inconsistent feel, which in turn will lead to indecision and anxiety before each shot – a recipe for disaster on the course.

Don't worry too much about scratches or even dents on the clubhead. But if anything looks distorted, steer clear.

Also try to examine the lofts (the angle the clubface makes with the perpendicular), lining each iron up to see if the loft increases gradually from one club to the next. In addition, holding a club up to eye level and looking down the shaft will tell you if the shaft is straight.

PROPER CARE

On steel shafts, check for rust spots, which indicate how well a set has been treated by

its previous owner. With graphite shafts, look for any dents. Graphite fibres damage easily and any imperfection here could limit the club's future playing life.

Apply the same techniques to judging metal woods. Again, too many serious dents can indicate that the clubs were not cared for properly.

Worn grips are less of a problem, since they can easily be replaced by a qualified professional. But if that is required, consider the additional cost when deciding if you are still getting a bargain by opting for used rather than new clubs.

Just like buying a child a pair of shoes, choose carefully for a youngster, have the clubs fitted and get them adjusted as they grow.

THE CLUBHEAD

◆ ◆ ◆ ◆ ◆

Modern science and even the space programme have contributed greatly to the variety of materials now used in clubheads — the only part of the club that comes into contact with the ball — and the way they are built. Once only made of wood, cast iron or steel, clubhead design and construction is now a highly sophisticated art, and one from which your game can greatly benefit.

IRONS HAVE either bladed or peripherally weighted heads. The traditional bladed head is still often seen in the bag of the tour professional — check out what your favourite pro uses the next time you watch a tournament on television — or the low handicap player who can hit most of his or her shots in the centre of the clubface.

But increasingly, the more modern peripherally weighted golf club — which came into general use about 20 years ago and which has an oversized clubhead with a cavity back — is replacing the bladed club. Originally designed to help beginners and golfers who do not possess a consistent swing and who are thus more liable to mis-hit shots, peripherally weighted clubs now find favour with such top pros such as Tiger Woods, Colin Montgomerie and David Duval.

INCREASED SWEET SPOT

With the weight distributed around the outside of the head, these clubs are more forgiving, much like larger tennis rackets which offer an increased sweet spot. Even when a shot is hit off-centre, the result is often a fairly reasonable strike.

As for woods, the clubheads these days are made of anything but wood, featuring such materials as steel, graphite and titanium. Metal woods — rather than the traditional wooden ones that dominated the game for decades — are now used by players at every level.

The clubheads are hollow and peripherally weighted, making them easier to hit and easier to maintain. Plus, they wear well.

As to the swingweight of the clubhead, that is an individual choice. A golfer should try out as large a variety of swingweights as

Lie angle can be adjusted on most irons and on some woods (often only when manufactured). If you want to test your clubs, make a straight line on the ball with a pen, place the line at right angles to the ground and hit the ball. If the club fits, the line will be transferred straight down the clubface.

Marking the ball to determine the lie angle of a wood

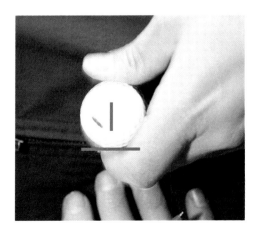  

Checking and adjusting dynamic lie angle

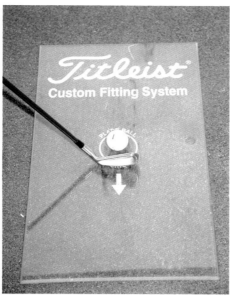

possible to determine which one suits him or her best. This is one area where there are no hard and fast rules.

DYNAMIC LIE

Lie angle is determined by the angle at which the shaft enters the head, and should be set by the manufacturer to suit a golfer's height, stature and arm length. But the only way really to determine the correct lie angle is by hitting shots. Merely holding a club to the ground, or taking up your address position with a club in a shop, will tell you almost nothing relevant about lie angle.

A number of factors have a direct bearing on the way the club returns to the ball at impact, so lie angle is an area where having clubs correctly fitted to you can make all the difference to your game. The wrong lie angle can lead to shots hit either left or right of the target, depending on whether the lie angle is too flat or too upright.

DETERMINING LIE ANGLE

To determine the correct lie angle for you, ask your pro to provide a number of clubs with different lie angles. The pro can then put some tape on the bottom of the clubs and let you hit shots off a hard board. The way the tape is rubbed off as you hit the ball will help him determine the right lie angle for you.

For example, if the tape gets worn at the toe, that means the club is too flat for you, and the ball could well shoot off to the right. Conversely, if the tape is worn at the heel, the club is too upright for you, and you may hit everything left.

Ideally, you're looking for a lie angle where the tape is rubbed off at the middle, indicating that the sole of the club is meeting the ground correctly at the moment of impact. That's called dynamic lie.

If your clubs do not have the right lie angle, it will have an adverse effect on how you hit the ball. The more lofted the club is, the more pronounced is the effect. Even 2 degrees off on a pitching wedge can be disastrous. So ensuring that your clubs have the right lie angle is yet another vital ingredient to playing that dream round.

Above and below: The dynamic lie angle of an iron can be measured either by the line method outlined for the wood, or by placing some tape on the bottom of your iron and hitting balls off a lie board (hard plastic). If the tape wears off the centre it's perfect – but if the wear is on the toe or heel end, get the club adjusted.

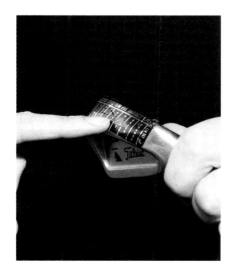

FLEX AND LENGTH OF SHAFTS

◆ ◆ ◆ ◆ ◆

Many golfers are of average height, strength and build compared with the rest of the population. Therefore, most store-bought clubs – which are manufactured to meet those averages – ought to suit them for flex and shaft length. At least in theory.

BUT CONSIDER this: if you're taller than some, shorter than others, nearing middle age, or unable to practise and play golf often enough to develop a consistent swing – more than once a week for both practice and playing – then you are not really average at all! In other words, although most of us are physically similar to our fellow men or women, we are not all the same when it comes to playing the game of golf. So you will want to give careful consideration to choosing the flex and length of your shafts.

THE RIGHT SHAFT

Shafts generally come in four very different flexes: L (ladies), A (quite flexible), R (regular mens) and S (stiff mens).

What's right for you? Obviously, L is meant for women golfers, though some stronger ladies would be advised to try the A or even R shafts to see if they suit them.

Alternatively, some men – especially as they age and lose some wrist and arm strength – feel more comfortable with the 'whippier' A shafts, rather than the traditional R or S.

Choosing the correct shaft for your game is so important. The shaft is literally the engine of the golf club; select the wrong one and it simply won't fire when required.

A set of clubs should be consistent in the way they flex. If you have a problem or a favourite club in a set, get it checked out – it may be different from the rest.

As for length, women's clubs have traditionally been built an inch (2.5cm) shorter than men's clubs when provided as standard manufactured sets. But again, with women's physiques changing through diet and more athletic training, it is best to have a pro measure you to establish the right length of shaft.

As a general rule, any man taller than 6 feet 2 inches (1.88m) needs a shaft that is a half to one inch (1.27 to 2.5cm) longer than standard, while men shorter than 5 feet 5 inches (1.65m) need a shorter length. For women shorter than 5 feet 2 inches (1.57m), the shorter length is best, while those over 5 feet 6 inches (1.68m) need longer shafts.

GRIP SIZE

Don't underestimate the importance of grip size, both for feel, comfort and its effect on shot-making. Grips that are too thick for a particular person's hands can actually result in a nasty slice or push (see definitions listed later in the glossary), while grips that are too thin can lead to pulled or hooked shots.

To check if a grip is the right size for you, place your left hand lightly on the grip, then close your fingers. Your two middle fingers should just touch the palm, or pad, of your hand.

Grips are made of leather, rubber or cord, though in recent years rubber has become the overwhelming choice for both standard clubs sold in stores and those fitted and built by a pro shop.

Keep your grips in good condition by regularly washing them with a mild soap and water solution, and have them replaced at least once a year by a qualified PGA professional clubmaker. The cost is minimal and the benefits enormous.

Grips come in different sizes, textures, patterns and much more. Try a few before deciding just which grip you would like fitted to your clubs.

CHOOSING A PUTTER

◆ ◆ ◆ ◆ ◆

*There are almost as many types of putter on the market as there are
golfers – which is quite appropriate. Putting is the most individual aspect
of the game and golfers approach this shot with a variety of pre-shot
routines, set-ups and grips. So it should not be surprising that the club
they use also varies to an enormous degree.*

PUTTERS CAN have shafts that are extremely short or as long as a broomstick. The blade can be flat on both sides of the head, partially rounded on one side like a mallet, heel-shafted, centre-shafted or offset. Some sport a flange, and many have an aiming line – or even two – to assist in sizing up the target.

THE SHORTEST CLUB

But a few things are constant about putters and how a golfer can use them. The putt is the only shot in golf where the ball does not travel at least partially through the air. The idea is to roll the ball over the short grass on the greens, although in some circumstances, you can also putt through the longer grass on the fringe of a green, from parts of the fairway, or even across the sand in a bunker.

But because the ball remains in contact with whatever surface you are trying to cover, the putter is designed as the shortest club in the bag (with the exception of the long-shafted varieties favoured by a minority of players), the most upright, and the one with the least loft – between 2-4 degrees. The head is small and thus meant only for relatively short distances, and the grip – although sometimes round like any other club – is often flat at the front, to accommodate the unique way a golfer holds this club.

PUTTER CHARACTERISTICS

Putters come with three types of clubhead positions: onset, offset and straight. Your hands will be in front of the club face with an offset putter, while the straight-headed putter face will be level with your hands when you line up. With an onset putter, your hands will be behind the club face.

It's vital to try all three types of putter before choosing the model that suits you, based on how easy you find it to aim

Putters are often marked
on the grip with their
length.

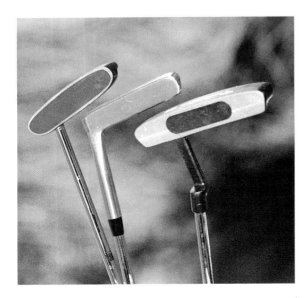

There are an enormous
variety of putters. Soft
face, titanium face, Ping,
Zing, Wild Thing – the
list is endless. But before
you buy, just ask one
question – do I believe I
can get the ball in the
hole with this?

correctly. Obviously, taking the right aim is the most important way to sink putts consistently.

Many putters also have lines on the clubhead to help you aim accurately. These line markings should be set precisely at right angles to the face. Some are also intended to reveal the putter's sweetspot, which can be a tremendous help to the average golfer.

But be careful when considering bargain basement putters. I have come across several models where the markings were less than accurate, and that flaw could affect how many putts you make. Anything that interferes with successful putting is a huge detriment to your game, since nearly half your strokes will be taken on the green.

BALANCE AND SWINGWEIGHT

A putter with good balance and the proper swingweight for you is vital to executing a smooth putting stroke. Balance refers to the distribution of weight in the clubhead, while swingweight is the weight distribution along the length of the whole club.

You may have heard the term 'heel and toe', which refers to the most popular form of balance in putters. With this type of putter, most of the weight is concentrated in the two ends of the blade. The idea is to prevent the putter from twisting in your hands when the blade strikes the ball. If it does, the ball will go off line.

The swingweight of putters can vary from very light to quite heavy, although many good golfers prefer a heavier club to assist making a smooth, rhythmic motion.

PRO TIP

Just like any other club in your bag, a putter also has a lie angle, and having the correct one for you is vital to playing successfully on the greens. Choose a lie angle that sets your eyes over the ball when you adopt your posture. That's the secret to aiming correctly.

Above left: The lie angle of a putter is also important. The head of the putter should sit flat on the ground.

Above right: As with other clubs, try a variety of clubs on a green before making any decision.

Left: When you've sampled some putters, you will develop a favourite. Now it's down to good technique and reading the line of the putts – so read on.

THE GOLF BALL

◆ ◆ ◆ ◆ ◆

After clubs, manufacturers spend most money marketing and advertising golf balls, promising that each new model is vastly improved and guaranteed to fly straighter, run further – or paradoxically – land softer, with the sort of spin you see great professionals like Greg Norman or Phil Mickelson achieving with a sand wedge to the green.

THE TRUTH is, like clubs, a golf ball alone cannot guarantee that dream round. But the right ball – at least for you as opposed to someone else – can certainly help your game, while the 'wrong' one can definitely hurt it. But how to choose?

The average pro shop or golf section of a favourite store confronts the potential buyer with a myriad of choices that can prove both exhilarating and/or dizzying – you are like the proverbial child in a sweet shop. And like sweets, golf balls come in so many different colours that it's impossible to choose the right one on that basis alone.

COLOUR AND PERFORMANCE

So let's make things easy. Colour has nothing to do with performance. Simply choose the shade you like best and proceed from there – with one bit of further advice. If you know you are likely to be playing in murky conditions – fog, drizzle or late on a cloudy day – a yellow ball is the easiest to spot, especially if you do not always hit the fairway.

Otherwise, it's what's inside – and to a lesser extent what's outside – a golf ball that really counts. Golf balls are made of one, two or three pieces.

One-piece balls are most often used at

Golf balls can be very different. The cover of the ball and its inner make-up determine how the ball will react in the air and when the ball lands. Experiment with different types of ball to find one that's right for your game.

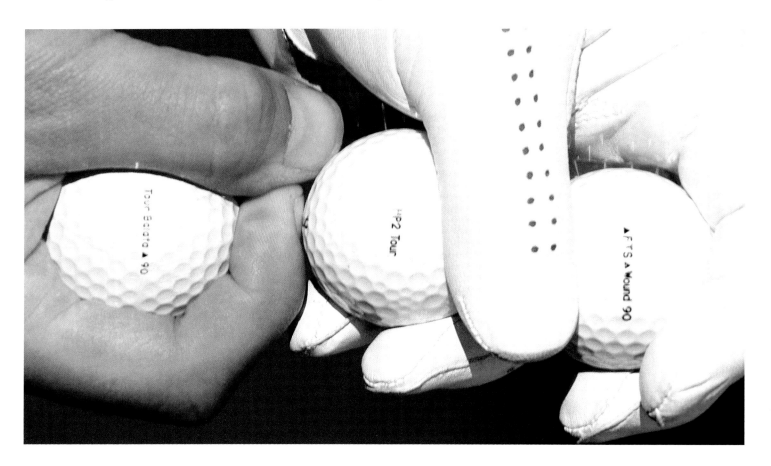

driving ranges, because they can withstand most of the the punishment dished out by beginners, and the occasional mis-hits of more advanced players. Constructed of a tough, rubberized plastic, one-piece balls are the cheapest to buy and therefore a good option for new golfers. The drawback is they do not fly as far nor as true as more expensive balls.

BETTER SUITED

The majority of golfers find that two-piece golf balls are the best suited for their game. The cover of a two-piece ball is usually made of 'surlyn' – an extremely tough and long-lasting material – and the inside is filled with various resins which expand and propel the ball forward when hit.

Most manufacturers of two-piece balls emphasize the endurance and extra distance these balls can achieve with a good strike, which is an advantage over both the one-piece variety and the three-piece. The downside is that two-piece balls do not have the exquisite control of a three-piece ball – the type favoured by most tour professionals.

But most golfers will take the endurance and distance as a reasonable trade-off, while also saving themselves money, since the three-piece ball is usually more expensive.

SPIN AND FEEL

The truth is, only single-figure handicap players and pros strike the ball consistently enough to get the full advantages of a three-piece ball, which has a liquid centre surrounded by wound fibres, and a cover of either surlyn or balata.

Balata is thin and soft, which gives the greatest feel and spin, but is also easily cut by the slightest mis-hit. As a result, even pros must replace their ball every few holes or so. In fact, some pros who are very meticulous, or who consistently hit down hard on the ball, replace their balatas on every hole.

Three-piece balls do not travel as far as their two-piece counterparts, which is hardly a disadvantage for most pro players, but certainly a consideration for the average golfer.

Finally, when choosing a golf ball, consider its compression factor, which is usually stated on the side of the box as '80', '90' or '100'. The 90 is best for the majority of golfers, although women and seniors might wish to experiment with the lower-compression 80s. The 90 performs well in less than ideal temperatures and weather conditions. The 100 is suited to pros and low handicappers, especially for play on warm days.

Above left: A logo on a ball can make it easier to identify. Otherwise make a mark on your ball with a felt-tipped pen.

Above right: Titleist have been the brand leader for many years, but now Callaway, Taylor Made and Nike are challengers.

If you want distance, choose a two-piece ball with a surlyn cover.

THE GOLF SHOE

◆ ◆ ◆ ◆ ◆

Choosing the right shoe for any sport is important, and it is certainly vital for golf, since the average round involves several hours of walking over often differing terrain – plus the threat of unpredictable and varying weather conditions. The correct golf shoe not only offers comfort and support, but provides the very foundation of the game – the anchor for each golfer's swing.

THE CORRECT set-up and stance depends on a secure footing, and a successful swing demands constant balance throughout. Golf shoes are built with a set of metal or hard rubber spikes attached to their soles, which provide grip and prevent sideways movement of the feet. When the ground is wet and slippery, that becomes doubly important.

A NASTY TURN

Just imagine trying to swing a golf club without your feet planted firmly on the ground. Suddenly, you're like a racing car with bald tyres, heading for a nasty bend.

Most golf clubs also have very strict rules about footwear. Without a proper pair of shoes – and the right type of spikes – you will not even be allowed the chance to play in the first place.

So how do you choose the right shoe?

• Wear thick socks when you try each pair on. Your feet will swell while playing, so you may need a size slightly larger than you think – or usually wear in other circumstances.
• Ensure that the shoes have cushioned inner soles, good arch support and a padded collar around the back. The collar prevents the sides from digging into your ankles when you lean into a shot.
• Always break your shoes in before playing. Remove the spikes and wear them around the house for a few days, or take some long walks. Remember, a round can last for up to four hours or more – quite enough time to raise some disabling blisters if your shoes are not supple. Stiff shoes and sore feet will impair your performance on the day.

WEATHER CONSIDERATIONS

The weather in your area may also be a factor influencing which golf shoe you choose to buy. If you expect to play often in the rain, you might consider one-piece shoes, which are constructed from a man-made material that is often guaranteed to keep water out completely. Such shoes are very light – which could help during a long round – and easy to care for, since they can be washed and rinsed with soap and water.

Shoes really are important. It's a long walk round a course in a variety of temperatures over awkward terrain. Your lower body needs all the support it can get.

Many courses these days insist on soft spikes as they are kinder to putting surfaces. If metal spikes are allowed at your course, they are better for winter conditions when it's slippery. Always check the regulations at the course you're playing.

But such shoes provide little ventilation and will make your feet perspire in dry and warm weather.

Traditional all-leather shoes are ideal for hot and dry conditions because they allow your feet to breathe. But they are heavier than one-piece shoes – which can affect your balance if you are not used to them – and need a lot of maintenance and care. Like dress shoes, leather golf shoes need constant polishing – and occasional waterproofing – to prevent damage and cracks.

A compromise is offered by shoes that have leather uppers – to let the feet breathe – and man-made soles to keep the water out.

SOFT SPIKES

In recent years – especially in the United States and now in Ireland – many golf clubs have moved to ban metal spikes. This is often the case at public courses and heavily-played private clubs intent on preserving the greens from the disastrous ruts caused by careless golfers 'skating' their spikes across the grass.

In place of metal spikes, golfers are required to put soft, plastic studs into their shoes, or to purchase new shoes with rubber-studded soles. Always check ahead to see if that's the policy when playing somewhere new. Nothing is more frustrating

than to arrive at the course and find that you have to buy new spikes and change them before going out. That time is better spent on the driving range, putting green or just relaxing and getting focused.

On the other hand, with soft spikes in your shoes or on rubber-studded soles, you might feel more comfortable on dry, hard ground. You are also free to wear your shoes indoors without fear of tearing carpets or getting snagged up and tripping. You can even drive to the course in such shoes, so saving valuable time.

When buying a new pair of shoes, remove all the spikes before you first play in them and grease each thread (Vaseline is ideal). This will make replacing spikes easier in the future.

Chapter 2

PREPARATION

◆ ◆ ◆ ◆ ◆

A golf swing takes around one second to perform. Therefore, the position you assume at the set-up is critical — it will either enable or disable your golf swing from the word 'go'.

PREPARATION – GOLF'S FUNDAMENTALS

◆ ◆ ◆ ◆ ◆

*At one time it was fashionable to think of golfers as anything but athletic.
After all, golf – even at the highest level – is played at a leisurely pace by
men and women of all ages, and, in some cases, by children. Endurance is
hardly a necessity, and no running, jumping or heavy lifting is required.*

IN FACT, it seemed that to play the game in a mere three to four hours, all one had to do was walk a few miles – or in some cases, not even that. Many courses (especially in America) provide – or even require – golfers to use a motorized cart or have a caddy to carry one's bag.

But watching a slow-motion video of golfers from the legendary Ben Hogan to current superstars such as Tiger Woods and Lee Westwood proves conclusively otherwise. Swinging a golf club in the correct way involves a series of finely tuned and very athletic moves, none of which is possible without the right set-up.

Mastering such fundamentals as the correct stance, posture and grip makes all the difference once a golfer finally lets it rip, leading either to a pure, clean hit – or any number of golfing disasters.

Gripping the club

Once you've aimed the clubhead, apply the hands to the club. For the right hander, always begin with your left hand followed by the right.

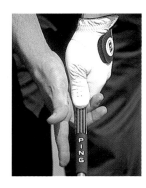

Begin by placing the club across the middle joint of the index finger of your left hand and under the palm pad of your hand. The left hand thumb should fall sightly right of centre on the club. Ensure the back of your left hand and the palm of your right hand point at the target.

THE GRIP

Most golfers think that the grip is one of the least glamorous aspects of the golf swing. But assuming the proper grip can be a thing of beauty – look at how athletic and powerful the grips of many professionals appear next time you watch a tournament. And forming a proper grip is certainly the essential starting point to playing that dream round.

Think of it this way. If the clubhead is the only object that comes into direct contact with the ball, the grip is the only part of a golfer's anatomy that makes contact with the club. In other words, a golfer uses the grip to transfer any power and skill he or she might possess to the object that propels the ball toward the hole. Have I got your attention now?

FORMING A PROPER GRIP

Here's how to assume a correct grip.

It has often been said that no two grips – like individual swings – are exactly alike, and I would find it hard to disagree with that statement. However, there are certain basics I can recommend. Once you understand and master those, you can adjust and experiment with your grip until it is comfortable and suits your swing.

But first a quick word of warning here. Forming the proper grip can take weeks, if not months, of practice before doing so becomes second nature to you. The golf grip is not a particularly natural positioning of the hands.

So I would suggest that dedicated golfers keep a club handy and practise taking their grip while watching television or, if possible, even while working in the office. And if you are in the process of changing your grip, I would caution you not to hit golf shots for as long as it takes to become comfortable with that change.

POSITIONING THE LEFT HAND

Allow your arms to hang naturally by your sides and then rest the sole of a club on the ground. Now place the grip of the club in the left hand leaving the top half-inch

A union of two hands

  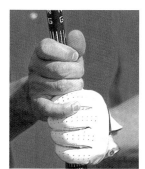

(1.3cm) of the club protruding from the top of your hand.

Position the club so that it runs diagonally from the middle joint of your index finger to the bottom joint of your little finger, then rest the club against the fleshy pad at the bottom of your hand. Finally, wrap your fingers around with your thumb falling slightly to the right of centre down the shaft.

Now take a look at what you've done. You should be able to see two knuckles on the back of your hand, and a 'V' – formed by the line between the first joint of the index finger and the thumb – pointing towards your right ear or shoulder.

Positioning the right hand

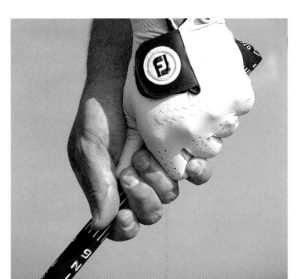

Now place your right hand on the golf club, positioning your club in the two centre fingers of your hand. It is essential that your club is held in your fingers and not in the palm of your hand. Your little finger should sit in the cleft between the index and middle finger of your left hand.

Now close your right hand over your left thumb so that it's covered by your right hand. The thumb and forefinger of your right hand should touch or almost touch.

THE RIGHT HAND IN THE GRIP

◆ ◆ ◆ ◆ ◆

It's time to add the right hand to your grip. But before you do, let me introduce a word of caution, especially if you are right-handed. Make sure the right hand does not try to take over the grip and dominate your left hand.

THE GOLF grip is different from many other things we do in life with our hands. In the case of the golf grip, both hands must work together, rather than separately. Think of it as shaking hands with yourself or as clapping. You want each hand to be an equal partner, working together so you can swing the golf club better.

By the way, when the complete grip is assumed, the image of clapping becomes even more appropriate. A good grip means

The natural position of the hands

A good grip will always ensure that the back of your left hand and palm of your right hand face the target.

essentially that both palms face each other, while the back of the left hand faces the target, and the palm of the right hand also faces the target.

ADDING THE RIGHT HAND

The right hand can be joined to the left in the grip in three different ways, depending on the position of the last or little finger. The three basic golf grips are:

• The traditional overlapping, or Vardon, grip where the little finger sits in the cleft between the index and ring finger of your left hand. (The Vardon grip, as you may know, was popularized by the legendary British golfer Harry Vardon.)

• The interlocking, where the right little finger lies between the first two fingers of your left hand and the left index finger is extended over the back of the right hand.

• The ten-finger or baseball grip, where each hand grips the club separately – the base of the right touching the top of the left – but with the fingers independent of each other.

Most golfers, pro and amateur alike, favour the Vardon grip for both feel and the effortless way it links the hands together as a unit. It can seem strange initially, however, and it takes getting used to for the beginner.

The interlocking grip is useful for golfers with smaller hands. Jack Nicklaus uses the interlock. The baseball grip is ideal for children and those with weak hands, although a former pro named Art Wall used it and was famous for hitting holes-in-one.

The three grips

Interlocking grip.

Overlapping grip.

Baseball grip.

Above: The three basic types of grip.

THE FINAL STAGE

Assuming the final stage of the grip is easy. Essentially, the right hand holds the club shaft in the fingers – never let it ride up into the palm. First, position the little finger of your right hand in the cleft between your left forefinger and middle finger, then wrap the rest of the fingers of your right hand around the club along the bottom joint, folding over your hand by fitting the vertical crease in your palm around the left thumb.

Meanwhile, your right thumb runs diagonally across the top, the tip resting near or lightly against the first finger of your right hand. The 'V' formed between the thumb and forefinger of your right hand should point between the right shoulder and chin.

GRIP PRESSURE

A final word about the grip. One of the most common faults of beginners is applying too much pressure with their hands, squeezing the club in a death grip. They often think that the harder they squeeze, the harder they'll hit the ball. Instead, it will guarantee a bad shot.

For years, golf instructors have searched for the appropriate analogy on how tightly – or not – to hold a club, suggesting that one should not grip a club any tighter than a fountain pen, an open tube of toothpaste, or a small, fragile bird.

NATURAL HOLD

My recommendation is simply to hold the club naturally, meaning not too tightly and not too loosely. Think again about the athleticism of golf. Your grip should be firm enough to ensure that the club does not slip out of your hands, or that your fingers do not come partially off the shaft at the top of the backswing or during the follow-through.

Passive right side

When placing your right hand on the golf club, ensure that your right shoulder is lower than your left shoulder. This will help establish your head and body in the correct position at the completed set-up.

But your grip should also be supple enough not to make you tense up, especially through the forearms. Any tension in the hands, arms and/or shoulders will destroy your ability to swing the club with the sort of fluid grace you see the best golfers use.

In other words, you want to exert only the amount of grip pressure that will let you swing like an athlete.

GRIPPING HONOURS

Harry Vardon did not invent the popular grip that still bears his name. That honour goes to Johnny Laidlay, the British Amateur champion in 1889 and 1891. But because Vardon was the most famous golfer of his time – winning a record six Open Championships from 1896-1914 – golfers everywhere sought to emulate him when he adopted Laidlay's innovation.

THE SET-UP

◆ ◆ ◆ ◆ ◆

Positioning the body in relation to the ball and target is known as the
set-up, or stance — and the key word here is balance. All athletic
movement takes place from a balanced starting position.

THINK OF a footballer preparing to take a penalty or a cricket player taking his stance at the wicket. The one thing they have in common is that their feet are positioned on the ground in a dynamic way that will allow them to shift their weight and use their body to propel a ball towards their target. Just like the golf swing.

PARALLEL RELATIONSHIPS

So where do we start in any discussion of the set-up? How about from the ground up. One of the unique things about golf is that we set our body up in a parallel relationship to an imaginary line that runs to our target.

In golf, we usually refer to that relationship as being square to the target, and we can visualize the set-up position along a set of railway tracks, with the golfer parallel to one rail, and the clubhead, ball and target line along the opposite rail. In the distance, both rails converge like lines of perspective at the target.

Any deviation from this parallel relationship will result in an attempt to correct any number of resultant problems during the swing, which eventually produces a swing fault. This could result in a loss of distance or directional accuracy.

But we'll cover that in more detail in the next chapter, the 'Pre-shot Routine', where we learn how to aim, set-up and swing down those imaginary tracks towards a spot on the fairway or the flagstick.

GOOD BODY ANGLES

Everything the golfer does in his or her set-up must conform to the goal of taking a stance in direct relation to where the ball will eventually fly — what the famous golf guru

David Leadbetter likes to call setting up good, level body angles. Of course, setting up any body angle starts with the feet.

For decades, golf instructors have debated the position of the feet in relationship to this line. Some, such as Ben Hogan, favoured having the back foot straight, or perpendicular, to the line of

Get in position to swing

The foundation of a good golf swing begins with the set-up. The time you spend developing good balance and position will make building your golf swing much easier.

flight, and the front foot angled out toward the target by about 20 to 30 degrees. This works for many tour professionals, but it also tends to shorten or restrict the turn of many less experienced golfers.

NATURAL POSITIONING

I prefer the approach whereby the feet are placed in the most natural, or athletic, position. In other words, both feet should be lined up with that imaginary railway track, but turned out slightly – again about 20 to 30 degrees – in relation to one another. Picture a clock with the ball at high noon. Your left foot should point to around 11 o'clock, while your right foot would aim at 1 o'clock.

This promotes the most balanced and natural position in which to anchor our set-up, giving our stance what Leadbetter calls 'dynamic balance'. Although it may seem an obvious point, remember that the feet are your only contact with Mother Earth while you swing the golf club. Positioning them correctly is the key to prevent you from swaying off the ball, or even coming close to toppling over as you bring the clubhead around your body at over 100mph (160km/h).

In other words, losing your balance means losing it. Period!

WEIGHT DISTRIBUTION

One key to balance in the set-up is an even distribution of weight between the left and right foot. Unless you are hitting a short pitch or chip, you should not favour either foot in your set-up.

Alignment of the clubhead and body

Ball position

Left: Begin by positioning the club so that the leading edge is at right angles to the ball-to-target line. Then align your feet, hips and shoulders so that they are positioned parallel to your ball-to-target line. During practice it's a good idea to put two clubs on the ground as shown parallel to your ball-to-target line.

Below: A club placed at right angles to the clubs indicating the ball-to-target line will help you to visualize your ball position.

Position of feet

Left: Turning your feet out as shown will help with maintaining your balance and assist your follow-through.

THE BALANCED SET-UP

◆ ◆ ◆ ◆ ◆

The width of your stance and where you position the golf ball in relation to your feet are important ingredients of a proper set-up. Almost everyone who has ever swung a golf club knows that one of the standard rules dictates that a golfer should position his or her feet roughly shoulder-width apart.

BUT WHAT many golfers forget – or don't ever realize – is this means shoulder-width as measured from the inside of the heels, rather than the outside of the feet. The width will also vary slightly according to which club is used, from the driver down to the sand wedge.

The shoulder-width rule begins with a standard 5-iron set-up. In this position, two parallel lines drawn from the outside of the shoulders would end at the inside of the heels. Widen the width a few inches for the longer irons and woods, and narrow it for the shorter irons.

TRADITIONAL ARGUMENTS

That brings us to ball position, which raises another time-honoured argument among dozens of so-called golf gurus. For years Jack Nicklaus advocated putting the ball on a line just inside the left heel for all shots, while others have insisted that the distance

of the ball from the front foot should vary, depending on the length of the club used.

I've seen both methods work well, so I would suggest experimenting with each variation until you find the one that works best for your game. Start with the ball opposite the instep of your front foot for the driver, then move the ball back by a quarter inch (0.65cm) or so as you use progressively shorter clubs until you get to the wedges, when the ball should be roughly in the middle of the stance. Or, like Nicklaus, try to hit every club off the left heel.

Of course, depending on whether we want to work the ball low under the wind, or high over an intervening tree, that rule will vary.

POWER AND CONTROL

Now it is time to move from the feet to the body, since keeping our feet in the right place is only part of the story, no matter how vital it is.

Short iron.

Medium iron.

Long iron.

Wood.

The three positions above show how to position your golf ball. Centre for short irons, middle for medium irons and inside of left heel for long irons and woods.

Experiment by placing the ball just inside your left heel for all shots – see what works and stick to it.

Balancing the swing

Left and above: The width of your stance increases as your club gets longer. As a rule of thumb, with a medium iron the outside of your heels should be at shoulder-width, whereas with your wood, the inside of your heels should be at shoulder-width.

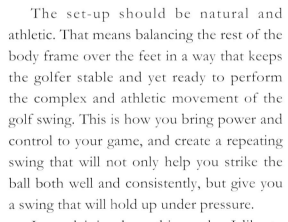

Above: Turning your body will soon show whether you are balanced, even without a golf club.

The set-up should be natural and athletic. That means balancing the rest of the body frame over the feet in a way that keeps the golfer stable and yet ready to perform the complex and athletic movement of the golf swing. This is how you bring power and control to your game, and create a repeating swing that will not only help you strike the ball both well and consistently, but give you a swing that will hold up under pressure.

In explaining how this works, I like to borrow an image created by another famous golf guru, Jimmy Ballard, in his book. Ballard asked his readers to imagine him standing on a platform, holding a large golf bag that weighed a great deal, with someone below ready to catch that load in his hands.

How would the recipient position himself do this?

BRACE YOURSELF

Obviously, as Ballard explained, anyone in such a position would instinctively spread their feet to about shoulder-width and brace themselves. With the feet well-grounded, and the body weight spread from the balls to the heels of each foot, they would also tend to flex their knees – like a boxer ready to receive or deliver a blow.

In addition, the posterior would naturally jut out slightly to straighten the spine, keeping the back erect. Meanwhile, the upper arms would be tucked into the sides of the chest to brace the upper torso.

In other words, the larger muscles of the legs, chest and shoulders would be angled and tied in towards the centre of the body like the supports of a bridge, and the person would be ready to catch that imaginary bag.

AGILITY AND STRENGTH

I like this image for what it teaches us about balance, agility and strength. But I want to stress a further point. Later we will add the actual golf swing to our set-up. So for now, don't get hung up on the idea of simply bracing to catch a heavy load someone might be throwing down to you!

The idea is to create a stance that is athletic, but not one that promotes any restriction or rigidity. In order to repeat a golf swing, it needs a firm, but flexible, foundation.

Above: Practise turning to a coiled position and assessing the foundation of your swing.

POWER POSTURE IN THE SET-UP

◆ ◆ ◆ ◆ ◆

The correct posture is the final ingredient that will help your set-up support the golf swing. In fact, posture can dictate how well a golfer swings his or her club. Standing too erect inhibits the shoulder turn and the free movement of the arms, while crouching too much forces the arms to lift up, often resulting in poor contact with the ball.

TAKE A 5-iron, assume a good grip, and hold the club out from the waist at about a 45 degree angle. Stand straight up – while remaining supple and at ease – then bend from the hips – not the waist! As you do, your rear end should jut out slightly into a semi-sitting position and your back, or spine, angle should stay straight.

SWING RADIUS

Finally, flex your knees slightly and ground the club, letting your arms hang naturally from your upper body, with your left arm forming an almost straight line from the top of the shoulder to the clubhead.

This line, by the way, will constitute the radius of your swing and you must strive to maintain it as a constant throughout that

Establishing good posture

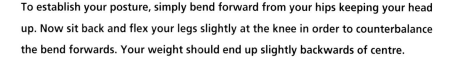

To establish your posture, simply bend forward from your hips keeping your head up. Now sit back and flex your legs slightly at the knee in order to counterbalance the bend forwards. Your weight should end up slightly backwards of centre.

MODEL SET-UPS

Next time you watch the pros on television, study their set-up position, trying to find the golfer closest to you in size. If you are tall, I would recommend focusing on Ernie Els or Nick Faldo, while shorter players would do well to emulate Ian Woosnam or Gary Player.

swing, which we will discuss further in chapters to come.

If you have done all of the above correctly, your weight should feel balanced from the balls of your feet to the heels, and overall, you should feel comfortable, centred, and yet dynamically positioned, in what David Leadbetter calls the 'sit-tall' position.

Now your set-up includes the correct posture and you can create the axis from which a powerful and controlled swing can be executed.

TRIANGLE AND STEEPLE

One final note on the set-up. With the left arm straight and the right arm also fully extended – but slightly relaxed – you should feel some pressure under the armpits or up around the highest reaches of your chest.

Later, we will see how this triangle – formed by the arms and chest – is tied together and functions in the swing as you begin your turn. Ben Hogan called this a triangle with the club emerging like the 'spire of a steeple'. That's not a bad image for something as beautiful as a well-executed golf swing.

Create space

Connection

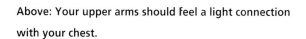

Above: Your upper arms should feel a light connection with your chest.

Position of weight

Above: With your posture complete, check that your weight is slightly backwards of centre.

When you sit back in your posture you create space for your golf club and achieve good balance.

Above: To sense just how your lower body should feel at set-up, throw something heavy up in the air and catch it. You will instinctively flex in the same way as you should at address.

Chapter 3

THE PRE-SHOT ROUTINE

◆◆◆◆◆

It's as easy as 1–2–3, but a set routine will greatly enhance your consistency.

THE PRE-SHOT ROUTINE

◆ ◆ ◆ ◆ ◆

Consistency is the key to golf. Having a reliable, repeating swing helps the golfer hit fairways and greens in the regulation number of shots. But when a shot is less than perfect, being able to get up and down from bunkers and off the fringe of greens is essential. Once on the green, a solid putting stroke is vital to avoiding three-putts — these are all aided by a pre-shot routine.

I F YOU can add all of the above qualities together, you will have a consistent game, which leads to lower scores and winning golf.

So why not incorporate that idea into the very act of stepping up to the ball, before taking each shot and putt? At the very least, you'll develop a pre-shot routine that helps you concentrate and deal with tension. At the very best, I can guarantee you will play better golf overall.

COMMON TRAITS

How can I offer such solid assurance? Because with a pre-shot routine, you have already played the shot in your mind, and having done so, you will know which club to select, how to hit it and where. Watch the pros. If they have one thing in common, it is that their pre-shot routine never varies, from shot to shot, from day to day — and often throughout their entire careers.

Consistency.

I can't say it enough. It's the key to golf. So develop your own pre-shot routine, and give yourself something to fall back on — something you can always rely on. It's the one weapon in your bag that should never vary.

VISUALIZING THE SHOT

The pre-shot routine is a blend of the physical skills you learned in the previous chapter on 'preparation' — including the proper posture, alignment and set-up or stance — and certain mental skills that will help you hit the ball to your intended target.

The latter concept is called 'visualization', a method of seeing not only where you want

Always be sure where you are aiming – choose your target.

Place your clubhead down so that the leading edge of the golf club is at right angles to the ball-to-target line.

Then position your feet, hips and shoulders so that they are parallel to your ball-to-target line.

the ball to go, but how you will get it there. Most beginners find visualization difficult. But that will improve with experience, especially after a golfer accumulates a mental gallery of good shots that he or she can call upon when confronted by a variety of situations. Some aspects of golf do get easier with time, and this is one area that is proof of that, as anyone who has played the game for more than a few years can attest.

You still may not be able to execute the shot perfectly every time, but you will at least know how to picture a good outcome, and that helps give you the confidence to approach each shot correctly.

CONFIDENT APPROACH

Obviously, positive thinking is a prerequisite here, especially if the shot you are trying to visualize is a tough one – say over a bunker or out of the rough. But at the same time, be realistic. It makes no sense conjuring up the image of a miracle strike – even if you have pulled a few off in the past – or a shot you simply are not capable of hitting. Even when visualizing, you should play within yourself.

MENTAL IMAGES

The pre-shot routine should start as soon as you walk on to the tee or when you reach your ball on the fairway.

First, try to gauge the difficulty of the shot by studying what lies before you on the course and assessing what the conditions are. Then decide on the type of stroke you want to play and how you will shape the flight of the ball.

Finally, see the shot in your mind, from the moment it leaves the clubhead until it reaches the ground – even down to mentally watching it roll up the fairway or towards the pin on the green.

Below: Visualization of just what you want to do with your shot is crucial. Seeing your shot in your mind will tell your body what you want it to do. Only once you have a clear image in your mind should you attempt to play your shot.

Once your club and body are in line, place your left hand in position.

Now place the right hand on the golf club – remember to lower your right shoulder when doing this.

A closer target can help your alignment. Choose a piece of grass, or a leaf, lying on your ball-to-target line no more than six inches in front of the golf club.

SIZING UP THE SHOT

◆ ◆ ◆ ◆ ◆

*One of the most important aspects of learning how to control your score
during a round – otherwise known as managing your game – is always
knowing the distance of every shot you will hit, and thus being able to
select the correct club to play it.*

BEFORE YOU ever play golf on a course, you should have practised enough on a range to know roughly how far you hit each club, distances which vary considerably from golfer to golfer.

Then, once you take your game onto the course, know where the distance markers are – often bushes, stakes or sprinkler heads that designate the distance to the green – and what club you need to reach your target.

Some golfers can estimate distance visually, but I always think that carrying a 'strokesaver' or 'course map' is an essential. If you cannot see the markers, or do not have a caddy, this will save you numerous strokes and allow you both to hit and think your way around the course, selecting the right club for each situation.

But even if you can see each marker, and do have a caddy, studying a representation of each hole before playing it is just one more way of aiding your preparation.

TAKING NOTES

Once you have determined the distance of the shot you intend to play, note the slope of the ground and any hazards that may come into play, such as an out-of-bounds line, intervening rough, ditches, trees, bunkers, hillocks and/or water.

Now judge the weather conditions. Is it windy, and if so, from what direction is it blowing and how hard? Is it raining, or has it been wet in recent days? Is the ground damp or dry? Soft or hard?

Given all that, you should be able to gauge how the ball will fly and whether or

Deciding on the shot to play

not it will run very far on impact with the fairway or green.

DECIDING TYPES OF SHOT

Now it's time to decide on the type of shot to play – draw or fade, high or low – and imagine the flight of the ball.

Again, the key to doing this is experience and knowing your own capabilities. However, if you are a beginner, you might seek advice from a caddy or playing partner – unless you are in a club competition. Seeking advice from a partner is against the rules of formal play, though no penalty is attached to asking a caddy for advice.

Now put everything together.

Perhaps there's a big tree on the left of the fairway about 100 yards (91m) down, while past that the ground slopes away from you in the same direction towards the green,

Above: Making the right decision as to the type of shot you are going to attempt is an essential part of playing a good golf shot. Spend some time evaluating your shot, especially when you are in trouble. And only play a shot that you have already practised.

Shot selection

Above: Some shots are inevitably more difficult than others. Be confident in the shot you choose.

BENDING THE BALL

In later chapters, I'll explain how to hit the 'draw' and the 'fade', essential shots for the advanced golfer. A draw moves from right-to-left with a low, penetrating flight and will run considerably after landing, leading to extra distance. A fade moves left-to-right, flies higher and lands softly, with less distance.

which is close to 160 yards (146m) from your present position.

Such a situation would ideally call for a draw, so you can bend the ball around the tree and take advantage of the run you will get from landing on the slope.

BEING CREATIVE

But if your natural shot is from left-to-right, or a fade, you might have to be more creative. Perhaps the solution is to take a more lofted club than you originally intended in an attempt to fly the tree and cut off the dogleg.

Now it's a matter of not only distance, but of getting the right height on the ball, and perhaps sacrificing a direct attack on the green, hoping you can then chip up and take one putt for par.

Visualize the shot in your mind, getting a real 'feel' for where the ball will go and how it will land. Then select the right club for you and take a few practice swings. Don't just brush the grass with your clubhead. Line up the way you will for the actual shot, and practise with an eye towards your intended swing path. That's where your set-up comes into play.

Above left: If you have a caddy, discuss the shot and agree that the one you have chosen is well within your capabilities.

The lie of the ball

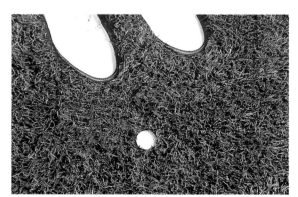

The lie of the ball can make a shot easier or considerably more difficult. Evaluate the lie before deciding on the shot you are going to play.

THE PRE-SHOT ROUTINE – THE SECOND PHASE

◆ ◆ ◆ ◆ ◆

The second and final phase of the pre-shot routine comes after you have sized up your situation on the golf course and decided what shape of shot you would like to play. Some golfers now think they are ready simply to take aim and fire at this point.

NO PRE-SHOT routine is complete without two more small, but vital, aspects – and, as I've said, a consistent pre-shot routine is the key to playing golf well. The two additional elements are:

1. Finding an intermediate target.
2. Relieving muscular tension.

Stand behind your ball and visualize the ball-to-target line, choosing some feature a short distance ahead to use as an aid to aiming your shot at the target. This might be a twig, leaf, divot or clump of grass. But the key is to find something that is only a few inches away. It's always easier to line up with something nearby, rather than something far away.

Moving around to the side to address the ball, hold the club in your right hand and place the sole of the clubhead behind the ball, aiming the face down the short ball-to-target line you have selected. Now take your stance, assuming the correct posture, flexing your knees, and lining up your feet, hips and shoulders – again, parallel to the short ball-to-target line you've selected – and just as in the railway track analogy I used in the previous chapter.

Finally, checking that the clubface is still aimed correctly, add your grip.

RELIEVING TENSION

But just a second! Here comes the toughest part of all, and I don't mean hitting the ball.

Just prior to starting the swing, pressure can become part of every golfer's game. If you're facing an important shot, or lack confidence in what you're about to do, muscular tension can creep in and potentially destroy your swing action.

Waggling

 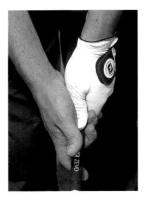   

Tension in the set-up usually begins in your hands. Waggling the club while setting up to the ball is the best way to relieve this tension and prepare to swing.

Relieving tension

Left: The nightmare scenario – don't let tension destroy your golf shot.

Below: Moving your feet up and down at set-up is also a great way to keep the body loose.

Waggling the club is done just with your wrists. The shoulders and the rest of your body do not move, otherwise you may alter your set-up position

Getting rid of that swing-strangling tension can make the difference between a clean, crisp hit that flies to the target and sets you up to score well – and a violent hook into the trees.

So rid yourself of any rigidity by lifting the club and giving it a waggle, or two. Then wiggle your toes inside your shoes, or move your feet up and down in a little tap dance. Flex your fingers on the grip, letting any tightness drain away, which will also help release any tension in the wrists and forearms. Finally, try to capture a feeling of lightness and relaxation throughout your arms, shoulders, legs and torso.

Now glance one last time at the target – focusing for a split second as if you were about to pull the trigger of a gun on that bad boy – before resuming your normal head position at address.

PRO TIP

The waggle is a vital ingredient of any pre-shot routine in order to relieve tension and groove the feeling of your swing. But some golfers take that a step further. Let's say you've decided to play a draw shot. I would suggest that in this case you use your waggle as another form of miniature rehearsal. Bring the clubhead back just on the inside as you waggle – the same way you will when you begin the in-to-out swingpath of the draw – then take it slightly out before assuming your final address position.

A MINI-REHEARSAL

You've now completed the pre-shot routine. If you learn to do this consistently, I believe you will automatically begin to play better golf. After all, the pre-shot routine is a mini-rehearsal for the swing itself, and thus a vital way of making that swing count.

Therefore, it has to be stressed once again, such a routine is every bit as important as the swing itself, and is a prerequisite to achieving overall consistency in your game.

Chapter 4

THE BACKSWING

◆ ◆ ◆ ◆ ◆

Like a sprinter leaving the blocks, a smooth, fluid beginning to the backswing is the key to a powerful, genuinely athletic swing.

THE BACKSWING

◆ ◆ ◆ ◆ ◆

It is always hard to make the first move. I don't have to tell you about the many situations in life where that axiom applies. But it is also a key in any sporting activity – and especially in the golf swing. Like a sprinter about to explode from the blocks, you have to be both poised and ready to go, but also relaxed enough to unleash your full power smoothly.

IN THE previous chapters, I explained how to assume a solid grip, a balanced and dynamic set-up – or stance – and a pre-shot routine that can help ease tension and serve as a mini-rehearsal for the real thing.

But now it really is time for the real thing. The first move in the golf swing – what is termed the backswing. Get this part right, and you have built the foundation for a powerful, athletic swing. But get it wrong, and nothing good can follow. The backswing is the key to the swing itself – which in turn is the central action of golf.

PROGRAMME YOUR BODY

So how should you approach the first move?

I believe you must fully understand what your body will be doing in the backswing, then programme it accordingly through hours of practice. Initially, much of this practice will not involve hitting any golf balls. Simply picking up a club and heading for the driving range is a recipe for disaster

So, don't go near a golf ball…at least for now. If you are a beginner and want to learn how to swing the club properly, this is the best advice I can give you. And if you are an experienced player – but have had limited success – it's even better advice.

MASTER THE BODY

You must first understand the role of your body in the swing – and please note that I said the body, rather than specifically mentioning the role of the hands, wrists and arms. Most golfers concentrate on the latter,

The first move in the golf swing is the most important part of it. A low, slow takeaway will help ensure that your arms, hands and body move in one coordinated movement.

The first move

DON'T FREEZE UP

Once you have gone through your pre-shot routine and assumed your stance, don't stop – as so many golfers do – by grounding the club behind the ball and going into a trance that leads to muscle tension. Pull the trigger as quickly – yet smoothly – as possible.

Exercise 1

Exercise 2

rather than the former, whether consciously or not. Unless you also fully comprehend the role of the large muscles of the upper torso, hips and legs in the golf swing, and how they work together with the arms, hands and shoulders – you'll never learn or master a proper swing.

But if you do understand this physical combination, I can promise you'll begin executing the first move in a way that will put you in the correct position at the top of the backswing. In turn, that will allow you to start the downswing – or what I prefer to call the throughswing – in the most efficient and powerful way possible.

The end result? You will propel the ball towards its intended target with both accuracy and length, setting up the possibility of a good score. But again, if you have not mastered the basic technique, the first move will cause you problems and lead to any number of golfing disasters

Left: In order to teach your arms and body to move together, try placing a credit card between your left arm and ribs. The right arm should not be held as tightly to the body, so a head cover should be placed under your right armpit.

Right: Ensure that when you initiate your takeaway, you rotate your body immediately.

The takeaway

DEVELOPING A REPEATABLE SWING

◆ ◆ ◆ ◆ ◆

You may know the feeling: you are standing on the first tee, and your playing partners are waiting for you…other people may also be standing nearby, watching and waiting as well, eager for you to get off so they can start their rounds…

AT SUCH times, it's very easy to get tense and even freeze over the ball, especially if you lack confidence in how to make that first move. If this happens, you are in big trouble. Add a faulty technique to the mix, and you'll really wish you had stayed at home.

THE REPEATABLE SWING

Here's how to avoid that nightmare scenario and hit a great shot – over and over and over again. By making the correct first move, you will prepare yourself for what's called the 'repeatable' (as in reliable) swing.

Once you have mastered this basic movement, you are well on your way to that goal, because the repeatable swing is just that – repeatable. It will not break down when you are tired, nervous or under pressure. You'll play better overall – and if your temperament is right – you'll even start winning competitions.

Now that dream round is closer to reality, but only if you can make the first move properly.

THE BASIC SWING

Let me pause here for just one moment, and add a note about how this chapter and the following one will be structured.

Of course, the swing is one continuous, athletic movement. But in order to understand best how it works – and how you can make it work for you – my approach will consist of examining the swing in two parts, breaking down each element of the backswing and throughswing, until you thoroughly understand each.

Then we'll put it all together and study the finished product – a swing that you can take to the course. A swing that you can start working on that will eventually produce consistently lower scores.

GOLFING SECRETS

Learning the proper swing is the only way to unlock the basic secrets of golf – which is equally true both for the beginner and the professional. Yes, even the pros are constantly learning about the swing, and re-tooling their basic movement. Some of the recent changes in the approach of Tiger Woods and Phil Mickelson bear out the truth of this.

In some cases, a few pros have even scrapped a successful swing and completely revamped their basic motion. Nick Faldo is the most famous example of that. Along with golf guru David Leadbetter, Faldo completely remodelled his swing, using many of the basic ideas and techniques that I am about to describe in this chapter.

The result, as we all know, was a better swing under pressure and increased success on the golf course.

You can do the same.

The repeatable swing

A repeatable golf swing is the result of a good set-up combined with a smooth, unhurried rotation of the body with the arms forming a wide arc throughout the back- and throughswings. Practised regularly, this will become a consistent movement.

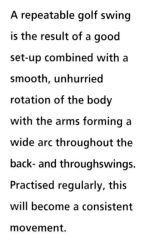

STARTING FROM SCRATCH

In the early 80s, Faldo was the top-ranked golfer in Europe. But Faldo knew his swing hid a multitude of faults that wouldn't stand up under the pressure of the world's 'major' tournaments. So he approached British coach David Leadbetter, who told him the refit would mean almost completely scrapping his swing, a process that could take at least two years – during which his game, and his earnings, would suffer. But Faldo was determined to become one of the world's best golfers, so he plunged into the task with relish, often practising such long hours that his hands bled. Faldo failed to win any tournaments in 1985-86. But in 1987, as he finally became more comfortable with his re-tooled swing, the discipline began to pay off. After capturing the Spanish Open, Faldo snatched his first 'major' triumph, coming from three behind at Muirfield to defeat American Paul Azinger for the British Open Championship. In the years since, Faldo has won a host of tournaments in both Europe and the USA, plus several additional majors, including two more Opens and three US Masters to rank him among the greatest golfers of his time

THE CONNECTED SWING

◆ ◆ ◆ ◆ ◆

Tee up the ball, take your grip, assume your stance, and go through a pre-shot routine. Now you are ready for that first move into the backswing.

TO START with, you want to conjure up a feeling of lightness throughout your body, but especially in your hands, arms, shoulders and upper torso. At the same time, you want your legs to be poised and stable – but never rigid – evenly distributing your weight in order to support a dynamic movement away from the ball.

Next, you want to think about making that first move with a nice feeling of rhythm and tempo, easing into the backswing in a way that builds towards a consistent, overall swing, and ultimately the release of maximum power into the ball.

Finally, you want to tie all of the above sensations together in what I like to call the 'connected' swing.

FEELING CONNECTED

Your hands, arms, shoulders and upper torso should move together, turning back and coiling behind the ball – partly in opposition to the lesser turn of the hips (more on that later) – while they are anchored by the stable foundation provided by the legs.

This feeling of connection is the secret to building a consistent, athletic golf swing that will repeat time after time – and, most importantly, under pressure.

By tying in the hands and arms with the larger muscles of the upper body, we can produce a motion that is fluid, coordinated and dynamic. In turn, that will generate the maximum amount of clubhead speed in the downswing, as you hit through the ball to a high and stable finish.

A light grip is essential to building good movement.

Assuming the stance and feeling connected

Here you can see the arms, hands and upper torso moving together, both on the back and forward swings.

Rear angle connection

A light connection of the upper arms and body aid a consistent movement.

But if you lose that feeling of connection at the beginning of the swing – I cannot stress this enough! – the entire action will fall apart and you will suffer a horrible experience when you hit the ball.

STAYING CONNECTED

The vast majority of golfers I see tend to move their arms and hands independently of the rest of their body, or upper torso. That is why they struggle for consistency in their swing.

Even those who have been taught or have read about the connected swing – and try to practise it – sometimes go to the opposite extreme. They interpret the idea of connection as meaning you must lock everything together, rather than just moving the various parts of the body together. Both variations ensure that a golfer will never reach his or her full potential.

ONLY HALFWAY

Connection will not work unless you are relaxed and can maintain a feeling of lightness throughout your upper body. And without good rhythm and tempo, you will have the lightness, but no dynamic movement.

Remember, the backswing merely sets up the full swing. Do it right, and you're halfway there. But only halfway. As Bobby Jones said, you don't hit the ball on the backswing.

LOW AND SLOW

The best advice I can give initially to promote the idea of the connected swing, while also establishing a nice sense of rhythm and tempo, is to start the takeaway – or what I like to call the first move – with the clubhead being taken back from the ball very low and slow. Start the club back low to the ground – about an inch or two above the turf – and move as slowly as comfortable, concentrating on a smooth movement. What this does is promote the idea of the arms, hands, shoulders and upper torso moving back together and the club staying on the proper line. A movement that is slow and smooth, rather than quick or jerky, keeps all your body parts together, avoiding the tendency of many golfers to snatch the club away with their hands. At the same time, taking the club back low to the ground helps widen your swing arc, and thus allows the bigger muscles of your body to impart more power to the ball later in the throughswing.

TRIANGLE-CENTRE DRILL

◆ ◆ ◆ ◆ ◆

I teach a certain drill to ingrain the idea of connection throughout the swing. Choke down on a club (i.e. grasp it further down the shaft than normal) and place the butt end against your body, somewhere between the navel and sternum – whatever feels most comfortable. Then practise moving the club away from an imaginary ball until the clubhead is about waist high.

IF YOU do this drill correctly, it will give you a strong impression of how the hands, arms, shoulders and upper torso ought to move away together from the ball – and how they work together as a unit.

But the most important part of this drill to note is that the last thing to reach a finished position at waist-high is the clubhead! Did that surprise you?

If it did, then you are like most golfers. You have been swinging with the hands and arms, rather than the body. But in this exercise, it is the connection that moves the clubhead to its destination. Probably, in the past, you have been moving the clubhead in a way that leaves your body catching up rather than driving the action of the backswing.

It is now time to reverse that damaging tendency.

TAIL WAGS THE DOG

Jimmy Ballard, the famous golf guru, describes this initial move as a way of maintaining a feeling of the 'triangle and centre'. He, and others such as the legendary Ben Hogan, have traditionally taught that, at address, the relationship between the shoulders, arms and hands should form a triangle that remains unbroken throughout the entire swing.

This simple exercise will help you understand just how the arms, hands and upper torso work together in the rotation back and through.

Triangle centre drill

Triangle centre drill – rear angle

With the butt of a club against your torso, you will sense how the body's 'centre' – or the middle of the upper torso – stays in harmony with that triangle.

In other words, the large muscles of the upper torso move in conjunction with the arms, hands and shoulders in the connected swing, pulling the clubhead back and through the ball.

Put yet another way by David Leadbetter, the 'tail wags the dog'.

THE ONE-PIECE TAKEAWAY

Perhaps you've heard the first move described differently – as the 'one-piece takeaway'. This is a term that I think confuses many golfers, because they inevitably interpret it by almost pushing the club back with the hands, arms and shoulder joints. Do that, and the only way to raise the club fully is by cocking the wrists too soon, and in a way that lifts the arms across the chest.

Thus, you are making the first move without the centre of your upper torso being involved, and you are breaking the connection I want you to strive to maintain. The first move in the golf swing must be made with the triangle of hands, arms and shoulders in unison with the centre of the upper body.

SUPPLE AND CONNECTED

When the club is waist-high in the backswing, the left arm should be comfortably extended and supple, so that if someone came along and pulled the club down to where you would normally grip it, you would remain connected and have a full extension of the clubhead.

At the same time, the right arm is starting to move away from the body and fold naturally.

If you were to continue the backswing here, the right arm would establish a triangle with the left up to the top of the swing, further mirroring our position at address when viewed from behind.

The triangle centre drill also helps you to appreciate just where the club should be halfway back and halfway through in your swing. Perform this exercise regularly to develop the correct movement of your body.

If the arms work independently of the upper torso and rotation does not occur, the result will be a choppy swing resulting in a sliced, pulled or skied golf shot.

PRACTISING THE CONNECTED SWING

◆ ◆ ◆ ◆ ◆

Now let's put triangle-centre drill to good use in the swing.
Swing the club back to the waist-high position and stop.

IT MAY feel odd having the butt of a club against your chest, while also assuming the position of such a short swing. But, beyond that, any discomfort or restriction you might sense is really because you've probably never swung a golf club in the correct manner before!

In other words, you have never taken the club away from the ball in the first move of the backswing with your hands, arms, shoulders and upper torso working together in the connected swing.

Now try doing the drill again without consciously keeping the butt of the club against your chest. Within a foot of moving away from the ball, I would bet the butt of the club has already parted company with your body. You are back to your usual swing. You are making the first move with the hands, arms and shoulders, while your upper torso lags behind or doesn't move at all.

Instead of a connected swing, if your movement is a series of independent moving parts, your swing will lack consistency.

PRACTISE CORRECTLY

So go back to practising the drill correctly, doing it over and over again to ingrain the idea of the connected swing. Use a long mirror if you have one, or better still, videotape yourself and note the progress you make.

I want you to concentrate on the idea of 'connectedness'. Think about how the body – in this case the upper torso – moves the hands, arms and shoulders, rather than the other way around.

Note also how your weight shifts back to your right foot and your left knee turns back toward the right – which I'll discuss further later.

COCKING THE WRISTS

Perhaps you are wondering why I have not mentioned the role of the wrists in the first move of the backswing.

If you are an experienced player, I'm sure you've heard golfers talk endlessly about how and when to cock their wrists in the

This is a great exercise to develop good rotation on the correct plane. Take your posture first and then practise turning while at the same time staying bent over. It is important not to lift up or dip down, just rotate.

Practising the connected swing

Connected swing close-ups

backswing. Or maybe they talk about how to manipulate their hands in the throughswing, especially at impact if they are trying to hit something other than their normal shot – say a draw.

You may have even been given some 'friendly' advice such as this during a round, delivered with the guarantee that it will improve your game immediately.

PASSIVE HANDS

Forget anything and everything you have ever heard about cocking the wrists and turning the hands!

The hands remain *passive* during a connected swing. They respond to everything else being done correctly. In a properly connected backswing, the right arm will begin to fold naturally as you reach

waist-high, and the momentum you are starting to build with the club will cause a natural hinging of the wrists.

If the club is gripped in the correct manner, and your swing is connected – with the triangle taken back with the centre – the wrists are set in the proper position automatically.

Never make a conscious effort to cock or otherwise turn your wrists during the golf swing. Never!

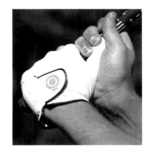

The natural hinging of the wrists will occur if you maintain a light pressure in your grip. As you rotate, your right arm will fold naturally as shown above.

Below left: The momentum of the swing will cause your wrists to cock naturally.

Below: In a perfect takeaway there should be no hand action as you initiate your swing.

Perfect takeaway

POWER AND CONTROL IN THE CONNECTED SWING

◆ ◆ ◆ ◆ ◆

Shifting your weight correctly is a key to building a powerful swing. In order to understand this, you should resume the position you had with the club waist-high in the triangle-centre drill (described in the previous pages) with its butt pressed against your chest.

THE CONNECTION you've established should have caused the left knee to break in well behind the spot where you would have set-up to the ball, and your weight should have shifted until it is predominantly on the inside of the right foot, or at least over the right foot from about the centre to the heel.

If neither is the case, go back and do this again until you feel the proper weight shift and can establish that position – while also keeping the right knee as flexed as it was at address.

Now swing through to a waist-high finish – or put another way, swivel forwards to face your intended target. You should feel your weight shift completely to your left foot – and that the weight has come off your right foot, which may have lifted off the ground, or could do so with little or no effort.

I hope that you will also now be starting to gain the sense that the throughswing *mirrors* the backswing.

CLUBHEAD POSITION

If you perform the triangle-centre drill correctly – including a proper weight shift – you will also see that the clubhead is in the right position, both when you take the club back, and when you swing it through.

Assuming that you had the clubhead square at address, and did not manipulate your wrists, you should find that at waist level in the backswing, the toe of the club points upwards to the sky, with the leading edge perpendicular to the ground. The clubhead should be in the same position at waist-high in the throughswing. In other words, the clubhead is square.

OPEN TOE

However, if you find that at waist-level in the backswing, the toe is open – or pointing behind you and facing up – you did not maintain your connection in the swing and you probably tried to dictate what your wrists were doing.

By the same token, if you find that the face of the clubhead is pointing towards the

Weight transfer

ground, or closed, in the throughswing, you have also broken your connection between the triangle and centre.

The important thing to realize here is that doing this will make any chance of returning the clubhead square to the ball at impact considerably more difficult. Plus, you will lack the proper coil behind the ball, because you have shortened the arc of your swing.

That almost inevitably leads to various mishaps – as you instinctively struggle to square the club with your hands. It will also certainly produce a lack of power in the swing.

BODY LEVERAGE

The point of all this is to introduce you to the idea of body leverage in the connected swing. By using your body to swing the golf club, you create power and consistency. This will give you a much stronger movement through the ball and you will not have to exert as much energy.

Watch the average golfer at the range. Within minutes, he's grunting and sweating. Does your favourite pro do that? When he or she swings, the effort looks minimal, and yet the result is a powerful, controlled shot –

essentially, what we mean by the phrase 'playing within yourself'.

LOSS OF CONTROL

But most golfers, whether consciously or not, think they can create power through their arms and wrists. They try to whack the daylights out of the ball, short-circuiting any input of the larger muscles of the body. This has several negative consequences, the most common one being a disconnection of the swing, and thus a loss of control over the clubhead.

If your swing is dominated by the hands and arms, the clubface will open and close too quickly and you will not be able to visualize where it is at any particular point of the swing. The tendency to try and compensate for a clubhead in the wrong position is extremely difficult to resist, and a lack of consistency will dominate your ball-striking.

When you use a connected swing, you are moving the clubhead in tune with your body, and it will open and close much more slowly and be in the proper place throughout the swing. In effect, there is less to do, and less to worry about, in the connected swing – and the result will be greater consistency.

The rotation of your body combined with the transfer of your weight from right foot to left foot is the engine of your golf swing. If you want a powerful, elegant and efficient golf swing, learn and practise good body rotation and weight transfer. Observe players like Tiger Woods – he is without doubt the best golfer in the world because he understands body leverage and connection.

HEAD POSITION IN THE CONNECTED SWING

◆ ◆ ◆ ◆ ◆

The first move away from the ball will break down if the golfer becomes fixated on the ball by trying to keep his or her head still or down. Your goal should be simply to allow your head to rotate freely with your body rotation.

DON'T ALLOW the ball to become the absolute target. Think about your swing, and where you want the ball to go, rather than the ball itself – partly by not staring fixedly at the ball, and partly by letting your head rotate slightly on the backswing.

SIMPLY TERRIFIED

But we often forget this. Standing over that little white orb, we are sometimes reluctant – or plain terrified in the case of most beginners – to turn the body, and thus the head as well, behind it.

We are afraid of losing visual contact. It's so tempting to remain with both eyes fixed on the ball, staring down in the hope that doing so will ensure we can bring the clubface back into contact with the ball and therefore hit a reasonable shot.

But the opposite will be the result, because failing to move the head at all will prevent the correct body movement – and destroy any hope of a connected swing. So forget everything you've ever heard about keeping your head still!

HEAD ROTATION

Not moving the head is one of the great myths in golf. In fact, the head must rotate slightly back, or to the right, along with the upper torso in the connected swing.

So, that feeling of lightness should extend to our neck muscles as well. They should be relaxed. They should be receptive to movement. Keeping the head in a fixed position, or square to the ball, will cause the swing to break down as the left arm folds up and collapses, reducing any chance of imparting real power to the ball. That's

In order for your body to rotate back and through, allow your head to move with your body. At the top of the backswing you should only be able to see the ball through your left eye, the head should then rotate through so that you finish looking at the target.

Correct head movement

Address.   Top of backswing.   Just after impact.   Finish position.

Head-down disaster

Forcing your head to remain still or down on a golf shot is the worst thing you can do.

because you will be unable to turn fully behind the ball and so you will reduce the width of your swing arc.

HEAD MYTHS

I wonder where the myth of the 'steady' head came from, or what other commentators sometimes refer to as keeping the 'head down'.

The correct practice has always been not to keep the head still, but to keep some visual contact with the ball – acting on the basis of that other old adage 'keep your eye on the ball'!

This maxim really does apply, although what we actually want to happen is to see the ball with only – and I emphasize 'only' – the corner of our left eye. You can test this by taking a practice swing and closing your left eye at the top of your backswing. If you can still see the ball, you've got a major swing fault, and there is certainly no 'connection' in your swing.

Again, you have not turned fully and your swing arc is narrow.

SWING TRIGGER

All the great players move their head in the backswing, some more than others – but certainly all of them! Jack Nicklaus often tells the story of his first teacher holding his hair to keep him from turning his head. But in fact, Jack does turn his head, though in his case, he moves it before he starts the backswing, pre-setting it so the corner of his left eye is over the ball before he starts his movement. For Nicklaus, that move is a swing 'trigger'.

LATERAL MOVEMENT

These days, several great players not only rotate their heads to keep their swings connected, but they also work on a slight lateral movement of the head. Tiger Woods is a good example. By the time he has set his powerful swing at the top, his nose is just over the inside of his back foot, with his head very much behind the golf ball.

So before you even start the swing, tell yourself that your head will move. Allow for the natural rotation of the head as the upper torso moves to the right and back, allowing the body to coil behind the ball. Then forget everything you have ever been told about trying to keep your head still.

Lateral movement makes good striking impossible.

NEW TOOLS OF THE TRADE

Having a friend videotape your swing is really the only way to check your head position during the entire movement. New computer software I now use in teaching my own pupils even allows for multiple images of your swing, including those shot from various angles, to be studied on the screen simultaneously. This marvellous tool also offers the option of comparing what you are doing with images of other golfers. I like to take shots of various golf pros practising on the range, then compare these images with those of my pupils, focusing on players who have a similar build and physique.

THE FOUNDATION OF YOUR SWING

◆ ◆ ◆ ◆ ◆

Another point that often gets overlooked before we even start our swing is the role of the lower body. As I described in the previous chapter on set-up and stance, your weight should be distributed from the balls of your feet to your heels, and it should remain this way to provide a solid, balanced foundation for the entire swing.

BUT MANY golfers get utterly fixated on their hands and the ball sitting below them on the tee or grass. And since they are holding the golf club in their hands – and the clubhead is poised near the ball – that's where most of their attention is directed.

They are concentrating only on what they can see right in front of them!

SUPPLE LEGS

I try to have a definite sense of my legs supporting me from below – supple, and yet firmly in contact with Mother Earth, and, of course, connected to the rest of my body.

If you do not have this feeling of support, your central nervous system is liable to interpret that as a sign of instability down below. And if that message is sent to the brain, the result will be a certain rigidity, as your body rejects any idea of cutting loose in a strong, athletic movement.

I liken this to standing on one leg. If you do that, your body will try to find a way to brace itself to overcome the feeling of instability, and this will certainly prevent you from doing anything as powerful and dynamic as swinging a golf club, for fear of the obvious result – you will lose your balance and topple over!

Your legs play a crucial role in anchoring your swing. Like a building, a golf swing needs a stable foundation.

Lower body

Legs and support

In order to maintain the plane of your golf swing and to brace the upper body rotation, your legs must retain the same flexed position as at address throughout the swing.

Below: If the lower body does not provide good support, loss of balance will be inevitable.

PUTTING IT ALL TOGETHER

◆ ◆ ◆ ◆ ◆

The correct backswing should feel more or less natural. The movement should be programmed into your mind and body. Let's go through the process together.

ONCE I know what my target is, I want to feel strong, relaxed and prepared to make all the right moves. Then I initiate my first motion in the backswing by trying to keep things very smooth, with a continuous, easy flow of the hands, arms, shoulders and upper torso away from the ball.

SIMPLE PICTURES

Picture the 'centre-triangle' image again, with your shoulders forming the base, your arms the sides, and your hands the apex of the triangle. You want to keep this triangle intact as you start the backswing, relative to the centre of your chest.

I trust that you've practised the essential parts of the first move for hours, days and perhaps even weeks or months! So, finally, it's time to simplify things. Just think in terms of maintaining the same basic position you had at address throughout the initial part of the first move.

In other words, you can now drop the idea of the 'centre-triangle' specifically, and merely picture a mirror image of a good address position being held throughout the backswing.

DYNAMIC RESISTANCE

Meanwhile, the lower body will be braced and supporting your movement, with the weight starting to move onto your right foot and the hips gradually being pulled around by the turn of the upper torso.

Please note that I said the hips are turned around by the upper torso. They follow, rather than move simultaneously, or lead the action. If this movement is done correctly, a slight tension will begin to build between the hips and upper body – and, in this case, the tension is good, rather than bad.

Such tension is dynamic, the resistance that actually balances the whole backswing, while later providing – by opposition – a powerful coil as the body moves fully behind the ball and begins to build up the power you will later unleash through the golf ball.

COILED SPRING

What do I mean by coil? Think of your upper body as a spring, turning against the resistance of your hips and legs. At the top of the backswing, that spring should be fully wound up, ready to be unleashed – or sprung – in a powerful throughswing that fires through the ball to a high and balanced finish.

But as you proceed through your backswing, keep in mind that your hips actually end their rotation at roughly one-half the turn of the shoulders and upper torso.

Remember also that it is the upper torso that pulls the hips around. They do not rotate at the same time or pace as the upper body. In fact, they are the last major part of the body to move in the initial phase of the backswing.

WEIGHT TRANSFER

Weight transfer is also a vital part of the backswing. I want to transfer most of my weight to the right foot as I rotate or turn back from the ball. By the time I finish the first move, about 90 per cent of my weight should be over the back foot, distributed from the centre to the heel.

At the same time, my right knee should remain braced and flexed, just as it was in my set-up. This provides the support I need to hold my position at the top, although that will only take a matter of a few split seconds in real time.

Meanwhile, my left foot has stayed on the ground, although for many golfers that isn't the case! A little lift of the foot here is acceptable, as long as you do not become unbalanced. Ben Hogan said that he did not care if a golfer raised his left foot in the backswing or not. And some of the great players had a pronounced lift in their front foot. But, if at all possible, keep your left foot planted. As you will see in the next section, it is one of the keys to a powerful, athletic swing.

To become a good golfer you need to study the previous pages so that your backswing can be produced automatically. Then, when faced with that pressure shot, you will instinctively believe in your movement.

THE ATHLETIC SWING

◆ ◆ ◆ ◆ ◆

*The basic golf swing has changed dramatically in recent years, becoming
more and more athletic. Players now have the ability to impart more
stretch and torque – or coil – to their swings, and that, in turn, gives
them considerably more power. In my opinion, great golfers in the future
will be professional athletes able to hit the ball up to 400 yards (365m)
with a driver.*

ONE OF the secrets of achieving this is keeping the left foot planted on the ground in the backswing – while completing your rotation. Doing so will add resistance, and therefore power, to your overall movement.

MAXIMIZING POWER

But what exactly do I mean by an athletic swing? I think of it as a strong, yet pliable and stretchy motion. Your body is used like a piece of strong elastic, which you stretch, then let go, the way you would fire off a giant rubber band or spring.

Making the body work in this way maximizes your power. Some golf instructors like to describe this as coil or torque, and that is the essence of the modern swing.

Today's players are trying to make a more powerful movement than ever before, while combining that approach with more consistency. This is the magic formula for success. If you can have great power with consistency, you have an unbeatable combination.

DRIVING AVERAGES

Look at the great players of this age, such as Tiger Woods, who can routinely hit the ball over 300 yards (274m) with accuracy. Only 25 years ago, the average driving distance

The athletic swing is the swing of the future. But remember that power is only an asset if it is combined with accuracy.

The athletic swing

among professional golfers was about 250 yards (229m). Yet now it's about 280 yards (256m). Advances in equipment have helped this surge, but so have more advanced training regimens.

Today's players are stronger and fitter. They are, in fact, true athletes, which they must be in order to compete in the modern game. To perform the swing of a Tiger Woods, you have to be both very physically strong and supple. And while not everyone can work towards an accurate replica of such a swing, the average golfer can produce a movement that is at least something like that of a Woods or David Duval – and which will maximize his or her potential.

SWING VARIATIONS

Of course, there are always variations on the basic golf swing – both among the pros and amateurs alike – that seem to work for individuals. For example, the Spanish golfer Sergio Garcia tries to think in terms of stretching his left arm to create more width through his left side.

I would be cautious about recommending this. I wouldn't try to emulate any other golfer's personal technique or traits. Garcia is a great talent for the future. But if the average golfer tries to stretch his left arm a bit more – in an attempt to get a lot more width – the likely result is that he will become too tense and so disconnect his swing.

For the mere mortals of this world, it is better to concentrate on what I have been trying to stress here – the connected swing, with hands, arms and body moving together, rather than just stretching one part of your anatomy. If you are going to try and copy another golfer in one particular respect, at least focus on someone who shares your height and build.

SHAKING HANDS

Here's one idea you can use, however. The American professional Tom Kite has a wonderful way of helping golfers visualize the movement in the backswing. He says you

should imagine you are turning around to shake someone's hand

Notice how much emphasis there is on the sheer opening of the upper torso in that description. You are almost literally turning around to face backwards. And if you can picture turning back to shake someone's hand who is in front of you, that is a nice impression of how we return to the impact position, and then move through to the finish.

That's the kind of opening in the golf swing that I would like to see most golfers strive towards.

Being strong and fit can only be an asset to a golfer of any age. Why not enrol in your local gym and develop a fitness, toning and stretching routine based around your golf swing? You'll be amazed at the results.

SWING PROBLEMS

◆ ◆ ◆ ◆ ◆

Many golfers interpret the idea of turning away from the ball on the backswing as an almost complete body turn. In other words, they move their hips along with their shoulders and upper torso — rather than allowing the upper torso to pull the hips around. When they do this, they fail to create any dynamic tension between the upper body and hips.

THAT IS all right in the beginning. In fact, if most golfers did that, they would be better off than not turning their bodies sufficiently. If you are going to overdo it, that's the way to go. But the real problem for the majority of golfers is that they do not open the body enough, if at all. In fact, the vast majority always underdo it.

OPENING FEARS

The fear of turning away from the golf ball is a persistent problem for most golfers. They simply do not rotate the body at all, or they do so to a minimal extent. In other words, they simply lift the club with their arms and hands. As a consequence there is a very limited opening of the torso, and a very small amount of weight transfer, and that is extremely damaging to the swing.

Most amateurs also overswing by using their arms and hands too much in the beginning of the backswing, and then they add a bit of rotation. But because they have used their hands and arms independently to begin with, before turning slightly, they end up with their arms and hands over the top of their heads, and the left arm inevitably breaks or folds.

If they had opened the torso correctly — and really been committed to that action at the beginning of the movement — their

When you're standing over the golf ball, it's vital that you are preparing your body to move. Too many golfers get stuck at this stage and end up like mannequins over the ball, unable to move freely.

Head down, straight left arm

problems would vanish. The crucial point is to make sure that the arms and hands are passive in the first move. In fact, almost totally inactive. I cannot stress that enough.

STRAIGHT ARMING

Another of the great myths about the golf swing is that you must always keep your left arm straight. Gary Player was a great proponent of this, but then he was one of the most coordinated and physically fit golfers who ever played the game.

But Player was also small, and in trying to find additional power, he devised a backswing technique that gave him more width.

LOOSEN UP

The idea that you should not break the left arm does not mean keeping it rigid or stiff. In fact, it certainly should not be rigid or stiff.

Let me emphasize that.

Many great golfers – Seve Ballesteros comes to mind – have played the game at the highest level with a swing that had a certain amount of give in the left arm. Remember, it is the big muscles of the upper torso that are really driving the golf swing and providing the power to hit the ball. So the arms really have a far lesser role to play.

There is nothing wrong with having some break in the left arm, as long as it is

not caused by independent movement of the arms and hands, a movement made without the rotation of the body.

The US PGA tour pro Calvin Peete is a great example to illustrate this. He actually has a withered left arm. But when he turns, he keeps everything together, and as a result he was one of the most consistent players on the PGA tour during the 1980s.

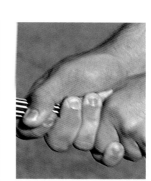

How often have I seen this? Head down, straight left arm – it's a disaster from which few recover. How can you possibly enjoy the game playing like this?

Tight hands will kill any chance of making a good swing or feeling the clubhead.

UNLOCK YOUR ARM

Slavishly trying to keep the left arm straight in your backswing can stifle any free, athletic movement in your overall swing and may even cause injury. When a golfer tries to keep his or her arm straight, they often twist the elbow inwards at address – rather than more naturally bowing the elbow out slightly. With the elbow twisted in, the golfer will struggle to return the clubface to square at impact and probably hit a hook. Even worse, some golfers smother the ball, slamming the clubhead into the ground, which not only results in a bad shot, but can also send shock waves up the arm – eventually damaging either the wrist or elbow.

SPINE ANGLE AND SWING PLANE

♦ ♦ ♦ ♦ ♦

When you take your position at address, you have effectively preset your spine in a certain alignment — what pros call the 'spinal angle'. As you rotate your body in the swing, it is absolutely essential that the angle you have created at address is maintained throughout the swing — so there is absolutely no lifting or lowering of the spine.

I F THE spine angle varies, it will have a very detrimental effect on your ability to bring the club back through the ball towards the target. So it's essential to maintain the spinal angle that you created at address.

FIXED AXIS

Picture an imaginary line drawn down your back, from the top of your head to your hips. As you begin your backswing, you are rotating your spine around that angle, or line, turning back and then forwards, simply opening and closing your body in relation to this fixed axis.

It is similar to a door hanging on an angle from a pair of hinges — opening and

closing. That is how the body turns along the spinal angle, both in the backswing, and as we unwind through the ball.

At the same time, your shoulder turn should remain perpendicular to your spine, and your shoulders turn on a level plane, with the hips on roughly the same line. This is what we call the 'swing plane', and it both follows from, and is connected to, the spinal angle.

IN THE SLOT

What do I mean by 'swing plane'? Ben Hogan was one of the most consistent strikers of the ball in the history of the game. But even he struggled to 'slot' his club into the proper position at the top of the

Above: Developing a consistent swing plane is very much part of becoming a consistent striker of the ball.

Left: Your posture will determine your eventual swing plane, therefore make sure you're in a good position before taking the club back.

A simple way to understand the swing plane is to swing the club at a target, in this case a caddy's hand, positioned at different levels, starting at head height and working down to the ball.

backswing until he understood the idea of 'plane'.

Once he grasped that concept and practised swinging the club along this imaginary line, he gained enough confidence to rely on his swing in the pressure of competition and eventually to become a winner of golf's most coveted trophies.

Imagine a pane of glass extending from the ball to your shoulders, with your head poking through a hole at the top. The angle of this plane will vary depending on your height and the distance that you stand from the ball, producing what we often refer to as either a steep or shallow plane.

STAYING ON PLANE

But one thing is constant. There is no such thing as a swing that is too steep or too shallow if the golfer consistently swings his shoulders along the line of the plane. Like the spinal angle, any variation above or below the plane will put the swing out of position and produce a bad shot. But staying on the same plane throughout the swing will groove an excellent movement.

Try to think about both your spinal angle and swing plane when practising your backswing. Getting both right is one of the essential ingredients to making that first move correctly.

Once you're confident you can make that first move, you'll be like a sprinter who is poised and ready to explode out of the blocks when the gun goes.

REFLECTIONS ON SWING PLANE

You can check to see if your swing plane is correct simply by looking in a mirror. Pick a spot on the floor where your ball would normally be in your address position, then swing a 5- or 6-iron back, holding it at the top. If an imaginary line drawn from the butt end of your grip to the ball falls across your left shoulder, your swing plane is too upright. This means you probably return the clubface to the ball in an open position, take deep divots, and often sky the ball. If the imaginary line cuts across your navel, your swing plane is too flat and you probably return the clubface in a closed position, resulting in many shots hit too low and hot.

The correct – or neutral – swing plane places the imaginary line directly across the right shoulder. From there, you will return the clubface square at impact and strike the ball more consistently.

Chapter 5

THE THROUGHSWING

◆◆◆◆◆

With the body coiled and ready to unleash the clubhead at high speed, the release of power into the ball on the throughswing can either be an exhilarating experience or an embarrassing hack.

THE THROUGHSWING

◆ ◆ ◆ ◆ ◆

Now it is crunch time. The transition from the top of the backswing to the start of the throughswing is the most crucial split second in golf – and the ultimate moment of truth.

EITHER THE golfer will take advantage of having achieved an excellent position at the top of the backswing – with the body fully rotated and powerfully coiled behind the ball – or the golfer will now destroy all his or her previous good work.

Done properly, the throughswing will unleash the clubhead at high speed – the pros hit the ball at over 100mph (161km/h) – smacking into surlyn or balata to send the object of our desire flying high and true towards the target.

TAKING SHORTCUTS

On the other hand – and I choose that phrase deliberately – the golfer may make a terrible hack of the job, not only embarrassing himself, but perhaps doing permanent damage to his score. How many times have you seen a fellow golfer make a nice backswing, only to snatch the club back at the ball or fail to hit through it?

Unfortunately, human nature is such that the failure of most amateur golfers is caused by rushing – they are trying to shortcut the downswing. They're nervous. They want to get to the ball as soon as they can. So almost instinctively, they fall back on old habits, bringing the club down with their hands and arms, rather than using their body.

LOOKING EASY

The transition phase from the backswing to hitting through the ball must be a dynamic, athletic move, fully utilizing the body in a coordinated fashion that is seemingly unhurried, and outwardly graceful.

Think of Ronaldo scoring a goal. Brian Lara hitting a boundary. Michael Jordan sinking the winning basket. There's no wasted motion, and no excessive exertion. In

A simple baseball type action is good practice when you are first developing the correct turning motion though the ball.

Practising the baseball swing

The throughswing – bad followthrough

other words, they make it look easy – even if it surely is anything but easy.

UNCOILING THE SWING

So, learning how to perform the throughswing is a case of disciplining the body and brain through practice. The golfer must know what is about to happen, and how he or she should proceed.

Simply put, the throughswing is a reverse image of the backswing, as the legs, hips, upper torso, shoulders, arms and hands gradually uncoil piece by piece. At the same time, there is a slight lateral weight shift to the left, as the majority of the weight moves from the back foot to the front.

In other words, the swing uncoils in exactly the same order as it was previously coiled up, so that the last thing to go back, is the first thing to come forward.

IMAGE AND FEEL

Think about that for a moment. Images and a physical feeling for what we do in golf are vitally important. Once again, I would suggest that you initially practise this motion in front of a mirror with a club, but no ball. That's the best way to help you prepare for what you'll do later on the practice range – and ultimately the course.

I like to focus on the impression of the backswing uncoiling like a tightly wound spring into the full swing. I firmly believe that if you can think of this move in that way, it will help to unravel any mystery attached to the throughswing – and help it unfold in a logical sequence.

Don't stay down with the ball too long, otherwise you'll get trapped behind the ball.

PAUSE AT THE TOP

One of the most common faults of the average golfer is the tendency to hit from the top – or initiate the throughswing with the shoulders, rather than allowing them to uncoil gradually after the lower body starts to move back to the left. The legendary Tommy Armour, a Scot who emigrated to America in the 20s and won 24 golf tournaments in two decades – including both the US and British Open – developed the most famous cure for hitting from the top – a split-second pause at the top of the backswing. In his 1953 book *How to Play Your Best Golf All the Time*, he wrote that adding this pause was the 'greatest single aid' to eliminating what he saw as the 'worst fault in the golf swing'.

Next time you are at the golf range, try Armour's technique and see if it doesn't help improve the timing of your throughswing.

THE FIRST MOVE FORWARDS

◆ ◆ ◆ ◆ ◆

*It can be difficult to keep the first move in the throughswing under control
– just as it was difficult to make that first move in the backswing. When
most golfers realize that they have arrived at, or near, the top of their
backswing, they suddenly want to get the clubhead to the ball as
quickly as possible.*

SO RELAX, there's no need to rush, the ball isn't going away. The throughswing has to be smooth, so that the body can uncoil fluidly and pull the clubhead through, rather than the other way around.

FIRST MOVE FORWARDS

Remember that as you coiled your body up in the backswing, your upper torso and shoulders rotated back, your weight shifted from your left to your right side, and your legs provided balance and support for the entire movement. At the same time, this coiling motion pulled in the left knee, inclining it towards the back leg, while the hips were gradually pulled around to half the rotation of the shoulder turn.

Therefore, the first part of the body that should come forward to start the throughswing is that left side. I believe that a slight lateral movement of the left hip towards the target is the ideal trigger for your throughswing. In the past, men no less eminent than Ben Hogan and Bobby Jones also thought that the forward turning of the hips was the trigger, or first move, that initiated the throughswing.

Other golf pros and swing gurus maintain it is actually a separation of the left knee from the right, the shift of weight onto the left foot.

It is difficult to focus precisely on individual actions, since they happen so quickly and everyone has their own way of sensing this motion. On top of this, any

A slight lateral movement with the left hip towards the target initiates the forward move. As your hips rotate to face the target, your upper body and clubhead will be pulled forwards developing tremendous centrifugal force.

The forward move

The lower body

Left: The forward drive of your lower body is an essential part of developing a powerful golf swing.

Below: In order to develop the correct motion through impact, practise turning your left hip to the left whilst at the same time swinging the right hand towards the target.

swing that is truly athletic will be partly instinctive, and therefore vary slightly from golfer to golfer. The way a golfer perceives the sequence of what happens will inevitably vary.

UNCOILING THE BODY

Suffice it to say that both the hips and the left knee move more or less simultaneously in the first split second of the throughswing and weight is transferred to the front foot. The essential point remains that the body must uncoil gradually, roughly from the ground up, in reverse order to the backswing coil – with the movement of the clubhead always coming last.

If you watch a slow-motion videotape of a good swing, you will see that indeed there is a pronounced separation of the left knee from the right in the initial part of the throughswing. Roughly at the same time, the hips and upper torso are beginning to uncoil as well, pulling through the shoulders and arms as the weight transfers smoothly from the right foot to the left.

The overall effect is that these actions allow the body to rotate around the left heel into the final part of the swing.

FORWARD POWER AND DRIVE

The way I like to think of this first move, and the way I teach it to my golfing pupils, is by telling them they are trying to develop a strong sense of forward power and drive, thus imparting that energy to the ball. This starts with a slight lateral movement of the left hip, which goes forward towards the target, then this translates into a rotational movement that pulls the body around, letting it eventually open up fully to face the chosen target.

But let me emphasize one thing in particular. This action must be done in the most non-violent way possible! The initiation of the throughswing should be an easy and fluid move, because if you turn the left hip – or anything else for that matter – too aggressively, the club will be thrown outside the correct line and you'll hack at the ball with an out-to-in swingpath, probably slicing it as a result.

Remember, the uncoiling of the body into the throughswing should be a natural movement that you do not force, hurry or try to push. A good way of thinking about this is to focus on the idea of simply *letting it happen*.

THE THROUGHSWING FROM IMPACT TO FINISH

◆ ◆ ◆ ◆ ◆

An essential ingredient of both the backswing and throughswing movement is the efficient transfer of weight. To initiate the throughswing, the golfer has to get his or her weight back over to the left side in order to unleash the swing and provide power to the clubhead.

USING A slight lateral slide as the hips begin to turn and the knees separate, you rotate over the left heel, holding the club lightly and simply letting it swing through. In effect, you allow the club to pull you. And if that happens, you're really in business. But if you start pushing the club in any way, you'll have serious problems.

HARD WORK

What do I mean by pushing the club? Instead of allowing the club to swing freely with light hands and wrists, many golfers try to muscle the clubhead into the ball, which inevitably means that they are holding the club too tightly and forcing all the action. In other words, instead of the club doing what it was designed to do – how many times have you heard this one – you do all the work!

Of course, your reward for all that hard work is a golfing disaster.

CLUB PULL

Try to hold the club as lightly as possible and allow the left hip to ease its way around in the throughswing. Don't try to be aggressive. Let your weight naturally move onto the left heel, and set the clubhead free.

If you have done this correctly, and allowed the club to swing freely, centrifugal force will come into play and pull the arms to full extension.

Yes, the club will actually pull you, and you might even be able to feel the right

shoulder being brought through under your chin to its finish point.

IMPACT!

What happens when the clubhead finally smacks into the ball?

The answer may surprise you – very little that you need worry about! In fact, if you've done everything correctly up to this point, the clubhead will merely zip through the ball and send it 300 yards or more – if you're Tiger Woods, that is.

In addition, any conscious effort to manipulate the hands or wrists will only lead to trouble. At the impact position, you can do precious little to control the clubhead, because everything is happening too fast. Rely instead on a sound grip, your preparation and the proper execution of your swing to allow the clubhead to do the work at this stage of the game.

PRACTICE IMAGES

I would suggest focusing on several images that you might conjure up when practising. These will help you to visualize your position at impact, and how you groove your movement through the ball.

First, you want to think of swinging through the ball as something like throwing underhand to a target, roughly like skimming a stone across a pond. The right arm is at first coiled backwards and raised, then swings forward with the wrist providing that extra momentum as the stone or ball is

Here you can see the throughswing in action. The hips are turning left and the club is released towards the target.

released. At the same time, the elbow passes close to the right hip and finishes with full extension or beyond.

Practise doing this with a tennis ball, a stone or whatever is available to give you the right feeling, then grab a club and swing it to waist-high. Think about the right hand turning over the left on the throughswing – once past impact.

As the body continues to rotate to the left, the club is literally pulling the golfer through to a complete follow-through.

TWO-HANDED PASS

Of course, you really want to swing as freely as possible with both hands through impact. One way of ingraining this idea is to practise with a medicine ball if you can obtain one, or at least a football, basketball or even a beach ball. The idea is to imagine you are making a two-handed pass with the ball, from the right side of the body to the left, with the object being to get the ball to a target. Doing this will resemble the motion of the golf swing.

Hold the ball in front of you and take your address position. Then begin a simulated backswing. You will automatically shift your weight from the left foot to the right, which builds up your power, then reverse the action as you fling the ball towards the target.

NATURAL POWER

This exercise will give you the idea of how you can naturally generate power in the swing through simple body leverage, with the hands and arms serving as conduits of that energy. In the end, your body rotation will carry you all the way around to the left, in exactly the same way as the club does in a good swing.

But remember that at impact, your technique is what you must ultimately rely upon. If you make a good backswing, and unleash your throughswing in the proper sequence, you will generate energy and power at the point of contact, with the centrifugal force I mentioned in the previous section controlling much of what happens through the ball.

THE FINISHED POSITION

How do we get to the finish of the throughswing? Simply put, the rotation of your torso and shoulders continues until your hips are fully turned and your chest faces the target, the body having fully rotated around your left heel.

That's the part that should be common to everyone. And yet every golfer has his own version of the finish, and they can vary dramatically. Some are unusual, and some are absolute works of art. Think of Arnold Palmer. Then think of Ernie Els.

The point here is that while no two golfers finish their swing in quite the same

Swinging a heavy object such as a medicine ball, or in this case a cool-box, helps develop the feeling of the arms and body working together throughout the movement.

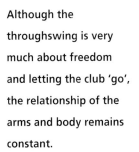

Although the throughswing is very much about freedom and letting the club 'go', the relationship of the arms and body remains constant.

way, they all tell us something about what went on before. They provide an insight both into a golfer's strengths and weaknesses. And they give us clues as to how we might enhance the good points, while fixing the faults, in our own swings.

MAINTAIN THE FINISH

I always tell the golfers that I teach to maintain their finished position for a few seconds. You want to do so because:

• If you anticipate finishing up with a balanced, controlled follow-through, that will have a positive effect right through your golf swing.
• Your swing faults will become apparent. If you fall forwards at the finish, for instance, you will discover that you did not shift your weight properly and you were not balanced.

COUNT TO THREE

Again, it is a matter of programming the body and brain to know what they are trying to achieve together. Such visualization techniques work on the subconscious. Thinking about balance and control will impart the proper idea while you are actually moving the club.

In addition, I suggest that at the end of the golf swing, you should hold the finish and count, 1-2-3. But rather than thinking of this as a finale, remember that the real action in golf is only just beginning. As you count, the imaginary ball has started to rise into the air and fly towards your target.

EXHILARATING SWINGS

If you have done everything I have described in this chapter and the previous one properly, the experience of hitting a golf ball *will* ultimately be exhilarating, rather than embarrassing. In short, you will have released the power in your swing, and found the key to unlocking your potential for the game of golf.

But before we conclude our examination of the swing – and you try to take my techniques to the course – please read the following chapter. There, I pull together everything I have explained about the backswing and throughswing, then round it off with a few more mental images. I also offer some final tips and thoughts on the central action of the game – your golf swing.

As the swing continues through, the pictures above featuring both cool-box and golf club show how the arms, hands and torso maintain the relationship that began at address.

Chapter 6

THE COMPLETE SWING

♦ ♦ ♦ ♦ ♦

Now it is time to draw all the bits and pieces together to form your own dynamic and athletic swing, free from conscious thought.

THE COMPLETE SWING

◆ ◆ ◆ ◆ ◆

It's so easy you could do it with your eyes closed. How many times have you heard that one? But, in truth, we often make life more complicated than it is, or has to be. That's especially true when you consider the countless decisions we make each day — from what to eat for breakfast to where we might be living next year — while also doing a multitude of tasks we have learned and conditioned ourselves to perform over time. Some are easy, and some are difficult. But that's life.

AT THE HEART of the game is one central action – the swing. Hand a golf club to a three-year-old, and that child will probably come up with a pretty good approximation of a proper golf swing. Hand the same club to someone who has been playing the game for years and they will begin thinking, tinkering…and, if they ever do finally take a swing, in all likelihood they will make a complete hash of it.

Now hand the club to a golf pro, and watch him or her make one smooth, seemingly effortless, pass at the ball that produces a drive that seems to fly forever, or a high fade that lands the ball softly on a green around 85 yards away – just a few feet from the pin.

INSTINCT AND PRACTICE

What's the difference between the three golfers?

Two of them *can* swing a club with their eyes closed, because they perform the action in what appears to be the most natural and instinctive way. Of course, in the case of the child, it *is* instinctive, while in the case of the pro, it's a mixture of instinct and about a million hours of practice.

For your swing to repeat you must learn to 'feel' your swing rather than 'think' your swing. Practising blindfold or with your eyes closed will quickly help you to understand just how a good swing should feel and help you to trust your movement.

Blindfolded swing

In the previous two chapters, I have broken down the backswing and throughswing into separate parts.

Now I am going to link the parts together and show you how to make it 'simple'. So simple, in fact, that it becomes natural – something you could even do from time to time with your eyes closed.

Which is how I want you to start.

REMOVE THE BALL

The first step to learning the complete swing is to remove the ball from the equation. Remember, you are trying to programme your body to move instinctively back from the ball, then through the ball to a high, balanced finish. But, invariably, the golf ball draws attention away from the real action of the swing, almost putting the average golfer into an hypnotic trance.

If that happens, any natural opening of the torso in the backswing will be inhibited and the swing motion might begin to disintegrate, destroying any hope of a properly executed, complete golf swing.

I try to counteract that tendency in my pupils by asking them to take slow-motion swings without the ball, swinging over and over again to build confidence in their movement. At the same time, I tell them to discipline their bodies to move properly, to ingrain an understanding of what they are trying to achieve.

LET'S SWING

Now comes the interesting bit. After you have swung the club slowly for a time, make some more swings with your eyes closed. In fact, make hundreds this way. And while you do this, concentrate on how the various movements in the swing feel, how they come together, and how they combine with the action of your body.

See? You *can* do it with your eyes closed.

Swinging in this way will also emphatically prove something else. In the previous chapters, we have broken the swing down into its various parts. But, in reality, it should be one continuous, flowing motion. With your eyes closed, I trust you will 'see' this vividly, as you build towards a better swing action.

Putting it all together is about developing one continuous flowing motion that is smooth, unhurried and consistent. Now you're ready to shoot those low scores.

REPLACE THE BALL

◆ ◆ ◆ ◆ ◆

As I've already explained, Nick Faldo spent the first two months of his golfing life developing his golf swing without a golf ball. When he began hitting balls, he had already created a swing that consistently propelled the clubhead towards the target.

WHAT IS the natural extension of the concept of removing the ball? My own golf instructor, Ian Connelly, used to repeat one basic rule over and over again to me. Only after you have learned how to swing the club properly are you ready to bring the ball back into play – and, finally, into its proper role.

In other words, you have now ingrained the idea into your mind and body that the swing is the central action of golf, and that it should be your principal focus – not the act of hitting at the ball. So after you've developed a dynamic, athletic swing – just put the ball in the way.

Let me repeat that: just put the ball in the way.

A good golf swing is one in which the ball is simply in the path of the clubhead. The ball is not your target – you merely swing through it, with no conscious effort to hit it. If you can master that concept, you have taken one of the biggest steps possible towards finding your own complete swing.

INSTINCTIVE GOLF

Like the little child who grabs the club and swings away with youthful abandon, you have to learn (or re-learn) how to be instinctive about your swing. An excellent swing links physical know-how and mental application, then tosses away the conscious mindset of the technician.

What do I mean by that? By now, your swing should be mechanically sound, but also programmed in your subconscious, with the whole process written into your muscle

A much improved swing

Exercise

Left: Repetition is the mother of skill. And remember quality is better than quantity so practise good swings again and again.

Above left: If you can't practise regularly, perform simple loosening exercises that remind your body of the correct movement.

memory and throughout your body. Of course, unless you continue to practise, any consistency that you have achieved up to this point will start to deteriorate.

REPETITION AND SKILL

Go back to what I said before. You must swing the club in slow motion, over and over and over again, without the golf ball. Far too many golfers fall into the trap of thinking they have learned something, and then immediately head out to the range, eager to whack a couple of dozen golf balls.

Avoid that trap like the plague. If you try to short-circuit the process, it will be disastrous for the development of your swing. You have to develop a pattern, and that takes hundreds of hours. Repetition is the mother of skill.

That is how to become both consistent, and to learn how to *not* think about the ball and the parts of the swing. In other words, how to make the swing instinctive again.

CENTRIFUGAL FORCE

◆ ◆ ◆ ◆ ◆

Everyone knows what centrifugal force is, and that concept is useful when it comes to understanding the complete swing. If you put a weight at the end of a piece of string and whirl it around, you will create motion in the weight that is much faster than your wrist can move as it twirls the object. We've all done that as children.

YOU MIGHT also think of figure skating, where the man spins his partner quickly around him, as if he were an axis point. Even though he does not move particularly fast, she will if they build up enough force and rotation.

Try to think of the golf swing in this way, with the clubhead the weight at the end of your string, or the skating partner at the end of your arm.

PULLING ARMS

Once I enable a golfer to create a good shape to his or her movement in the swing, I tell them to keep their hands as light as possible and try to sense the feeling of spinning that weight around them, the force coming from the centre of their body, which in this case serves as the axis.

If they can harness this strength and force properly, the clubhead will literally pull their arms to full extension. But any tension will destroy the effect. The arms will narrow and the swing arc will lose its width. This is like moving your wrist when you are spinning the weight on a string. The weight will drop out of its orbit and slow down or even stop.

If you allow your club to swing freely, your arms will be pulled to full extension by the centrifugal force developed by the swing.

The same happens in the golf swing when you don't allow the club to swing freely, or you move out of plane. The hands and arms take over, the power and momentum you have created is reduced, and your shot will lose distance and accuracy.

RADIATING POWER

What is the secret to maintaining centrifugal force in the golf swing? Remember that you must coil and then uncoil your body in a smooth, efficient manner to produce a good swing. Do that, and you will radiate power out from the centre of your body – or torso – while at impact you will be able to whip the club through the ball.

Let me re-emphasize that the hands and arms must be passive in this scenario. They conduct force and energy, but do not generate it.

Think of how a discus thrower uses his athletic skill to propel the object he is trying to hurl a great distance. He winds his body up in a circular motion from the ground up, concentrating and shifting his weight. His hands and arms merely serve first to hold the discus, then eventually to transmit the energy he is slowly building. Finally, he uncoils his body fully and seems to explode, the discus hurtling from his grasp.

ROTATE AHEAD

How can you relate this to your golf swing? Keep in mind that the discus thrower is always turning ahead of his discus, and that everything involved in his physical technique happens before the discus leaves his hand.

That's what you want to do in the golf swing as well. You turn or rotate your body ahead of the clubhead, in effect keeping the clubhead behind your motion, so that the lag builds up tremendous force and drive into the ball.

The ball then goes a great distance.

As you can see in the top left picture, by this stage the club has taken the initiative and is pulling you to the finish position shown in the final photograph.

ANCHORING THE SWING

◆ ◆ ◆ ◆ ◆

*What is the axis of the golf swing? On the previous pages I described how
a golfer can generate force and energy in the swing from the centre of the
body, and how he or she can rotate around that as an axis point. But the
axis point of an individual's golf swing is not like the fixed position of the
wrist when a weight is spun on the end of a string, or the upright partner
in the graceful movement of a figure-skating pair*

IN A SENSE, we have more than one axis in the golf swing. At address, our weight is evenly distributed between the left and right side. But when we move into the backswing, we shift our weight to the back foot, then transfer it forward to the front foot in the throughswing. This shift, plus the coiling of the upper body against the more static hips and legs in the backswing, produces power that is imparted to the ball.

So the axis, or anchor, of the swing is really two contact points – our feet.

PIVOTS AND TURNS

Golf guru David Leadbetter calls the basic motion of turning back and through in the golf swing a 'pivot'. Others simply call it a 'turn' or 'rotation'. Whatever term you prefer for the basic movement of the golf swing, the one constant is the role of our feet. If they don't provide a solid foundation for the swing, we will become unbalanced and the entire action will unravel.

The golfer should always keep his or her weight distributed between the middle of the feet back to the heels. When you move your body in the swing, think about rotating around each of your feet.

Putting that in the simplest way possible, your axis points are your right and left heels. On the backswing, you first shift your

When you make your backswing, feel yourself rotate round the right leg. Here my colleague ensures that my right knee remains flexed throughout my backswing. Do the same with your left knee on the follow-through.

Anchoring the swing

Left: Good support in my lower body ensures that my coil will be secure so that I can realize my full potential when swinging the club through the ball.

weight to the right foot, then you should start thinking about swinging around the left heel on the throughswing.

COILING BEHIND THE BALL

Tell any golfer that you can grant three wishes and what would he or she ask for? Distance. Distance. Distance. But if you asked most golfers to demonstrate how *they* think increasing their distance can be accomplished, they would probably produce a swing that is mostly hands and arms, in a vain attempt to muscle the ball down the fairway.

The secret to executing a powerful, dynamic swing is a coordinated physical effort that starts with the move away from the ball. At the top of the backswing, the body must be fully coiled like a spring, ready to snap back and unleash the clubhead through impact with the ball.

In other words, most golf swings are only as good as the backswing the golfer uses to set up his motion. The key to understanding how to do this well is knowing how far to move behind the ball.

REVERSE PIVOT

Imagine a short wall behind your right leg. Now swing back until you have fully coiled your upper torso and hips behind the ball. If you have done this properly, your leg should be snug against the wall. However, if you have gone too far back, you have swayed past the wall and have lost the effect of using your right leg as a brace for your weight, and a help in enhancing the athletic energy of your coil.

On the other hand, if your right leg never moved into the wall, you have probably produced a reverse pivot, the 'cardinal sin' of golf. In a reverse pivot, the weight actually tilts forward onto the front leg, so that when you start your downswing, your weight will then move back onto your right foot. The result will be any number of variations on a bad shot, and a dramatic loss of distance.

Below: Remember – turning the feet out slightly will aid the opening of your body both back and through the swing.

PRO TIP

As an aid to body rotation, think about how your right knee, although flexed, should swivel slightly during the backswing. If it points to 12 o'clock at address, it should have turned to 1 o'clock as the body moves back from the ball. The knee rotates slightly to allow the body to turn.

If the back foot is slightly opened up (i.e. turned outwards), that helps rotation as well, aiding the opening of the body. The same is true for the front foot. Both can be slightly open, despite what you may have heard in the past about the back foot needing to be perpendicular to the target line, while the front foot is open.

Having both feet angled out is a more natural set-up for most players.

REVERSING A REVERSE PIVOT

◆ ◆ ◆ ◆ ◆

How can you avoid the reverse pivot and make a proper backswing?
Take your stance with the ball roughly opposite your left heel and start
your backswing. Now imagine a vertical line running from the centre of
the ball up to the sky. If, at the top of the backswing, you are totally
behind that line, your coil is correct.

THE FAILING of most golfers, however, is that they become anxious as they move away from the ball and never fully turn behind it – or fail to 'complete' their backswing.

Remember that a good backswing means first turning the triangle of the hands, arms and shoulders back from the ball in conjunction with the centre of the upper torso. At the same time, there is a slight lateral movement to the rear as the weight shifts and the hips and left knee are pulled back by the chain reaction set up by your upper body – until everything settles into the brace of the right leg.

THROWING A PUNCH

The throughswing then starts in reverse sequence to the backswing, from the ground up, as the hips turn back and the weight moves to the left heel, pulling the upper torso, shoulders, arms and finally the hands – which should remain passive throughout, following the orders being issued by the body.

This, in turn, lets the clubhead lag behind slightly, building up tremendous power and centrifugal force until it whips through the ball and on to a high finish. Think of this as an uncoiling of the body. After winding up the dynamic tension in the body, you are now unwinding it – in much the same way as a boxer throws a punch.

Of course, he does not start his move with his weight forward. Rather, he subtly winds himself up by shifting his weight back, then moving towards his target with the stored energy of that weight shift.

MULTIPLE SINS

The failure to coil properly behind the ball creates a multitude of problems. If a golfer does not complete the backswing, he or she will have a tendency to begin the throughswing from the top, rather than the bottom up, and so cut across the swing plane.

In doing this, the swing becomes disconnected, and the relationship between the centre of the body and the triangle of the hands, arms and shoulders is destroyed. Now the hips are swivelling with no real role to play and the club is thrown or almost cast like a fishing rod.

This generally guarantees that the clubhead will return to the ball in an open position (i.e. pointing to the right of the target line) and the golfer will hit a weak

Convincing a player to move behind the ball is the most difficult part of my job. Imagine throwing a punch or skimming a stone – the move backwards is the 'power move'.

Throwing a punch

PRO TIP

Many golf instructors stress turning with some lateral movement to get weight onto the back foot. But how much is enough? As a practical matter, a full movement behind the ball almost never happens anyway. Everyone who has ever taken a golf lesson knows about turning behind the ball, but few golfers necessarily get all their weight shifted to the right side, then back to the left on the throughswing.

Simply put, try to get as much weight transfer as you can. Don't worry about swaying off the ball, since you are probably doing the opposite. If anything, the body has a tendency to get stuck over the ball. So fight your fears and you'll achieve a better overall swing.

slice. But, given this scenario, the hands might also turn over, and then a dead pull is produced.

In better players, the swing path of the club will not be quite as badly affected, but the disconnection will certainly prevent an adequate release through the ball. Distance and accuracy are always sacrificed because of this faulty move.

Below: A good finish position generally indicates a good backswing. A swing should mirror itself on the back- and throughswing.

Wrong and right

Above: Reverse pivoting simply means moving your body weight the wrong way round. In a good move your weight should move to your right foot in the backswing and the left foot on your follow-through. So if your weight is on your left foot at the top of the backswing – start to worry.

SWING KEYS

◆ ◆ ◆ ◆ ◆

Certain aspects of each golfer's swing will be as individual as his or her personality, physical appearance and mannerisms. But there are common traits in every good golf swing, and they should be studied and practised over and over again in order to groove a repeatable swing.

HERE ARE some of the most important factors that you should bear in mind as you prepare to swing your golf club

• In the set-up, the feet are spread to shoulder-width – measured from the inside of the heels – and the hands, arms and shoulders should form a triangle, with the left arm and club extended in virtually a straight line.

• The knees and hips should be level, but the right shoulder will be slightly lower than the left because, in the grip, the right hand is under the left on the club.

• The spine should form roughly a straight line from the top of the head to the hips, with the backside jutting out slightly as a balance point.

• A little flex should be present in the knees – giving the golfer the feeling of standing tall to the ball.

• The body – and especially the hands and arms – should be free from tension. A smooth, controlled waggle (or two) will help achieve this, along with a wiggling of the toes or slight lifting of the feet to drain tension from the lower body, just before the ball is struck.

Kick start

Making the first move is never easy, as we all know. So try kick-starting your swing by moving your right knee towards the target in conjunction with a slight rotation of your hips in the same direction.

KICK START

Initiating the first move of the swing is always tough. Through the years, golfers have used a variety of ways to start off their swing, such as the once traditional forward press. I think David Leadbetter's more modern approach is the best one. He suggests a 'kick-start' from the right knee towards the target, in conjunction with a slight rotation of the hips in the same direction.

But don't just go out on the golf course and try this the next time you play. The key is to practise this move until it becomes ingrained in your swing routine. Then, when done correctly, it should enhance the tempo of your overall swing.

A BRIEF PAUSE

Some golfers have an almost perceptible pause at the top of the backswing. In fact, the body is really moving in two different directions at this point. As the backswing reaches its fullest turn, the lower body is starting to move forward.

However, thinking about taking a brief pause at the top will help steady your swing and make it more consistent. If you do this correctly, you will also aid your rhythm and tempo, and most probably keep your swing in the proper plane. In turn, that will produce a better shot.

STANDING TALL

With the proper emphasis on the body moving first in the throughswing – rather than the hands or arms – the impact position will resemble that of the address. The golfer will appear to be standing tall again, with the left arm fully extended.

Any dip or break of the left arm at this juncture will wreak havoc with the flight of the ball.

MIRROR IMAGE

A good swing should mirror itself in the way the body turns back and through the ball. Try to recognize this and develop a feel for how the swing reflects itself by practising

slowly in front of a mirror, or with the use of a video camera.

At the same time, try to think about how to simplify all the various parts of the swing into two basic moves – the body turning away from the target, and then the body turning to the target. This principle is adhered to in all good golf swings.

Try especially to think about how the body dictates the swing, with no thought given to the role of the hands, arms or the ball.

A brief pause at the top of the backswing can help to maintain a good rhythm and tempo in your swing and aid consistency.

HOW TO PRACTISE

◆ ◆ ◆ ◆ ◆

Most golfers cannot wait to start letting fly with a bucket of golf balls after they have read one magazine article on swing technique, taken a few lessons, or tried a new grip. That's a surefire recipe for failure.

EVEN IF you do hit a few good shots, it would be a mistake to believe you have mastered a new swing, or some aspect of a new swing. More than likely, you'll probably hit a lot of indifferent shots after the initial excitement wears off. And again, it would be a mistake to think that fact means anything, either good or bad.

You have to practise each new aspect of the swing for a considerable period of time before you can incorporate it into a practise routine, and certainly long before you can take it to the course.

DRIVING RANGE TIPS

Do go to the driving range, although, once there, try not to hit too many golf balls! Take lots of practice swings instead. And use an easy club like a 6-iron, rather than the driver, for an extended time. After you have built up some confidence, and an understanding of what you are trying to accomplish, then you can pull out other clubs, trying to groove the same swing aspect with each.

Always aim at something when hitting balls on the driving range, and vary the targets. When you play, you are constantly confronted with a variety of situations, so why turn practice into a mere bash of the ball into the unknown?

Develop and practise a pre-shot routine at the range. All the top pros have a consistent routine that helps them visualize the shot, take aim and relax before hitting the ball. Doing the same is a key to playing better. In addition, developing consistency in one area will work into other parts of your game.

TIME FOR SUCCESS

Pick a target, decide on what club to use and how to shape the shot, then visualize the ball moving along your target line and landing where you want it to go.

Move behind the ball to find an aiming point, using something a few inches ahead on the mat or grass.

Take your stance and give the club a waggle to loosen up before starting your backswing.

Finally, step back and see how many other people at the range are doing the same thing. Not many, I'll bet – out of shyness, impatience or whatever – which is their mistake, not yours.

Now you're ready to take a shot. Go ahead, and succeed.

Left: The only person you never see in golf is yourself! That's why you need a good teacher.

PRO TIP

Several famous golf gurus have suggested a shoulder turn of about 90 degrees to the target, with the hips turned half that amount. I agree with that basic ratio, as long as we keep the numbers approximate. Some players can turn only 75 degrees, and others 110 – it depends on individual flexibility. Big hitters such as John Daly turn more than 90 degrees. But even the pros turn less as they get older. Roughly speaking, the hips will turn half the amount that the upper torso does.

Below: Practise with all your clubs hitting a variety of shots. This keeps it interesting, helps you to become more creative and encourages you to play and learn a variety of shots.

How to practise

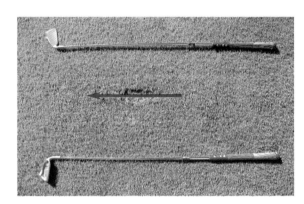

Good = straight shot.

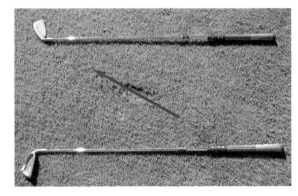

In-to-out = slice or push.

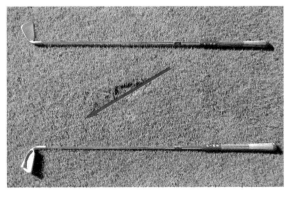

Out-to-in = hook or push

Above: Learn from your divot pattern – with clubs lined up on the ground it's easy to see if your swing path at impact is good or bad.

Chapter 7

CHIPPING AND PITCHING

◆◆◆◆◆

*Devote 50 per cent of your
practice time to these shots and
your scores will improve
dramatically.*

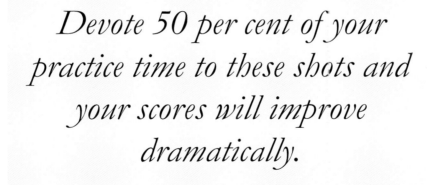

CHIPPING AND PITCHING

◆ ◆ ◆ ◆ ◆

Have you ever played a round with a golf pro? If you have, you know what separates his or her game from yours. No, it's not that the professional golfer is generally two clubs better than you, that they can hit a driver nearly 300 yards, or even that their putting stroke is just that much more silky.

YOU KNOW the real difference. What makes the pro a better player is their short game. Put another way, it's how they correct errant shots. How they get the ball up and down for par after making that occasional, but inevitable, mistake. Meanwhile, when you go into a bunker, miss the green by a few feet, or face an awkward 40-yard (37m) pitch, you know you're probably heading for bogey (one over par) – at best.

The same holds true for the pros out on the various tours around the world. Think of today's leading stars, and who do you come up with? Men – and these days increasingly women – who combine awesome power off the tee with an exquisite short game. Pros like Tiger Woods, Ernie Els, David Duval, Colin Montgomerie, Laura Davies, Annika Sorenstam and Karrie Webb.

They're all considered 'long', but also have 'touch' around the greens.

THE REAL SECRET

Now you know the real secret of golf. In this chapter, and the following two (Bunker Play and Putting), I will show you how to play better from close in, a skill which can dramatically lower your scores.

But there's a catch. You'll have to practise these shots more than you probably do now, because here is where feel, and to some extent, imagination come into play. That does not come easily, though I guarantee that any extra time you spend perfecting these shots will more than pay off in the long run.

As Gary Player – one of the great short-game artists of all time – often says: 'The more I practise, the more I get lucky.'

THE STANDARD PITCH SHOT

This is a crucial shot for the average golfer for all the reasons stated above, but for one more in particular. Most high- to medium-

Below left: Pros often carry different types of wedges from the rest of their irons (3–9 irons). These wedges are often made of softer metal to help control the golf ball from short range.

Below: There are even different shafts made specially for wedges that are stiff flex and that maximize the feel of the clubhead.

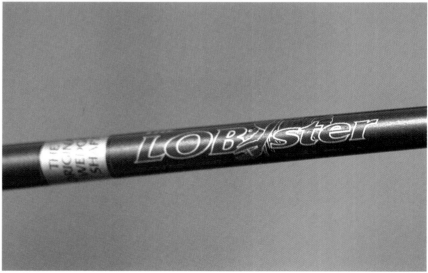

range handicap players will generally miss at least 50-60 per cent of greens in regulation, and might have problems hitting the green in two on long par fours and certainly most par fives.

In each situation, the golfer is often faced with a third shot which a pro never has to play, which quite literally accounts for the 18 or so extra strokes that the average club player is given in the form of a handicap before his or her first tee shot on the first hole.

But here is where you can cut that margin down and start threatening the club championship, or at least move up in your local rankings. With a solid pitching stroke, you can start turning bogeys into pars, and pars into birdies.

FLOATING PITCH

How many times have you found yourself with 200 or more yards (185+m) to an elevated green for your second shot on those

Right: Ball position will vary depending on the height that you require on the pitch shot.

Right: The chip and run shot can be used if no hazards lie between you and your target.

Below: Practice will help you determine the length of swing required for various distances.

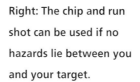

long par fours? And how many times have you faced an 85-100 yard (78–91m) shot on a par five for your third?

In the first case, most golfers would be advised to forget trying to hit the green in two and put that problematic fairway wood back in the bag, opting instead to hit a comfortable 7- or 8-iron to a spot around 100 yards (91m) or less into the green. Alternatively, with the modern development of utility woods, other players may opt to try a 7- or 9-wood and try to land within 40-60 yards (37–55m).

In both cases, you are now ready to float a high pitch shot onto the short grass. With practice, you should be able to land that pitch close enough to the pin to have a chance at making the putt.

PREPARATION FOR THE PITCH SHOT

◆ ◆ ◆ ◆ ◆

The pitch shot is really just a miniature version of a full swing. The ball is hit high because of the loft of the clubhead – usually travelling between about 35 and 100 yards (32 to 91 m) – and goes further in the air than it does along the ground.

THE MOST commonly used clubs to play the shot – depending on the distance to carry – are a sand wedge, pitching wedge or 9-iron. In recent years, many golfers have also added a lob wedge to their bag, which is ideal for shorter pitches off a good lie.

SHORT BUT SWEET

Now for the tricky part, and the reason why you must spend more time practising this shot than most others. The pitch is hit with an abbreviated version of the full swing, but the ball must still be hit firmly.

Put another way, although you are not swinging the club as far back as you would for a normal shot, you must still accelerate at the bottom of the swing, just as you would for a normal hit!

Without an authoritative swing, you will pull your punch, and the result will be a disastrous hit, a shot skulled over the green or one that trips along the grass seeking out a hazard. Now, instead of that par or birdie you envisioned, you're looking at bogey, double bogey, or even worse.

As a result, many golfers fear the pitch shot as much as any other in the game. But there's no reason for that fear if you understand how to execute the pitch.

THE STANDARD SET-UP

The key to making a good pitch shot is first to set-up well to the ball. Here, the stance is

Set up with your ball in the centre of your stance and your hips and feet pointing slightly left of the target (open stance); your shoulders should remain parallel to the ball-to-target line. Your hands should be ahead of the golf ball and you can choke down on the club (by how much depends on the length of the shot).

Pitch shot technique

also a miniaturized version of what we use for a longer iron or wood, with some important differences.

The first difference is that the stance is 'open', which means you pull your lead foot back from parallel to the target line by a few inches. At the same time, the back foot, hips, chest and shoulders remain square, or parallel to the ball-to-target line.

The second difference is that the stance is narrower, with the outside of the feet at about shoulder-width for the average pitch. You'll remember that for a 5-iron, an imaginary line would run from the outside of your shoulders down to the inside of your heels, this distance widening slightly for the woods.

The third difference is that you position your hands in front of the ball, and that you choke down slightly on the club, leaving about two inches (5cm) of the grip protruding from the top of your linked hands.

WEIGHT AND POSTURE

Now you are ready to distribute your weight according to the type of shot you are about to play. If you are hitting a pitch from 80 yards (73m) or more to the green, you should favour the left side with about 55 per cent of your weight, and the right with 45

per cent. If the shot is from 35-70 yards (32–64m) out, then the weight is even more towards the left foot, at about 60/40 ratio.

As for posture, that is determined by the club you have selected for the shot. With a sand wedge, for instance, you will be more bent over than if you were using a 9-iron, because the wedge has a shorter shaft. Therefore, you will need to sit back more – or stick out your rear end – to keep your balance throughout the swing, simply because your spine angle is more inclined.

BALL POSITION

Where do you put the ball for a standard pitch shot?

Position it in the middle of your stance or even slightly further back, depending on how high you want the ball to fly. I shall explain this further in another chapter – along with variations on the standard pitch, such as the lob over a hazard, the low-flying pitch under the wind and pitching from the rough.

But for the average pitch, setting the ball halfway between the feet is the ideal.

Above and below: When you play the pitch, your weight should favour the left with less weight transfer. This will help you control the shot and get the ball close to your target.

MASTERING THE PITCH SHOT

◆ ◆ ◆ ◆ ◆

Now that I have shown you how to assume the proper set-up for the pitch shot, let's take a look at the basic swing action.

THE TECHNIQUE used for a pitch shot is very similar to the normal golf swing but there is less weight transfer, the back and throughswings are more compact and the emphasis is on accuracy.

Your left hand is one of the keys to the throughswing. This hand must stay ahead of the clubface, then remain ahead of the right hand for as long as possible. At impact, keep your left wrist firm – but not rigid – and focus on striking the back of the ball. It's important not to scoop or chop at the ball as you move forward into a balanced finish.

GAINING FEEL

The standard pitch calls for about a three-quarter backswing, and a follow-through of equal length. But the shorter the pitch, the shorter the backswing and follow-through. That is where 'feel' comes into play and this is a skill that cannot necessarily be taught easily. That's why you must practise this shot

as often as possible to get the hang of it, while also fighting any tendency to decelerate the clubhead at impact.

Try hitting pitches at a variety of distances when you go to the range, picking out a target at 35 yards (32m), then 50 (46m), 70 (64m) and so on – until you can comfortably land the ball to within 'makeable' putting distance. Or set up an open umbrella – upside down, top spike into the ground – in your backyard or garden, and pitch balls into that.

VARYING THE LENGTH

Another key to varying the length of the shot is to narrow your stance slightly for the shortest shots. This naturally cuts down on your turn, while keeping most of your weight on the left side will also help produce the desired effect.

It can also be useful to imagine a clock mounted behind you, and hit different increments on that clockface for each shot.

Placing your hands down the grip is one way of controlling distance on your pitch.

Good tempo is crucial in mastering the pitch. The first move should be low and slow.

Tempo is key

Left: The length of your backswing will be the governing factor as to how far you will hit the ball. When you are practising these shots, experiment with differing lengths of backswing and note how far the ball travels.

Left: The length of your follow-through should mirror the length of your backswing. This will ensure you don't quit on the shot.

Below: As with all shots, a balanced finish indicates a controlled swing and will help you gain consistency.

For example, a three-quarter swing for a pitch of 85 to 100 yards (78 to 91m) would mean the club stops at about 10 or 11 o'clock on the backswing, and hits the 1 to 2 o'clock mark on the follow-through. A shot of about 50 yards (46m) would mean hitting the 9 o'clock slot on the backswing, and the 3 o'clock mark on the throughswing.

TEMPO IS THE KEY

Even with the shortest pitches, you must be positive or you will commit a multitude of sins. Maintaining a smooth, even tempo is a key factor in the pitch shot. Despite the compactness of the swing, a steady pace is necessary to ensure that the clubhead swings firmly through the ball, just as with any other shot – but perhaps more so with the short irons.

Finally, don't forget what I told you in the chapters on preparation and the pre-shot routine. With pitch shots, it's essential to 'visualize' the shot before playing it. Pick a spot on the green and imagine the ball flying through the air, then landing softly and rolling up to the flagstick.

Now you're ready to hit a solid pitch and shave strokes off your score.

CHIPPING

◆ ◆ ◆ ◆ ◆

What if I guaranteed that you could save six strokes a round by learning just one basic technique? That's right, tomorrow you can finally break 90, 80 or even…well, not so fast. It will not happen tomorrow, because the technique I am now going to explain how to execute – like the pitch – demands a few weeks of practice to learn. But compared to perfecting the full swing, it is easy.

I'T'S CALLED chipping, perhaps the most humble – and yet important – stroke in the game. And even though it's often been said that you drive for show and putt for dough, few golfers consistently hit the green in the required one, two, or three strokes regularly to threaten par.

However, as we get better and better, we do get closer to the greens with most shots – and that's where chipping comes into play.

surface. The goal is to get the ball close enough with your chip to have a tap-in with your putter on the next shot.

Along the way, you might even hole a few chips, and then that miracle round you have always dreamed about may start to become a very real possibility.

This is another shot that calls for a maximum of 'feel' and imagination. And that means practice, practice…and more practice.

MAXIMUM FEEL

The chip is a stroke played anywhere from a few feet to 30 yards (27m) off the putting

IN A NUTSHELL

Here's how you do it. Any club from a 5-iron to the sand wedge can be used for chipping, depending on the position and lie of the ball relative to the pin, the amount of green you have to work with, and whatever ground you have to carry the ball over to get it rolling on the green. That's the key thing. Get it rolling on the green.

Your first objective is to choose your weapon.

PRO TIP

In recent years, golfers such as Tiger Woods have popularized the idea of using a 3- or 5-wood in certain situations to chip from off the green. Woods uses this club to keep the ball even lower than when chipping with an iron, reducing any risk of a bobble or bounce with the slight initial elevation on a chip shot. The key is to be confident and take an even, smooth stroke.

When you're practising, try rolling the ball underarm towards your target. This will help you visualize the shot rolling towards the hole.

As Ray Floyd, one of the finest short game players ever and winner of both the US Open and Masters tournaments, said in his book *From 60 Yards In*, this shot 'is simply putting with a lofted club'. Essentially, that's the whole idea in a nutshell, and you'll see why as I describe the technique in the next four pages.

JUDGMENT CALL

First, visualize your shot. If you are on the fringe of the green, with say about 30 feet (9m) to the cup, pick a spot where you want the ball to land. Take into consideration the break on the putting surface and any other factors that might come into play – such as the slope or the wind.

The key to executing this shot successfully is your ability to judge distance and how the ball will roll, just as if you were about to hit a putt.

Again, this will take some preliminary practice to get a feel for if you are a beginner, while the more experienced player will have the advantage of being able to conjure up the memory of a similar shot from the past.

But a good rule of thumb is that when you use the standard chipping stroke, and strike the ball with a medium to short iron, the ball will travel about a third of the way to the target in the air and the rest of the way along the ground – depending on the situation.

Conversely if you throw the ball in the air, you inevitably find it more difficult to get the ball close to the hole.

A feel shot

The chip shot can be played from a few feet to up to 30 yards (27m) off the putting surface. When playing the shot, your head should stay very still and your weight should favour the left foot. Feel is the essential factor when playing this shot, and feel can only be developed through practice.

THE BASIC CHIP SHOT

◆ ◆ ◆ ◆ ◆

Now it's time to select your club. Some golfers like to use the same iron for all chip shots, and that's often a pitching wedge or a 7-iron. If you are a beginner, that's probably not a bad idea.

BUT IF you have played the game for a time, you will know that each club produces a slightly different effect, and that club selection is crucial. Picking the right club – in combination with a solid chipping stroke – can make the difference between a long, difficult putt for par versus a short, easy one.

In general, the farther away from the green your ball is lying, the more lofted a club you need to carry the intervening grass or hazard. The added height such clubs naturally put on the flight of the ball will also help impart the backspin needed to check the ball when it hits the green and prevent you shooting past the hole.

ELEVATION AND ROLL

In other words, as I described in the first example above, if you are on the fringe – say only about two to three feet (c.1m) off the green – and the pin is about 30 feet (9m) away, a 6- or 7-iron is ideal, since it will elevate the ball onto the edge of the green, and then let it roll the remaining distance like a well-struck putt.

However, if you are about 15 feet (5m) further back, you'll probably need a wedge with enough loft to keep the ball in the air about the same distance, and then land the ball on the green and let it roll up to the hole.

Any farther back than that and you would be playing, in effect, a pitch or possibly a lob shot, which will be described in later chapters.

THE SET-UP

Now you're ready to take your set-up. Position your feet about a foot (30cm) apart in an open stance, angling the front foot out some 20 degrees – just like you did for a pitch – while keeping the rest of your body and the clubhead parallel to the target line. Now concentrate most of your weight on the front foot and position the ball towards the back of your stance, just inside the big toe of your right foot.

Choke down on the club until your lower hand is at the bottom of the grip near the shaft – you can use your putting grip (see Chapter 9) if that feels more comfortable – and push your hands ahead of the ball, so you can hit the shot with a slightly descending contact.

Choke down on the club and ensure that your hands are ahead of the clubhead at address.

Take the club away with the arms and hands.

Regulate the length of swing in relation to the distance of the ball from the target.

Keep your hands ahead of the clubhead and swing through with the back of the left hand moving towards the target.

Setting up a chip shot

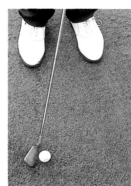

Left: Set-up – begin with your normal pre-shot routine: aim the club, align the body, position the ball, grip and posture.

BRUSH OFF

Finally, in order to execute the shot, think about your putting stroke. Keeping your hands, wrists and arms fairly passive, start the backswing with the same, smooth pendulum motion – arms forming a triangle with the shoulders as the base – that you use for putting.

As you come through the ball, just brush it off the grass, making sure your follow-through is the same length as your abbreviated backswing. And just as you do while putting, keep your head down until the ball is well on its way to the hole.

With any luck, and a solid chipping stroke, by the time you look up, the ball will be disappearing from sight and you'll have a par or birdie on your card.

Right: You will be confronted with many situations where a sand or lob wedge are necessary to lift the ball over a hazard and land the ball softly.

A putter is a real option when you are close to the green. Remember that the grass you're putting through should not be too thick and it must be dry.

Chipping with a wood

This is the 'Tiger' shot. Played from just off the green, the 3- or 5-wood can be highly effective in lifting the ball over the apron and rolling the ball towards the hole.

Practice makes perfect.

Chapter 8

BUNKER PLAY

◆ ◆ ◆ ◆ ◆

The bunker shot — which strikes terror into most high handicappers — is actually the easiest shot in golf since it leaves the player the highest margin for error.

GREENSIDE BUNKER PLAY

◆ ◆ ◆ ◆ ◆

On most weekends, my golf club is crowded with people using the driving range, playing the course or enjoying a meal in the restaurant. But the area in front of the clubhouse, where we have a practice bunker and green, is usually deserted — so much so that I often park my car nearby since it gives me easy access to my office.

I KNOW I needn't worry about stray golf balls. Parking there is practically safer than on the street near my own house, since hardly anyone ever uses that bunker. So far, I've yet to suffer a dent, scratch or smashed window from what would be only a slightly errant shot out of the sand.

MENTAL CAPITULATION

Now why is that? Especially since many golfers are terrified of landing in sand traps, and, once there, are often ready to capitulate mentally. Assuming they will not get up and down for par, they have already resigned themselves to making bogey or worse.

In this chapter, I'll show you how to gain more confidence when you end up in sand by demonstrating what is really one of the easiest shots in the game. As with any fear or phobia, taking the mystery out of things can go a long way towards solving the problem.

For proof, ask any pro or low handicapper whether he'd rather be in a trap or in the rough, and he will tell you it's no contest. If you're going to make a mistake around the greens — and you will during any round — sand is the best place to find yourself.

From a bunker, you have a large margin of error, you can usually put some spin on the ball, and your chances of getting down in two shots should be better than 50/50.

But like chipping and pitching, practice is the key to mastering this vital shot — although once I convince you of that, I may have to start moving my car to a less convenient parking spot.

Taking the fear out of bunker play comes down to practice. If you fear this shot, read the next few pages and then stay in the bunker until you believe me.

Getting a feel of distance, where you will land the ball, and how the ball will fly is especially important before going into the sand, as often you may be unable to see the flag when playing from a deep bunker.

PREPARATION

The key to playing successfully from the sand is to be positive before you even step into the bunker. How many times have you left the ball in the trap once – or even twice – or bladed it over the other side of the green and into more trouble?

Being afraid of this shot will paralyze your swing and stifle your momentum. And, as with most shots around the green, a smooth but crisp tempo is essential. When a golfer goes into a mini-panic, or is unduly worried, he often fails to swing through the ball, which is the cardinal sin in bunker play. Leaving the clubhead in the sand ensures the ball will stay there as well.

SHOT REHEARSAL

Let's go back to the idea of always rehearsing a difficult shot before hitting it. In the case of bunker shots, this takes on added importance, since this is a unique shot, and it is against the rules of golf to ground your club in the hazard before you take your bunker shot.

First, visualize the shot before getting into the sand – actually conjuring up a mental picture of how the shot works (which I'll explain in a moment) – then imagining the clubhead sliding into the sand, and the

ball lifting up on a wedge of sand to the green and trickling towards the hole.

Secondly, I would suggest that you take a few practice swings outside the bunker, using the same set-up and swingpath you will use once inside. When you do go into the bunker, move your feet from side to side to give yourself a firm footing as well as enabling you to assess the depth and texture of the sand.

Now it's time to climb into the bunker and go for that par.

Basics of set-up

Your feet and hips should point left of the target (open stance).

Position your ball on the inside of your left heel.

Keep your weight principally on your left foot throughout your stroke.

THE SAND WEDGE

◆ ◆ ◆ ◆ ◆

In the 1930s the legendary Gene Sarazen invented the sand wedge, a club that changed the way golf was played. Before that, golfers had to improvize when they found themselves in a bunker, using a variety of clubs in a variety of ways to escape from trouble. So consider yourself lucky to enjoy the benefits of the Squire's creation, and don't neglect to take advantage of it.

THE SAND wedge will always do the job in a bunker if you know how to utilize it, which may seem like an obvious and even laboured point. But it isn't. Many golfers never practise this shot. As a result, when they are forced to hit out of sand, they have no idea what this unique club can do, nor how to make it do what Sarazen had in mind – even more than 70 years later!

More surprisingly, some golfers do not even carry a sand wedge in their bags. If you are one of them, remedy that situation immediately – although I would hasten to add that you should first consult with a PGA pro before making a purchase. Choosing a sand wedge with the correct design for the conditions where you play is essential – they do vary.

UP AND OVER

The sand wedge should not to be confused with the pitching wedge, although many beginners tend to mix up the two clubs. With 56 degrees of loft, the sand wedge is designed to lift the ball upwards and impart spin, which also makes it handy on the fairway from 80 yards (73m) and less to the green. In addition, there is a wide flange on the sole of this specialized wedge that helps encourage the clubhead to slide through the sand and prevents the leading edge of the blade from digging in – what golf pros refer to as 'bounce'.

I believe the most important aspect of the bunker shot is the follow-through. Too many players stop at impact, so don't get trapped – make a big throughswing taking lots of sand.

Bunker play

That's important because the bunker shot is the only one in golf where we do not strike the ball directly. Instead, the golfer hits one to two inches (2.5 to 5cm) behind the ball, the clubhead passing through the sand and under the ball to lift the ball up and over the forward lip of the bunker and onto the green.

AGGRESSIVE STROKE

Notice I said that the clubhead passes under the ball! In effect, it is the momentum created by a positive stroke that is transferred from the club to sand to the ball. Thus, the sand wedge allows us to hit an attacking shot that imparts spin and stops the ball quickly on the green.

GETTING OUT OF A RUT

A forerunner to Gene Sarazen's modern invention of the sand wedge was a variation on the mid-19th-century club known as a 'cleek' (there were also driving and even putting cleeks), which had a lofted iron blade. Used to play off tight lies and sand, the cleek was ideal for hitting out of cart tracks! In those days, especially along the links land of Scotland, the townspeople had the right of way to cart off sand, gravel and seaweed, and whatever they could salvage from items routinely washed up on shore from passing ships.

Make your mark – in practice!

When you're practising (you're not allowed to do this in a game), draw a line in the sand a couple of inches either side of the golf ball. Once you've hit the shot, ensure that all the sand was taken.

But how is it possible to hit aggressively, never touch the ball – and yet get it to travel only a few feet with backspin?

That's where the set-up comes into play. And once you master that, hitting the basic sand shot should become second nature.

Removing sand before the ball is your safety margin that will guarantee success playing from the sand.

The ball is lifted by removing a wedge of sand underneath it

THE BASIC SAND SHOT

◆ ◆ ◆ ◆ ◆

Assume an open stance — with feet, knees, hips and shoulders angled left of the target line — and with the clubface open to your stance line, but square to the target. The ball should be positioned in the middle of your stance, with the majority of your weight (about 60 per cent) resting on the front foot.

AS WE shall see later, depending on the height you need to achieve to clear the forward lip of the bunker, and the pin placement, these alignments will differ slightly. But, as a general rule, the more height and spin you need, the more you should open your stance and the clubface while also moving the ball farther forward in your stance.

DIGGING IN

Now give yourself a secure, balanced footing by digging your spikes into the sand, twisting your feet until your movement is restricted, the sand about as high as the soles of your shoes. This will also provide more clues about the texture and density of the sand.

With practice and experience, you will learn how to adjust your swing for differing conditions. For instance, with wet, coarse sand, your ball will come out hot and fast, so you may have to shorten your swing. On the other hand, fine, powdery sand will demand more speed and a longer swing to avoid burying the clubhead. I'll go into more detail about this later.

GRIP AND CHOKE

Now you are ready to grip the club, and although I recommend using your normal grip, some golfers prefer to weaken theirs for a sand shot — to ensure the clubhead stays open. I believe this is a personal preference, but if you normally use a slightly strong grip to help avoid a slice and get more distance, I'd suggest moving to a neutral grip for bunker play to avoid any tendency to dig the clubhead into the sand.

The sand wedge is shaped differently from other clubs in the set as it is made with a flange on the sole to prevent the club digging in.

Far left: Sand wedges do vary in shape, some having a larger flange than others. It pays to hit some different trial sand wedges and find one that suits your game.

Left: Taking your stance in a bunker requires you to dig your feet in. Therefore you need to grip down the club to compensate.

Left: Move your feet in the sand to get a firm footing.
Below left: If you need extra height, open your clubface.

Below: Confidence is the key to good bunker play. Keep your tempo smooth, take sand before the ball, and follow-though.

Bunker play

But whatever grip you use, choke down on the club. By twisting your feet into the sand, you have shortened the distance between your hands and the ball, and, as with any shot, you will want to maintain a full extension of your left arm through impact.

POSITIVE HIT

Finally, you're ready to hover the club over a spot on the sand about an inch and a half (4cm) behind the ball, and start your backswing along the line formed by your feet – or along an out-to-in swingpath.

Break your wrists early and take the club back smoothly – good tempo is the key to any bunker shot. As for the length of swing, that will vary with the type of shot required. Consider a three-quarter backswing as about average.

As you begin your throughswing, keep in mind that the crucial element in any bunker shot is not to leave the clubhead in the sand. Hit with a positive blow, slicing through the sand to a full, finished position.

If you do that, I guarantee that the ball will rise high out of the bunker and land softly on the green.

SLOPING BUNKER LIES

◆ ◆ ◆ ◆ ◆

The round, bowl-like design of most bunkers means we usually are lucky enough at least to find a level lie, since the ball will often trickle down to rest on the flat part of the sand at the bottom of the hazard. But if the golf ball ends up parked on a slope, we have to make some adjustments before we can hit it with the standard technique.

ALWAYS ALIGN your body with the slope. That's the starting point for these types of shots. On an upslope, the ball will travel higher, but cover less distance than one played from a level lie. Confidence is a vital ingredient here, since this shot calls for hitting with a longer swing than normal from a bunker, so the ball will not be left short.

The opposite line of flight will characterize a lie where the ball is resting on the downslope. This is a tougher shot because the golf ball will tend to come out lower and run farther on the green.

Your backswing may even be impeded by the rear edge of the bunker. Again, approaching this situation with confidence, and a firm grasp of the proper technique, is vital to executing a good shot.

UPSLOPES

Set up with an open stance, the face of the sand wedge square to the target and your hands just ahead of the clubhead, making sure the ball is just opposite your left heel. With your weight concentrated mostly on your back foot – which should be securely dug in – set your shoulders in line with the

With the ball lying beneath my feet, I concentrate on stability in my lower body and staying down with ball. Remember, be positive with your stroke.

Sloping lie

Above: Follow through.

Left: If you're on a uphill slope, your shoulders at set-up should follow the line of the slope. Take a firm footing.

contour of the bunker and think about swinging up along the slope.

Start your backswing with an even tempo, making a fuller swing than normal. As you start the throughswing, maintain that pace, letting your left wrist and arm lead the club. Hitting the sand about an inch and a half (4cm) behind the ball, avoid the tendency to stab at the ball that this sort of lie seems to induce, especially in the less experienced, or jittery, golfer.

Remember, the slope and the loft on your clubhead will send the ball high over the nearside bank – you do not have to try and help it along! But the slope may also prevent a full follow-through – though in this case, that's not a problem. Your momentum should carry the ball up and onto the green.

DOWNSLOPES

Again, set your shoulders with the slope, this time angling them downward, with your weight firmly on the front foot and both feet dug well into the sand for balance. Open the clubface as much as possible to gain height on the ball and try to stop it more quickly on the green. Your stance should be open and the ball positioned from the middle to the

back of your stance, depending on the severity of the slope.

On the backswing, break your wrists immediately and lift the club up sharply. This will help you to clear the back of the hazard and provide a steep angle of attack on the ball to force it up. Remember, you can incur a two-stroke penalty by grounding the club or hitting the sand on the backswing.

On the throughswing, hit into the sand about one inch (2.5cm) behind the ball and pull the club through to a high finish in order to ensure that you have lifted the ball up and over the face of the bunker. The ball will probably run on landing more than you would like, but at least you will be out and on the putting surface.

STAYING POSITIVE

Hitting from an upslope naturally makes the ball fly higher and stop shorter, so you can play this shot more positively than the downhill shot. Take a positive swing and watch the ball shoot up towards the top of the flagstick, then fall like a rock to the putting surface.

This is one of the most difficult shots in golf. Practise this shot from various situations and lies until you have the confidence at least to get on the green.

PLUGGED LIES AND LONG BUNKER SHOTS

◆ ◆ ◆ ◆ ◆

Golf balls have a nasty habit of finding fiendish ways to plug in bunkers, and playing them from such a lie makes sand shots that much harder. But with the right approach, you can extract a ball from almost any plugged lie – even ones that have settled into the sand so far you can barely see the top of the ball!

BUT REMEMBER – as with any shot out of the sand – you are never striking at the ball directly. Rather, you must find a way to let the club get into the sand *and* under the ball, then lift the ball out on a bed of sand, somewhat like blasting your way out of trouble.

With a normal lie in the sand, you can achieve both height and backspin this way. But the opposite is true for most plugged lies. The ball will come out low and with topspin – since you'll often be hitting it with a closed clubface – which makes it run when it lands. Try to allow for that, if possible.

SHARPLY DOWN

Many plugged lies occur on the front edge of a bunker, when we come up short trying to hit a pin positioned close to the near edge of the green. For this shot, set up as you did for a ball on an upslope, with your shoulders parallel to the slope. Square up or slightly close the clubface and hit sharply down, causing it to enter the sand just behind the ball. You may leave the club in the sand with this shot, but if struck properly the ball will pop up and might even stop quickly on the green.

For a more conventional plugged lie elsewhere in the bunker, try to hit sharply down just behind the ball with the clubface square or closed, and try to limit your throughswing so the clubhead does not pass your hands. In this case, the ball will again rise up on the sand, but roll farther on the green.

Your grip pressure on all shots from plugged lies should be firmer than normal, to allow for the harder impact of the clubhead hitting into the sand.

LONG BUNKER SHOTS

It's often said that a bunker shot of 40 yards (37m) or more is among the toughest in golf. That's because it's so hard to get the correct feel for the distance the ball must travel, no matter what the lie in the bunker or position of the pin on the green.

The plugged lie is not as difficult as it looks. Keep your shoulders and clubhead square to the target and hit down into the sand. The ball will pop up but allow for the ball to roll, as backspin cannot be applied from this lie.

Long approach bunker shot

I try to play this shot as close to a normal hit off the fairway as possible, much like a pitch. First, consider the height of the lip of the bunker. If it is low enough, and the ball is sitting back far enough, you might consider using a pitching wedge, a 9-iron, or even an 8- if you think it will clear the edge of the hazard.

Square up the blade of your club, play the ball off your left heel, and think about nipping it cleanly off the surface of the sand. Then swing with conviction!

GIVEN A CHANCE

The same applies to fairway bunkers (which I cover more extensively in Chapter 11), where the shot might be 150 to over 200 yards (137 to 183m). In such a case, and with an ideal lie, you might even try hitting a wood. Again, the key is experience and practice. The first few times you try shots like these, the results might be near-disaster.

Remember, the first priority in hitting any bunker shot is to get out! If the ball is plugged, too close to the lip for comfort, or the rim of the trap is too high to clear, simply forget about reaching the green and go back to your sand wedge. Then try to land your ball somewhere on the fairway that will give you a good second shot, perhaps playing the ball out of the bunker sideways or even backwards. That way, you will at least give yourself a chance with your next shot.

When playing a plugged bunker shot, keep the clubface square, allow for the ball to roll on the green and hit down into the sand. Oh, and good luck!

The plugged bunker shot

Chapter 9

PUTTING

•••••

Putting accounts for at least 50 per cent of the game, or a possible 36 strokes taken in an even-par round of 72. Here's how to start working towards cutting your score dramatically by more effective putting.

PUTTING

◆ ◆ ◆ ◆ ◆

Drive for show and putt for dough. If a more familiar axiom exists in golf, I don't know what it is. But this one does bear repeating, because like many axioms it contains a crucial element of truth. Putting adds up to 50 per cent of the game, or 36 of the 72 strokes you might take in a round of even par.

PUT ANOTHER way, if you routinely miss just a handful of makeable putts per round, it will mean a major difference to your score and handicap. Instead of playing to an average of around 18 strokes over par, you are in the very mediocre range of the mid-20s duffer. So rather than consistently threatening – or actually scoring – in the 80s, you're struggling to break 100!

VITAL GAME

Does that sound like your game? If it does, then this chapter is for you – not to mention everyone else who currently plays the game of golf. Name the last player to win a major tournament on any tour on the planet who did not putt well. Or name a great player from any era – from Harry Vardon to Tiger Woods and Colin Montgomerie – who was a poor putter.

Putting is the most vital game within the game of golf, and all the great players are great putters.

CONSISTENT STROKE

Putting well demands a precise physical and mental approach that in some ways is far more demanding than any other shot in golf. As I have stressed in this book, the secret to playing well is having a 'repeatable' swing. The same holds true when you take the putter from the bag.

Simply put, there is little margin for error in this phase of the game. Learning to strike the ball with the same, consistently smooth putting stroke is the only way to start really improving your scores and consistently playing well.

Beyond good mechanics, you also need feel and touch, plus the ability to judge distance. In addition, you must bring that other, less tangible, quality to your putting game that I have also mentioned before – confidence.

NATURAL OUTCOME

The object of every putt is to hole the ball, or at least to leave the next putt within the 'gimme' range. Anything more than two putts on any green is a waste of strokes that will have a significant impact on your scorecard, and may well influence your mood on the next tee with negative consequences.

So let's work first on how to putt more successfully. Once you can do that, the

A consistent, repeatable putting stroke is just as important as a good golf swing. Time devoted to this part of your game will be well rewarded.

natural outcome will be an increase in your confidence. Putt better, and you'll gain confidence. Gain confidence, and you'll putt better. It's a magic circle. In other words, if you approach every putt thinking you can make it, you're halfway there.

Bob Charles – the left-hander whom Jack Nicklaus once called one of the greatest putters ever – said that his putter was the 'life-line' to his game, and the key to every victory he ever achieved – with confidence providing the crucial link between technique and execution.

Remember, the last stroke you take on every hole is a putt, and in many cases – whether it drops in the hole or not – it's often the most significant.

Left: When lifting the ball out of the hole do so at arm's length so as to avoid unnecessary wear around the hole.

Below: One of the reasons that soft spikes are often insisted upon is that metal spikes can cause marks on the green that affect adversely the roll of the ball.

Left: Never up, never in – it's a common saying but so true. Always aim to roll the ball past the hole.

THE PUTTING GRIP

◆ ◆ ◆ ◆ ◆

Golfers use a variety of grips when they putt. Whether pro or amateur, the grips of players I teach are almost as individual as each golfer is. Some use the same grip they employ for the woods and irons – whether the Vardon, interlocking or ten-finger 'baseball' grip.

OTHERS REVERSE the position of their hands on the club, which is called 'cross-handed' (or 'cack-handed'). A few even putt from the opposite side to the one they use for their normal golf swing. In addition, golfers may choose to set their grip strong, weak or neutral.

COMMON AND SOUND

But the most common grip I see used today is what is called the 'reverse overlap'. It's the one I prefer, and the one I recommend to most golfers I teach. It is the most fundamentally sound putting grip, and offers the average player the highest chance of success. With this grip, the hands are positioned on the club in a way that naturally binds them together as a unit, while removing any tendency to get 'wristy' in the putting motion.

In the reverse overlap, the palms are positioned in opposition to each other, which also provides stability. Combined with the proper set-up and stroke, this grip gives the golfer the best chance of keeping his putter square – or moving it straight along the imaginary target line to propel the ball forwards on the correct line to the hole.

ASSUMING A GRIP

Here's how to assume the reverse overlap grip:
• Place your left hand against the grip handle of the putter, leaving a gap at the top of at least an inch (2.5cm). Now grip the club lightly with the middle, third and little fingers of your left hand. Keeping your forefinger off the shaft, point your thumb straight down the grip.
• Place all four fingers of your right hand on the club, aligning the grip along the pads at the base of the fingers. The little finger of the right hand should be resting snugly against the middle finger of the left hand and the right thumb should also be pointing straight down the grip handle.
• Finally, position your left forefinger in one of the three following ways:
1. Around the little finger of the right hand.
2. Crooked around the ring finger of the right hand – overlapping the last two fingers.

Take time forming your putting grip. Just as in the full swing, the placement of your hands makes a big difference to your final stroke.

The putting grip

 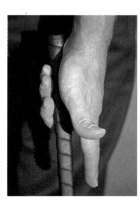   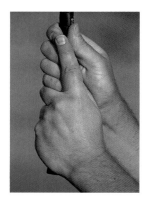

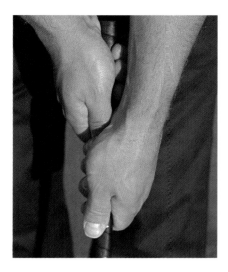

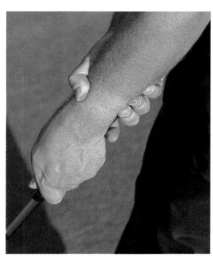

Right: The cross-handed grip – the right hand is below the left hand – is worth trying.

Far right: The Langer grip, developed by Bernhard and used to great effect. Only try it if you're desperate!

3. Or run it straight down across all the fingers of the right hand.

Any of the variations described in this final step will form a good reverse overlap grip. Try each one to see which suits you. But remember, only do that when practising. Never experiment on the golf course!

GRIP PRESSURE

Again, grip pressure is a matter of individual choice.

Tom Watson, one of the best putters ever – even though he's had problems with that aspect of his game in recent years – believes in varying his grip pressure. Watson favours his left hand, so he can guide his stroke with the leading hand. He exerts more grip pressure with the last three fingers of the left hand, plus the index and middle two fingers of the right hand.

Personally I favour keeping the pressure from all the fingers and two thumbs constant throughout the stroke. Hold the club firmly, and yet lightly – much the same way as I recommend you grip both the woods and irons.

FOCUSING GUIDE

When I'm having trouble with my putting, I often try to focus on my left hand for a time, in effect just slightly tightening my grip pressure with that hand in an effort to use it as a guide in stroking the putter towards the hole. I think about keeping it firm throughout the stroke.

Consistency is the key. Experiment with every possible variation in your grip pressure on the practice green. But when putting on the course, make sure you maintain the same pressure throughout the stroke. Any change while playing will distort your feel for the putting motion and may even pull your stroke off-line.

PUTTING YIPS

Some golfers, especially pros and those with more experience, develop the 'putting yips' – a vague, anxiety-related condition that causes a player to stroke across the ball with a short, jerky stab. Often, a golfer can not pinpoint just where or when he or she first developed the problem. But such famous players as Ben Hogan, Tom Watson and Bernhard Langer have known the agony of suffering through the yips at one or more points during their careers. No absolute cure exists for the yips, because the problem is often psychological and far too complex to analyze. However, overcoming the yips is possible, as both Watson and Langer can attest. The first step to a cure is to experiment with several options, at least for a time. The cross-handed grip – reversing the position of the left and right hand on the putter – that Fred Couples has used is worth trying. A broom-handle putter has also helped Langer and Sam Torrance. Of course, it's impossible to estimate how long someone should adopt a novel approach in trying to overcome the yips. Simply consider any method you choose as a way of getting back to some form of normality and re-gaining confidence. Keep in mind as well that the yips can come from having too much intensity over the ball, much like the idea of 'keeping the head still' during the golf swing. Discipline yourself to take one look and then hit. Spending too much time over the ball causes you to freeze up, and then you will barely be able to move, which can produce a very jagged and irregular stroke. Trust your instincts and try to keep it short and sweet. Finally, when you're practising before a round, don't hit 20- and 35-foot putts. Instead, hit several short ones. Putting the ball into the hole is the best way to cure the yips, and the yips tend to affect the short putts more than the long ones. Tom Watson has had the most problems with three- to four-foot putts over the past several years, and the greater majority of golfers suffer from the same malaise, finding it easier to deal with a 40-foot putt than a crucial short one.

THE PUTTING SET-UP

◆ ◆ ◆ ◆ ◆

*The putting stance is another area where golfers show how different —
rather than alike — they can be when playing the game of golf. Some set up
slightly open to the ball, while others use a closed stance. Some bend low,
and some stand almost straight up. The arms may be tucked in or flared
out. The feet may be close together or spread wider than shoulder-width.*

WHY ALL the differences? Because of two factors common to all putting styles. When putting, every golfer tries to get as comfortable over the ball as possible — which, in turn, ought to breed the confidence needed to make the putt.

Secondly, they are trying to position their eyes directly over or just inside the ball-to-target line.

EYES LINED UP

You can argue the merits of the first case — and I shall in a moment — but there is no disputing the second. Unless your eyes are

lined up above the ball or just inside it, it's extremely difficult to stroke the ball successfully on a line to the hole. In the case of right-handers, this means the left eye specifically.

On the other hand, if your eyes are lined up outside the ball, you will get a distorted view of the target line and will probably pull the putter back on an outside path, which may result in a putt missed to the left.

EVERYTHING SQUARE

So how do you position yourself to make the most putts? I'm all for being comfortable over the ball. But unless you can claim

When I practise my stroke, I choose a flat putt and set up guide lines as shown above.

The putting set-up

Left: Alignment of the clubhead is always rule no. 1 – take time to line up your leading edge.

Opposite left: Now ensure your shoulders, hips and feet are parallel to your ball-to-target line.

Opposite right: Finally complete putting your hands on the club in your chosen grip.

almost flawless success with your current set-up position – assuming it's somewhat different from the classic one I'm about to explain – try my way for a time.

In watching Bob Charles and Ben Crenshaw over the years – and now Tiger Woods and Jose-Maria Olazabal – I have become convinced that the best putting stances are those where everything is absolutely square to the ball and line of putt – feet, knees, hips and shoulders.

The ball is forward of mid-stance – or inside the left instep – and the eyes are directly over it, with the arms hanging naturally, forming an almost perfect triangle with the shoulders.

From this position, these pros seem to move the putter effortlessly – first back, and then through the ball – in a rhythmic, pendulum motion. The result? They sink more than their share of putts to capture the big tournaments.

WINNING FORMULA

Here's how to assume that winning formula in your set-up:

• Positioning the ball inside your left heel, set yourself so that your left eye is directly

PUTTING IN A STIFF BREEZE

I always widen my stance – and even crouch a bit – when putting in a stiff wind to gain more stability. If you were taking a full swing with this set-up, it would restrict your turn. But since you're putting, you want to minimize any body motion and anchor yourself against swaying off the ball. By the way, don't underestimate the effect of the wind on the line of your putt. A stiff cross-wind can blow a slowly turning putt off-line by several inches. That's why I always recommend that new golfers hire a caddy when playing links courses, where the wind can be especially tricky. A caddy's advice on how a putt will break in the wind can save you several strokes per round.

over the ball. You can test this by dropping a ball down the sight line of your left eye. If you are lined up correctly, that ball will hit the ball on the ground below you.

• Now do try to get comfortable by letting your arms hang naturally, flexing your knees and bending forwards from the hips. Wiggle your toes inside your shoes until you balance your weight evenly between both feet – with your feet set at a distance of about 12 inches (30cm) apart.

• Finally, align your body parallel to the line of the putt.

Above: Your left eye should be directly above the golf ball – if you drop a ball from your left eye, it should land on the ball below.

THE PUTTING STROKE

◆ ◆ ◆ ◆ ◆

The basic putting stroke is like the motion of a pendulum, with the hands, arms and shoulders moving as one unit. There is no body rotation – the shoulders simply move back and forth. That's why it is important to align yourself correctly at address.

HOWEVER, HERE again many golfers use highly individualistic approaches. Some are very wristy, some jab at the ball and some even hook it across the target line.

I recommend using the pendulum motion to reduce any variables and take your hands out of the game – which, as we have seen from the driver to the sand wedge, increases the chance of a properly executed shot.

As I have stressed all along, in modern golf the hands serve as a conduit, not as the beginning and end of the swing. The pendulum motion is a long, sweeping action that strokes the ball with topspin towards the hole. Because the hands are passive and work together, the tendency to hit or flick at the ball is greatly reduced.

LOW AND SLOW

Here's how it works. Take the putter back with your hands, arms and shoulders working together – firmly but without rigidity – the length of the backstroke dictated by the length of the putt.

The clubhead should come back low and slow, just above the ground, and appear to be moving in a straight line – although it will in fact eventually move slightly inside the line on longer swings.

Developing the stroke

Far left: Keep your arms, hands and shoulders working together. Your putter should be low to the ground – your head must remain very still.

Left: Always accelerate through the ball. Your hands should remain passive throughout – and keep your head still.

Follow the same swingpath into impact – letting the clubhead naturally accelerate from the motion of the swing – until your left shoulder rises slightly and the throughswing is equal in length to the backswing.

The overall feeling should be one of pace, fluidity and rhythm. Never force the pace, or you'll knock the putt off line. You are stroking through the ball, not hitting it!

ANXIOUS LOOKS

Finally, it is important to realize that many golfers almost complete the putting stroke in fine style, but then look up too quickly, anxious to see how their ball is doing. If you do that, you will miss the putt more often than not. It's like failing to reach a good follow-through position on a shot with a longer club. Injecting a note of anxiety into any golf stroke, especially before completion, will inevitably lead to problems.

Never look up until well after striking the ball. This stops your head from lifting or turning. When you raise your head too soon, or too abruptly, you can cause your shoulders to move and so send your putt off the target line.

As your swing the putter forward, allow the left shoulder to rise slightly – keep smooth and listen for the ball to drop. Remember, don't look up too early.

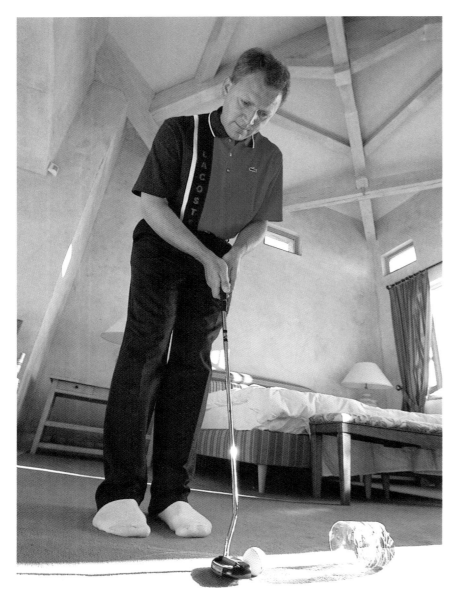

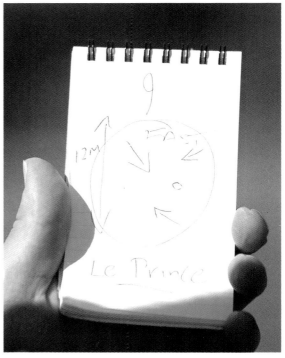

Left: Practise whenever and wherever you get the opportunity – even in the bedroom!

Above: If you have a chance to play a practice round, or you play a course regularly, make some notes about the shape of the green and how the ball rolls.

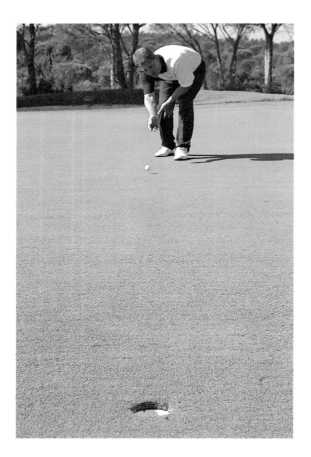

Left: When practising, roll a ball underarm across the green. It helps you to judge distance and pace more accurately.

Right: Practising putting to a tee makes the hole on the course look huge.

Right: A miniature slice – the ball will spin right if you swing out-to-in.

Below: Trapping an object between your arms can help to keep arms, hands and shoulders working together as a unit.

Above: After marking and cleaning the ball, replace the ball with any straight lines parallel to the target line.

Below: Allowing the wrists to flex in the putting stroke is generally disastrous.

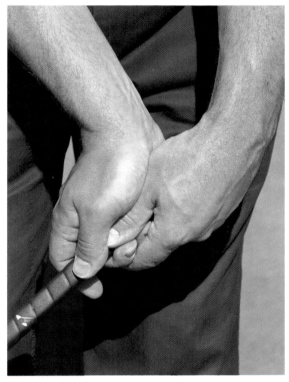

PRO TIP

The great American pro Sam Snead had the classic cure for raising your head too soon after the putting stroke. He advised golfers to listen for the sound of the ball plopping into the hole before they looked up! For those who just cannot wait that long, I recommend at least counting to two before allowing your curiosity to get the better of you.

THE PRE-SHOT ROUTINE FOR PUTTS

◆ ◆ ◆ ◆ ◆

I believe that having a consistent pre-shot routine is one of the most important aspects of putting. And no matter what your routine consists of, it should be repetitive. In other words, each time you step up to a putt, do exactly the same thing before striking the ball. This is vital to both your mental and physical preparation – and thus is the key to holing more putts.

WATCH THE professionals. Their routine never varies. And when they are distracted and forced to back off a putt, they always go back to the beginning of their pre-shot routine, doing the same thing over and over and over.

STEADY AIM

The first thing I do is to walk behind my ball and study the line that I think the putt will take – I'll explain about how to decide on the line and how to read the green in the next sections. I can usually get the best perspective on that line by squatting down on my haunches.

Then I approach the ball. Standing to the side of my line and setting the putter down, I aim the face parallel to the target line. Finally, I set my body, aligning my hands, arms and shoulders square to the line and the head of the putter.

Notice I said aim the putter first, then align the body! Doing the reverse virtually guarantees that I will be out of sync with my target and miss the putt.

LINE AND PACE

Now it's time to take a practice stroke or two along – or rather parallel to – the intended line, not at the target. If I were to aim directly at the target, I'd be setting myself up to hit right of the hole later when I address the ball.

Below left: Stand to the side – between the hole and the ball – to help estimate the distance of the putt.

Below centre: Always go to the lower side of the hole to help establish the line of a putt.

Below right: Mark and clean the ball.

The number of practice strokes is up to you, but my advice is not to overdo it – one or two is about right. Each stroke should be a mini-rehearsal for the real thing. I'm trying to get a feel for the pace, or speed, of my putt, and to groove my actual stroke.

Lastly, I step up to the ball, keeping everything lined up by sliding the putter forward without changing its alignment and moving both feet up an equal amount. Now, with the putter blade right behind the ball, I look down the target line towards the hole, this time trying to assess only the pace – the speed at which I will hit the ball – rather than the line.

I might check the line once or twice, but the absolute rule of thumb here is to swivel the head when doing so – rather than lifting or turning it. If I do the latter, I lose the visual sight line and may even affect the alignment of my body and/or the putter.

DEADLY FREEZE

Once I'm positioned over the ball, and confident my overall set-up is correct, I start my stroke.

Don't hesitate here! Freezing up over the golf ball is as deadly as doing the same thing over a tee shot. Tension starts to creep into the hands and arms, and the result – even at the short distance of a putt – is always a shot that goes off line.

So trust your preparation – or pre-shot routine – and let her go.

Once you've decided what you're going to do with the putt, don't waste time as this will often cause confusion and doubt, as well as annoying your playing partners. Take aim and fire!

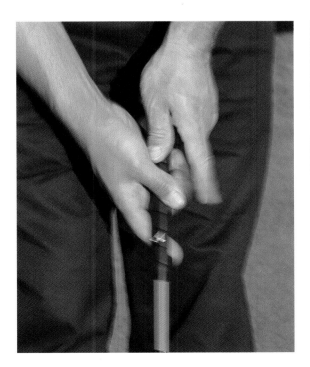

When standing over the ball in the those final moments of preparation, ensure that you stay loose and keep focused on a mental image of the ball rolling into the hole.

READING THE GREEN

◆ ◆ ◆ ◆ ◆

From the moment I hit a shot into the green, I start to size up how I shall go about sinking the putt. As I walk up the fairway, I try to judge the surrounding land to get an idea of the slope and the general lie of the land.

IS THE green on flat land, or part of a ridge that falls away from a hill? Is there water nearby, and do the natural contours lead in that direction? If it were raining heavily, which way do I think the land would drain?

Once I get closer, I start to analyze the slopes on the green itself, plus the colour and coarseness of the grass to gauge the speed of the green. On hot summer days, or in warmer climates, I might even consider the time of day to give me a clue about that speed. The later it is in the afternoon, given such conditions, the longer the grass and possibly heavier the air will be, which will slow a putt down.

Finally, unless I'm putting first, I spend any free time I have practising my stroke. Then I watch how others hit their putts. If I can, I also walk around as much of the green as possible – without causing any delay to my partners or the golfers behind us – getting more of a feel for the texture and grade of the putting surface.

COMBINING FACTORS

Of course, everything I have just described constitutes a method for judging the speed, slope and run of the green I'm about to play – information vital to making my putt.

Those are the three key words in learning how to read greens, and becoming a good putter – speed, slope and run.

PICTURE GALLERY

As I've stressed about every aspect of the short game, before you can hope to lower your scores significantly, you have to put in the time on the practice range. This is certainly true of putting above all else.

By the time that you reach any green during play, you should have logged countless hours hitting putts uphill and down, along left-to-right breaks or vice-versa, and on slow, fast, wet or windy surfaces.

That way, once you take the first look at your putt in any circumstance, you'll have some experience to fall back on. You will have compiled that mental picture gallery that I have referred to in previous chapters – although that's only half the battle. Here's how to handle the other half.

Reading a green is an art in itself. But there can be no doubt that if you can read the slopes on a green, you will hole many more putts. If you can visualize how water would flow on a slope, that's how the ball will roll too.

Above left: Visualize the roll of the ball before playing the shot.

Left: Always aim to get the ball past the hole – don't leave it short.

Above: With long putts speed is so important – try to get the ball inside a 3ft (1m) circle around the hole.

FIRST GLANCE

How much will your putt break? If at all.

All three factors – speed, slope and run – could come into play here, so start by squatting behind your ball and taking a visual cue. You can also walk to the hole and try to visualize the line from there back to the ball. Returning from the hole to the ball will also help you to get a sense of what lies between, not to mention allowing you to pause to look at the putt from the side.

USING VISUAL AIDS TO LINE UP A PUTT

What are the professionals doing when they mark their ball, crouch down, and then seem to fiddle with the ball before placing it back on the green? Many times, they're trying to line up the manufacturer's name with the target line to the hole. This visual aid can help both in aiming your putter blade correctly and instilling confidence, since you are giving yourself a specific cue that's easy to focus upon. Just imagine the ball rolling end over end – with the manufacturer's name holding steady at the equator – down the line to the hole. Another way of using the maker's name is to place it at the back of the ball, where the putter blade will strike first. Again, this gives you something to aim at and a way of concentrating on bringing the putter into the ball cleanly, before sweeping it away. It's easy to let your concentration drift when putting, especially if you lack confidence on the greens. Using either of these methods will get you into a sharper frame of mind and thinking about a positive result.

Once you have a sense of how far the ball will break, overplay that break. One of the most common errors I see is golfers who underread breaks. At least if you overread the break, you still have a chance to get the ball in the hole, since you will be coming in from the high side of the hole, rather than the low one – where you have no chance.

What do I mean by this? Consider a putt that breaks from right-to-left. That means the slope rises from left to right, or falls from right to left, depending on how you wish to view it. Thus, overestimating the break will probably put you above the hole when the putt starts to die, with a chance that the ball can still fall into the cup.

Underhit this putt and you end up below the hole falling away down the slope.

LAST TURN

Next, consider the speed. The ball will break more on fast greens than slow ones, because there is less friction to slow it down. So play more break on a fast green, and watch how the ball starts to curve more as it dies near the hole. Of course, if you are putting downhill, there will be even more speed and break.

In the above example, you should always try to hit the ball past the hole, even if that prospect frightens the life out of you. Above all, don't be so tentative that you freeze up and stab at your stroke. And don't try to finesse this type of putt, hoping it will die into the cup on the last roll. Even if you run well past the hole, you'll at least have a simpler uphill putt coming back.

DISTANCE DICTATES

When playing uphill putts, you must tell yourself to hit the ball harder. That is often quite difficult, and is rather similar to going from playing on fast greens to slow ones. Often, some mental or physical inhibition just will not let us loosen up in these situations, and some golfers consistently leave such putts short.

So again, try to visualize hitting the ball past the hole, or charging it. Of course, by that I do not mean hammering the ball.

Always putt with a smooth, rhythmic stroke, letting the length of the putt dictate the distance the ball travels.

I find that the best way to overcome this problem is to concentrate on my follow-through. Think about stroking the putter fluidly toward the hole and the rest will fall into place.

COLOURFUL CLUE

Finally, consider the grain, or the direction in which the grass lies on the green. The longer and thicker it is, the more it will affect your putt.

How does grain affect your play? A putt hit downgrain will run faster and farther than one hit upgrain. And if the grain runs across the line of your putt, the ball will break more in the direction the grain is running, and less so the other way.

You can tell which way the grain is running by its colour. If it looks light or has a sheen, you are looking down the grain, as opposed to upgrain, where the grass will appear more dark and coarse.

Another way to determine the grain is to examine a golf hole. If one edge looks slightly frayed – what you're seeing is the actual ends of the grass projecting over the hole – that's the way the grain is running.

The colour of the grass will help you to decide how the ball will run. A shiny light colour will indicate you're putting down the grain – a quick putt. A darker colour signifies that you're putting against the grain – a slower putt.

If you're playing early in the morning, you will often see dew on the grass. If others have preceded you, they will have created marks that clearly show how the ball will move across the green. This can be very useful in judging your putt, but remember that the dew will slow the ball dramatically as the putt loses speed – so be bold with your stroke.

LINE OF PUTT

◆ ◆ ◆ ◆ ◆

This is the real secret to putting. Despite how a putt may break, you should visualize each one as a straight line, and think about hitting it only along that straight line.

LET'S SAY the green slopes from right to left. To compensate for this, pick a spot to the right of the hole. The line from your ball to this imaginary hole is the line of your putt. A ball hit down this line will curve with the slope and drift down to the actual hole, providing you hit it with the correct pace.

PICK YOUR SPOT

That's the only tricky part. Depending on the speed of the green and the severity of the break, you have to make a judgement about how far from the actual hole you visualize your line, and then how hard you hit the ball down that line.

The beauty of this method is that all the putts you hit are straight, rather than bending, which is a hard concept to deal with mentally. Also, once you pick a spot along the line where you think the ball will begin to curve towards the hole, you've simplified things. Aim at that mark, making sure you hit the ball hard enough to reach it and then get beyond to your imaginary hole.

Of course, the rest is down, once again, to practice and feel. You will probably also have to consider other factors, such as uphill and downhill slopes and the grain.

LONG PUTTS

You should approach every putt with confidence. But a measure of reality is essential as well. Even the best golfers miss more than their share of putts over six feet (1.8m) in length, and once you are over the 20-foot (6m) range, the odds of making more than a handful are down to luck more than skill.

So on very long putts, think in terms of getting the putt close, rather than holing it. The important thing is to remain confident, yet sensible. Knock a good putt up to the hole, and then sink the next one. Now you've probably made par, or bogey at worst. But a three-putt is too costly, no matter how many strokes you took to get up to the green.

From over 20 feet (6m), visualize a circle around the hole of about three feet (1m) in diameter, and aim to leave the ball in that area. Thinking that way takes a great deal of pressure off your stroke, and should you make the long putt, consider it a bonus.

Visualizing a putt can only be learned with serious practice. Every putt you hit on the practice green should be treated as if it's for The Open Championship!

CHARGE OR DIE

◆ ◆ ◆ ◆ ◆

It is always important to know when to attack, and when to defend, whether in life or in sport. But on sloping greens, this knowledge becomes essential for success.

AN UPHILL putt aimed at the back of the hole, struck firmly and aggressively, is called a 'charge'. A downhill tickler, struck with a cautious but well-calculated hit, is called a 'die' putt – the idea being to roll the ball gently up to the hole so that it topples in on the last revolution.

The key difference between these two putts is how hard we hit them and the line we take to achieve success. You will take a straighter line to the hole with the charge putt, so you must hit it with more authority to get it up the slope.

By contrast, a die putt will take a wider berth because it is struck almost delicately, and thus has more time to come under and respond to the pull of gravity.

ADDED LUXURY

Deciding whether to play a charge or die comes with experience and practice. You should take a moment to consider the speed and slope of the green, your own ability with this sort of shot, and what you need – or don't need – to score.

In other words, if you need a birdie to win a hole in matchplay, or to avoid elimination from a competition, you might even charge a downhill putt. On the other hand, if you have the luxury of two putts for a win, you would probably play the die, even on an uphill putt.

The immediate condition of the greens is also a factor in deciding whether to charge or die a putt. Let's say a green has just been mown and is very slick. In that case, even with a slightly uphill putt, you might want to play more break and die the ball into the hole.

By the same token, if the grass is long and slow, you could charge a downhill or across-the-slope putt, knowing that even if you run the ball past the hole, it won't go that far.

FIGHTING TENSION ON DOWNHILL PUTTS

A steep downhill putt can strike fear into even the most experienced of golfers. But don't let that fear turn into tension that restricts your putting stroke and guarantees you will stab at the ball, running it many feet past the hole. Try to maintain a feeling of real lightness in the hands, arms and shoulders during your pre-shot routine, then concentrate on stroking through the ball, just as you would for any putt. Any attempt to trickle the ball down to the hole by restricting your follow-through will have the opposite effect! The ball will shoot off the putter blade and fly past the hole, leaving you in three-putt territory. Simply control the speed of your putt by taking a shorter backstroke, which will automatically shorten your follow-through.

In putting, as in life, one has to decide when to attack or defend. Tiger Woods and Arnold Palmer have both been advocates of attacking the putt.

THE MENTAL SIDE

◆ ◆ ◆ ◆ ◆

Now that you know how to execute the basic putting stroke, and how to judge distance and break, let me address the idea of confidence. I believe that the art of building faith in your putting stroke starts on the practice green, and that even if you only have a few minutes to spare before teeing off for a round, this is the place where you should spend that time.

START BY hitting only short putts of under three feet (1m) – in other words, the sort that once on the course you might consider 'gimmes', and that might even be conceded to you by your playing partners.

But how many times have you seen other golfers – or even found yourself – standing over such short putts and losing it? The knees turn to jelly, the arms and hands start twitching, and pretty soon a putt has been missed that most people could normally make in their sleep. From that point on, your entire round may go south.

Believe me, it happens to the best of us.

POSITIVE SOUNDS

So confine yourself to positive action before each round. Hit at least a dozen short putts, striking each ball firmly and with conviction, using your basic stroke, and listening for the sound of the ball striking the metal pin in the hole, or rattling into the cup.

Now you can head for the course feeling decisive, the memory of each sweet, well-struck putt carrying over to your game.

TRUST YOURSELF

Once on the course, trust yourself. Here is where the hours of practice, the experience, and your natural instincts should take over.

Far left: Even if you only have a few minutes before a round, use the time constructively by hitting some short putts and building confidence for your round.

Left: This is one of the many exercises I use and teach – start close to the hole, knock the putt in, and then move back to the next ball. Continue until you have holed all the balls.

Above: See the putt in your mind – and then feel it in your arms and hands.

Remember, the first glance you take at the line of a putt should tell you almost everything you need to know about the shot, and be enough to let you proceed to play it.

You aren't building a bridge. You don't need a calculator to figure the angles. This isn't rocket science. Feel the putt into the hole.

POSITIVE IMAGES

You can also try conjuring up a positive picture to help you prepare for the shot.

Relax and imagine the ball rolling down the line, then plopping into the cup. Visualizing a successful putt is halfway to making that putt. On the other hand, letting negative thoughts intrude into your mind will almost guarantee you miss the putt. And the next one.

But remember, if you have played even one really decent round in your life, you know you can sink a lot of putts. You know you're capable of making more putts than you miss.

So go ahead. Trust your ability and strike the ball.

Above: Learning to trust your stroke is the most important part of putting.

EQUIPPED WITH CONFIDENCE

Having confidence in your equipment is a sure way to instill more confidence when putting. If your putter has a flattened grip on the front side, have it checked frequently by a qualified PGA pro or clubmaker to ensure the grip is precisely angled at 90 degrees to the face of the putter blade. Any minor discrepancy here can seriously affect your alignment and lead to consistently missed putts, though you are not likely to know the reason – and thus will start blaming your own technique. If that happens, you might eventually lose confidence in your abilities and miss too many easy putts during a relaxed round, and bunches under competitive pressure. So have the grip examined – and if need be re-aligned – on a frequent basis. Then you will approach each putt with at least one more positive in your bag.

Chapter 10

FAULTS AND CURES

· · · · ·

Perfection in golf is
unattainable, but the best
players know how to correct
a fault quickly.

FAULTS AND CURES

◆ ◆ ◆ ◆ ◆

Golf is a game of managed imperfection. What do I mean by that? In golf, we essentially try to limit and/or control our bad shots, rather than eliminate them entirely — which is impossible. In other words, as a golfer, you are only as good as your least successful hits.

BUT DON'T take my word for it. The legendary Ben Hogan once said that not even the greatest golfers – himself included – could hit the ball perfectly every time, and that, therefore, the game was really one of near 'misses'. The secret to playing well, Hogan insisted, was to learn how to reduce the severity of your mistakes, so that a less-than-perfect shot is still a reasonably well-hit shot.

DECISIVE STRIKE

Think of the rare hole-in-one. If you've ever enjoyed such a decisive strike, you have probably come as close to hitting the perfect shot as possible for any human being swinging club to ball. But even David Duval, during his miraculous Sunday round of 59 early in the Spring of 1999, did not achieve a hole-in-one. And yes, Duval's swing can go bad from time to time, just like that of any club golfer.

So the trick becomes not how often we deliver a textbook movement, but how quickly we can cure some of the faults that will inevitably creep into our game.

BACK TO BASICS

Curing faults often means going back to basics. Assuming a proper set-up – including a good grip, alignment, ball position, posture and balance – will go a long way towards avoiding a slice or any number of other swing faults.

Even if our set-up is near perfect, learning how to adjust for problems in our swingpath – while maintaining a good spinal angle and swing plane – will help to reduce other problems that can crop up.

Left and above: If things go wrong, check your fundamentals first, starting with the aim of your club, your grip, and the alignment of your body. Nine times out of ten, the fault will originate from your set-up.

GRIP PROBLEMS

The greater majority of swing problems emanate from the grip, and often occur without anyone noticing that something has gone wrong. Grip problems can lead to a reduction in clubhead speed, less power and tremendous directional problems.

So spend time working on a proper grip, and have a certified PGA pro examine yours on a routine basis. Perhaps as many as 65 per cent of all swing faults can be traced back to how we hold the club, so curing this problem will go a long way towards fixing a swing.

But be careful. When making any dramatic grip changes, avoid the urge to start hitting golf balls immediately. Harvey Penick suggested that golfers spend several months getting used to an overhaul in their grip by practice-swinging the club with their new hand position as often as possible – but never at a golf ball.

GRIP TENSION

Grip problems often stem from exerting too much pressure on the club and, unfortunately, the majority of golfers suffer from this tendency. Our basic instinct is to hold the club tightly in an effort to be in absolute control of it with the hands. At address, as the golfer initiates the backswing, he or she tends to grasp the club far too hard, trying to use the hands and arms – especially the hands – to dictate the whole golf swing.

Invariably, this leads to restriction in the movement of the clubhead. Rather than letting the weight of the clubhead dictate a free-flowing movement, the golfer is trying to lead and control the action of the club.

The result is usually a shot blocked off to the right, or occasionally pulled left.

Above: Grip faults can cause numerous swing problems. Check hand position and pressure.

Below: Clubs set parallel to the ball-to-target line enable you to check your alignment and ball position.

EASING TENSION FROM THE BACK

Most golfers are aware that if they tense up their grip, their wrists, forearms, and even shoulders may also become rigid, leading to a restricted swing and lack of power through the ball. As a result, they try to relax these areas during their pre-shot routine, but later find that they were not successful as a shot pulls off-line and they feel tightness in their upper body. What happened? Maybe they haven't gone to the actual source of the problem. Next time you line up to the ball, try visualizing the middle part of your upper back, between the shoulder blades. Often, this is the centre or even source of muscle tension. Taking a deep breath, try to pinpoint a spot equidistant between the shoulder blades and relax the muscles there. I guarantee you will feel a lightness in your shoulders, arms and wrists as a result – and that you will subsequently hit the ball better.

CURING GRIP PROBLEMS

◆ ◆ ◆ ◆ ◆

*Remember that the clubhead should open and close in synchronization
with the rotation of the body during the swing. In the backswing, the
clubhead is gradually opening, then closing until it is square at impact –
before closing completely in the follow-through.*

BUT WITH too much tension in the hands, the golfer prevents the clubhead from reacting naturally to the path of the swing. As a result, the clubhead stays open at impact, which is why the ball will veer off to the right.

FREE AGENTS

Holding the club too tightly may also cause more immediate problems in the backswing. When the swing is initiated with the hands – rather than a synchronized movement of the hands, arms and upper torso – a quick breakdown in the overall swing occurs. The upper body gets left behind, and the swing is destined to fail because it is no longer a co-ordinated movement.

What is the cure? It is essential that grip pressure remains light, so the wrists can remain free agents and work in unison with the rest of the body in the golf swing – allowing the clubhead to flow correctly through impact with the ball.

Too much tension destroys that harmony.

FAULTY HANDS

After tension, the second major problem in the grip usually comes from the positioning of the hands on the club. The upper, or left hand, will often tend to creep around to the right, while the lower, or right hand, moves to the left. When that happens, the hands are working against one another, rather than as a solid unit.

Why does this occur? Most right-handed golfers unconsciously try to dominate and control the club with their right hand. The right forefinger and thumb can become

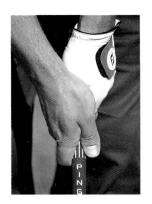

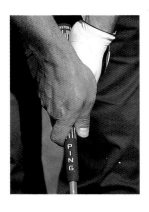

Above: If your hands are too far to the left on the club (bottom), a slice will be inevitable. The correct hand position is shown (top).

Left: When placing your hands on the club, ensure the back of your left hand and palm of your right hand are facing the target. This is the position to which they will naturally return.

Above: Place your hands lightly on the club. Nearly everyone who slices holds the club too tightly.

Right: A good grip enables you to swing back correctly.

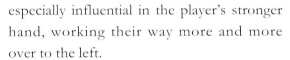

Above: The strong or hooker's grip is certainly one to avoid.

especially influential in the player's stronger hand, working their way more and more over to the left.

Ben Hogan called the right thumb and forefinger the 'pincer' fingers. If they press in, all the tendons up to the top of the shoulder will tighten and even lock up, preventing a decent backswing. Additionally, the right arm will not fold properly as you go back, and the right arm will swing the club across the ball, producing a pull or slice.

CREEPING HANDS

At the same time, the left hand often tends to creep to the right, or go underneath, because it seems more comfortable in that position. As a rule I am less concerned with the left hand creeping under – into what is known as the traditionally strong grip – than I am with the right hand moving over.

The more the right hand comes around the club, the more that influences the positioning of both hands, and thus the way they present the clubhead to the ball at impact. This will also influence the positioning of the arms and shoulders in the set-up.

If the right hand gradually creeps around to the left, then the right shoulder becomes more and more dominant – the shoulder is actually pulled out of alignment. And the more the right shoulder moves out, the more likely the golfer is to swing from out-to-in.

Unfortunately, once again, this produces a slice or pull, a common fault among most golfers.

CLAP AND CLOSE

To overcome this tendency, try to assume a more 'natural' grip. Simply allow your arms and hands to hang down naturally, with the back of the left hand and the palm of the right hand facing the target – as if both hands were about to clap together, saluting your excellent grip position. Then just close the hands around the club.

Any other positioning of the hands will cause some degree of artificiality in the swing. You will have to manipulate your hands to get the clubhead back square at the point of impact.

Above: A weak or slicer's grip will cause you to swing across the ball and so cause it to pull or spin off to the right.

PRO TIP

Many top players now try to keep the right thumb and forefinger apart for fear of squeezing them together during the swing. This can tighten up the muscles of the arm and shoulder, so don't let that happen to you – it will overpower your swing. Instead, lay the thumb and forefinger on the shaft, but just leave them there, with a small gap between the two.

CURING ALIGNMENT PROBLEMS

◆ ◆ ◆ ◆ ◆

Proper alignment is crucial to developing a consistent golf swing. But, unfortunately, the average golfer often sets his or her body at the target, rather than aligning it parallel to the ball-to-target line.

WHY? IT is natural to associate lining up to a target in much the same way as one would aim and fire a rifle – which is down the shoulder line, bringing along the feet and hips.

This is totally wrong in golf!

When you swing a golf club, you are moving the clubhead at right angles to the ball-to-target line and the body must be parallel to that target line. Remember, it is the clubhead that hits the ball – not the body.

PULL AND SLICE

If you get in the way of your swing, you'll have a serious problem. With your body pointed directly at the target, it will be aligned too far to the right and you will be blocking the clubhead from swinging through to the target, and the resulting swingpath will be out-to-in. Generally, the golfer who commits the fault will pull their short irons and slice their longer clubs.

PRACTISE CORRECTLY

What is the cure for poor alignment? Practise with a purpose. When you go to the driving range, don't just set up in line with the edge of the mat or any other marker in your hitting area. Instead, pick a defined target and align yourself properly with that. Otherwise, you will probably set up incorrectly and start practising a fault, then ingrain a bad habit in your swing.

The best way to practise correct alignment is by putting some golf clubs on the ground to help you aim correctly. Place one club behind the golf ball, pointing straight to the target. Then put another one down just to the right of that and parallel to the target line.

Finally, place a third club parallel to the first two, but left of the ball – or nearer your feet. Now take away the club behind the ball and you are left with the proper alignment pattern indicated by the two parallel clubs.

To check your alignment – first place a club next to the ball pointing at your target, next place two clubs either side of the ball as shown below. Now you can check all aspects of your set-up starting with your clubhead and moving on to your body. Note any differences from the way you normally set up on the course and you've found your problem.

Your hips and shoulders need to be checked as well as your feet. They should all be running parallel to the ball-to-target line – that means that your body is pointing slightly left of your target, not at the target as most golfers believe.

Aiming the clubhead at right angles to both of the clubs on the ground, set your feet along the target line. Now you have a perfect set-up.

ON-COURSE ALIGNMENT CURES

Golf course architects are very clever. When they design a hole, they often make the tee box (teeing area) point right or left of the target, towards the rough or other problem areas. In such situations, you must remember to aim across the tee, which is difficult. Fairways can also be cut to tempt you off to the right or left of the hole.

The way to overcome such problems is relatively simple. Walk behind the ball and choose a target a few inches in front of the ball. Focus on a piece of grass, a divot, a twig or anything you can find that is along the correct ball-to-target line. The same goes for putting. You should always find something in front of the ball with which to line up.

BODY LAST

Now comes the most important part. The key to aligning properly is first to position the clubhead correctly along your chosen line, then set your body parallel to that line.

Don't ever do it the other way around! In other words, don't ever line your body up first. If you do that, your body will generally be misaligned.

Finally, on the course, if you are not playing in a competitive situation, you might try putting a club across your shoulders, hips or above your feet to check your alignment.

But in a practical sense, you cannot spend much time on such methods during a round. And, of course, any practice devices you might use on the range are strictly illegal on the golf course.

Use a short target in conjunction with the clubs you've laid down parallel to your ball-to-target line. This will show up any swing problems.

PRO TIP

Don't be embarrassed to practise proper alignment and aiming on the range. Golfers don't do that enough, and then they take their faults to the course. I've seen Jack Nicklaus practise many times, and, unless he is forced to do a very quick warm-up, he regularly puts clubs on the ground to promote proper alignment and practises with them in place through every club in the bag.

CURING PROBLEMS WITH BALL POSITION

◆ ◆ ◆ ◆ ◆

The position of the ball in your stance is also important to hitting good golf shots. If you put the ball in the wrong place relative to your set-up, you will make it difficult to achieve a decent strike.

WHEN THE ball is too far forward in your stance, or even in extreme circumstances outside your left foot, it ends up pulling your shoulders around because you have to reach for the ball. The right arm now becomes extremely dominant, which will lead to a variety of problems.

Quite often, the golfer who does not place the ball in the proper position will also have a bad grip and alignment. He or she may aim to the right, then put the ball miles too far forward in the stance.

COMMON NIGHTMARE

This can produce a nightmare scenario, though it is a common fault in many golfers. Now the player is so turned around that the feet are aiming to the right, and the shoulders are aiming to the left of the target line.

Given that set-up, there is no possible way to make a decent golf swing. The golfer will generally pull shots with the short clubs, and produce a big slice with the long clubs.

OPEN AND PUSH

Putting the ball too far back in the stance is much rarer, but it also causes numerous problems. Such a position will cause a push, or the ball flying straight to the right. Remember that body rotation in the swing

A ball placed too far forward in your stance will cause you to pull or slice the shot.

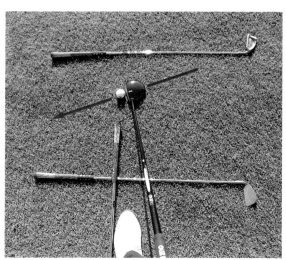

Far left: If your ball is too far forward, it will often lead to a closed club face and an out-to-in swingpath.

Left: A ball placed too far back in the stance will cause the club face to be open and an in-to-out swingpath.

Ball too far forward

opens and closes the clubhead, so if the ball is too far back, you will hit it too early in the swing, when the clubhead is still open.

Because the club is still coming in on an inside track, you might also impart unwanted spin to the ball. If the ball is not pushed off to the right, you might well send it off to the left with a hook spin.

The cure? In the previous section on alignment, I suggested putting two clubs on the ground that are parallel to the ball-to-target line when you practise. This should establish you in the proper set-up position. It's also an excellent way to check for proper ball position.

Put another club behind the ball, but perpendicular to the other two clubs. That

will tell you exactly where your ball is situated in your stance.

Practise this consistently, and you are halfway to achieving a proper ball position.

An out-to-in (slicer's) swing is the result of the ball being too far forward in the stance.

PRO TIP

I do not mind if a golfer plays every shot off the left heel – which is what Jack Nicklaus advocates – as long as they are relaxed with that and can place the ball properly. On the other hand, the more traditional way of positioning the ball is also correct for many golfers, with the woods and long irons played off the left heel, the medium (5, 6 and 7) irons played midway between the centre and the left heel, and the short clubs (8, 9 and wedges) played from the middle of the stance.

It's very much an individual preference, and either choice is acceptable. I teach both, depending on which works better for each person. However, as with anything in golf, the key is to be consistent – and always to place the ball in the proper position relative to the clubhead and body along the target line.

Below: If the ball is too far back in your stance, an in-to-out (hooker's) swing is likely.

Ball too far back

CURING POSTURE PROBLEMS

◆ ◆ ◆ ◆ ◆

Good posture is the cornerstone of an athletic golf swing.
The correct posture gives your swing balance, which will enable your
overall movement. But poor posture can interfere with balance, and then
everything can start to go wrong.

I BELIEVE YOUR body weight should be slightly backwards of centre, towards the heels of your feet. If a golfer's weight moves forward of centre, an out-to-in swingpath will result causing the club to cut across the ball. When your weight moves forwards, your upper body will generally begin to sway forwards as well.

If this happens, the golfer is putting his or her body in the way of the swing, especially as he or she comes through the ball. The golfer is then forced to move the club farther outside the normal swingpath – or farther away from the body – hitting across the ball with a glancing blow that starts it spinning. The common result is a slice to the far right of the target with the longer clubs, and a pull with the short clubs.

SWING AROUND

One way to maintain good posture and balance is to keep your weight slightly back of centre. Throughout the movement of the swing, you want to rotate around the pivotal points of the right heel on the backswing, and the left heel on the throughswing.

While doing this, you must keep the body exactly the same distance from the ball at all times. Only then can you allow the club to swing truly around you.

If you move the body either closer to the ball – or farther away from it – you will experience a loss of balance, which will upset everything in the swing. The golfer is then in a different position at impact from that at address, and the swing can never be consistent.

Indeed, you will be struggling to rebuild your movement while trying to swing the club correctly.

SWING PLANE

Another way to focus on posture and balance is to think about swing plane. If the upper body's position lifts during the

Most posture problems are caused by trying to get too close to the ball. Be bold, stand tall, bend from the hips and sit back – it's simple.

The athletic posture

The 'head up' position

backswing, it creates a swing plane that is too flat. And when the upper body drops dramatically, it sets up too high a swing plane, with the arms lifting in the air, independently of the body.

Remember that swing plane is formed by the initial posture at set-up, and that the angle of the spine dictates the plane. We want the spine to stay in one place throughout the swing, and if that angle remains constant, then the club can move around the body on a consistent circle.

But if the spine moves up or down, it will take the arms, hands and club with it, dramatically altering the swing plane and thus the golf shot.

MIRROR CURE

How do you cure posture faults? One way is by using a mirror. Check your posture in this way as often as you can, examining your spinal angle from behind. Better still, capture yourself using a video camera, or get a friend or golf pro to take a look regularly. While practising this, close your eyes and try to ingrain the feeling of correct posture in your mind.

How do you know what the ideal posture is for you? That's dictated by your height and the length of your arms and clubs. The shorter player will be more upright, the taller one more bent over.

Here's how to take up your particular posture correctly:

1. Using a golf club, bend your upper body forwards from your hips – not from your

waist – keeping the head high and the chin nicely clear of the chest. Try to retain the integrity of your head position vis-à-vis a reasonably straight line down to the base of your spine. When you bend forwards over the ball, you must retain that line – that's your spine angle.

2. Now let the clubhead touch the ground.

3. Your weight will be somewhat forward, so you'll need to counterbalance that by sticking your bottom out. Adding a little flex to the knees will help to push your bottom out until you feel you're almost leaning against the back of a chair.

Exactly how the above moves are accomplished will vary somewhat with every player, and with every club that is used.

A very tall golfer with a short club will have to stick his or her bottom out quite a bit – because otherwise too much weight will remain forward. On the other hand, a shorter person with a long club will scarcely need to bend over at all, or consequently stick their rear out very far.

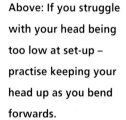

Above: If you struggle with your head being too low at set-up – practise keeping your head up as you bend forwards.

If your legs are too straight, you will have to bend forwards excessively.

Too much flex in your legs and you will be too erect in your upper body causing a top shot.

CURING THE SLICE

◆ ◆ ◆ ◆ ◆

In order to cure the slice, you have to start with the set-up. Check your grip, alignment, ball position and posture. If the set-up is wrong, you cannot fix your golf swing. Generally, the swing itself is the last thing that is wrong.

BUT ASSUMING you have a perfect set-up, what other factors can we look at?

One is the swingpath through the ball. That will be very influential. If you are slicing, you are swinging across the ball from out-to-in, imparting sideways – or clockwise – spin to the golf ball.

DO THE OPPOSITE

What's the cure? Once you are reasonably sure your set-up is correct, try to do the opposite of what is causing the problem. In other words, you should try to swing along an in-to-out swingpath and make sure you are freely releasing the club.

Try only halfswings at first, in an attempt to gain a feel for that movement and establish it as your swingpath. Remember, if you are slicing, you have become used to swinging from out-to-in, and often you will not even realize you're doing it.

DEFINED TARGET

Then pick a defined target on the golf range, place some clubs on the ground to ensure your alignment is correct, and try to make the ball move from right to left. In other words, you must literally try to draw the ball.

As slicing is caused by swinging the club to the left of the target, practise swinging the club more to the right of the target.

It's the one I've seen so often – the out-to-in swingpath can only cause a pull or slice.

Bad swing

Out-to-in swingpath

PRO TIP

Hit some shots from a sidehill lie, with the ball several inches above your feet. This can help you to produce a better swing plane and promotes an in-to-out swingpath.

Above: The out-to-in swingpath illustrated in detail.

Below left: Ensure your hands are lightly placed on the grip.

Below: Check your ball position is not too far forward in the stance.

In addition, make sure your hands are light on the grip so your wrists are free and the clubhead can release. Holding too tightly helps create a slice.

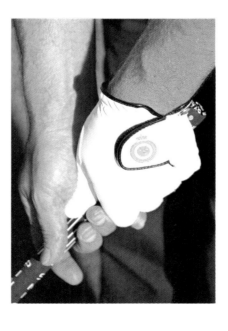

Below: Here I demonstrate the correct swing. Note the differences at set-up, top of backswing and through the ball.

Good swing

CURING THE SHANK

◆ ◆ ◆ ◆ ◆

*Is there a more dreaded word in golf? I will not even repeat it, except to
say that this sometimes contagious 'mis-hit' happens when we strike the
ball with the hosel of the club, or the spot where the shaft joins the
clubface. The ball will then career off wildly, usually at right angles
to the target line.*

THE CAUSE can often be attributed
to the player standing too close to
the ball, or shifting his or her
weight too far forwards. But most of the
time, the 'shank' (there, I said it!) is caused
by tension.

The arms and hands lock up and the
body takes over, with the shoulders pushing
the clubhead down the wrong swingpath.

SHARPER STRIKES

The cure for this fault is to practise sharper
strikes with your feet close together. This
exercise restores timing and promotes better
feel for weight transfer and the free swinging
of the hands and arms.

And lastly, take a deep breath to make
sure your breathing is relaxed and steady,
and then lighten your grip pressure.

The shank is when the
ball is struck in the heel
of the golf club and is
often caused by
standing too close to
the golf ball.

Practise half swings

Left: An instant cure – address the ball on the toe of the club.

Above left: The most common cause of shanking is too much tension, a head-down position at address and being too close to the ball.

Above: If you get rid of the tension at set-up, you'll almost always cure your shanking.

Practising half shots is a great way to get rid of shanking and sharpen your strike on the golf ball. Keep your hands light and allow the club to swing freely – enjoy yourself and things will improve.

CURING THE HOOK

◆ ◆ ◆ ◆ ◆

The hook is often the result of any number of set-up problems. Generally, the hands have crept too much to the right, a position which is known as a strong, or hooker's, grip. And as the hands creep round, the shoulders tend to get more and more closed, until they are aiming too much to the right.

WHEN THESE faults occur, the golfer might also begin to position the ball too far to the back of his or her stance.

In this situation, it's also common for the golfer inadvertently to open the clubface far too much. Why? As the ball begins to move more and more right-to-left, the golfer becomes petrified of the left-hand side of the golf course, and will do anything to stay right. So, they tend to open the clubface, aiming to the right of the target line.

Of course, most golfers do not realize the clubface is opening. In fact, they would bet their life they're aiming straight, when they are actually aiming as much as 30 degrees right. Now the ball can only go right and the swingpath gets increasingly in-to-out, aggravating the tendency to hit a hook.

TROUBLE ZONE

But if the golfer swings in-to-out and hits the ball with the clubface square, the ball will start spinning right to left. Now the ball will start straight, and then begin to veer off to the left. By contrast, if the ball is hit with the clubface even only slightly closed – say one or two degrees – that will produce a duck-hook, or snap-hook.

In this case the ball hardly gets airborne, flying very low and rapidly curling left. As Lee Trevino says, you can talk to a fade, but you can't talk to a hook, because once the ball starts spinning low and left, it will bounce violently and spin off into trouble when it hits the ground.

INITIAL FLIGHT

What is the cure? Look at your set-up first, examining the grip, alignment and ball position. Then check the clubface. If it's wide open, square it up behind the ball. Finally, put some clubs on the ground to check your alignment and pick a defined target, working on the initial line of flight of the ball.

If you can get a friend to stand behind you at this point, that will be helpful. He or she can tell you if the ball is starting right, and spinning, which you will not be able to see yourself.

Using the clubs for proper alignment, work on starting the backswing in a straight line, trying to get some initial width. Then as

CHECK THE LINE OF YOUR DIVOT

One of the telltale signs of an excessively in-to-out golf swing will be shown in the divot you take. Look carefully at your divot after you've hit your shot. If it's pointing to the right of the target you're swinging too much in-to-out, thus causing the hook shot.

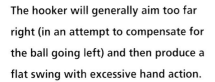

The hooker will generally aim too far right (in an attempt to compensate for the ball going left) and then produce a flat swing with excessive hand action.

you come through the ball, think about pulling the club through with your left arm, keeping the left arm and hand ahead of the clubhead, swinging out-to-in in a way rather like hitting a bunker shot.

You are literally trying to cut the ball, or move it from left to right, trying to hit a slice.

ON AND OFF

Fuzzy Zoeller once said that he had the easiest job in the world striving to be a good golfer because he only suffered from one fault, and that was hooking the ball. So what he tries to do on any shot is to slice it.

But as with all hookers, they may be on form one day, and off the other. The American big-hitter John Daly is another classic example. He is long and extremely powerful, but tends to hook the ball. On a course such as St. Andrews – where he won the British Open a few years ago – he is relatively all right, because there's little trouble on the left. But put him on a course with danger on the left, and he has a serious problem.

As with curing the slice, you have to attempt the opposite shot to fix a hook. Try to visualize slicing the ball. Try to start the ball to the left of the target and make it spin to the right. That's the quickest way to cure a hook.

Left: Once again check your body alignment – so often this is the root of the problem.

Below: A great cure for the hook: give control to your left arm and try to cut across the ball as though you are trying to fade or slice.

CURING THINNED AND TOPPED SHOTS

◆ ◆ ◆ ◆ ◆

Thinning, or topping, the ball can be caused by a number of factors, but the most common one I see among golfers is their tendency to keep the head rigidly down during the swing, preventing proper body rotation.

WHY IS that? The average golfer often strives to look squarely at the ball. But remember, you don't have to stare at the ball with both eyes forever! For the most part, you only see the ball out of one eye as you take the club back, and keep watching the ball until until you strike it.

FREEZING UP

But many golfers are so keen to stare the ball down – while making sure their head does not move – that they freeze. Then, when they do try to swing back, the head does not rotate as it should, and the upper body is prevented from opening up, or making a full turn.

This will often lead to a second error, especially if the idea that 'you must keep your eye on the ball' and 'keep your head down' is constantly moving on a loop through your brain. Because your head has not rotated properly, and your initial move has not been correct, you will now inadvertently force yourself to move your body down towards the ball – which is a disaster.

BREAKDOWN

This produces a drop in the spine angle, and from there, you cannot hope to rotate the body correctly behind the ball. The arms will also break down, and you will lose width in your swing. In addition, because you are now closer to the ball, your balance will also be severely affected, since your weight is probably too far forwards.

Now you have a tenth of a second from the top of the backswing until you hit the ball, and yet you are three or four inches (8

GETTING OFF THE GROUND

Concentrate on grooving your swing and transferring your weight correctly to avoid thinning or topping the ball. Put a tee peg in the ground and take half-swings, gently sweeping the tee out of the turf to ingrain the idea of a correct swingpath and hitting through the ball in a way that lets the loft of the clubface do its job properly. Now replace the tee with a ball and resist the temptation to try scooping the ball off the ground. Secondly, focus on the idea of moving your weight back, then forward, by swinging slowly, concentrating on how your weight shifts back to the right foot, then forward around your left (see picture right). If your weight shift is timed correctly, and fully executed, the clubface will simply brush the ball off the turf, striking it at the centre – rather than on the upper half (see picture above).

Bad form resulting in topped or thinned shot

Ironically the topped shot is often the result of trying too hard to keep your head down or rigidly still.

A good swing to prevent topping

A fluid swing starting from a good posture and position will rarely cause you to top the ball. And rather than telling yourself to keep your 'head down', simply tell yourself to 'watch the clubhead strike the ball'. This will result in less intensity and thus no restrictions in your movement.

to 10cm) closer to the ball than you should be, or were at address. What are you going to do? You have to come up. As you swing through, you have to lift your body to get decent contact with the ball. But that is very difficult, and at that point, you are generally destined to do one of two things:

1. You will lift up too much to compensate, and thus you will top or thin the ball – also known as skulling it.
2. Or you will not lift up enough, and you will hit the ground way behind the ball – what we call hitting it fat.

MIRACULOUS MISHAP

But what will your friends say when you ask for advice? They'll say you lifted your head, and that maybe your left arm is breaking down!

So on the next shot, you'll try even harder to stay down, which makes you drop even lower and further increases your difficulty. Once again, your body will not turn correctly, you will lose all the width in your swing, and even if you manage miraculously somehow to hit the ball – it will be without any power.

FULL TURN

The way to cure this fault is to allow your head to rotate naturally behind the ball and to complete a full turn by not fixing your gaze on the golf ball with both eyes. At first, you may feel as if you are swaying off the ball, but if you transfer your weight properly and keep your spine angle intact, you cannot help but make a decent backswing.

Practise this motion in a mirror to convince yourself.

CURING FAT AND SKY SHOTS

◆ ◆ ◆ ◆ ◆

Fat shots (when you hit the ground behind your ball) are directly related to topped shots. If your head goes down, and then you do not compensate by pulling back up on the throughswing, you will hit fat. But the second reason for hitting fat — and it's a very common fault among golfers — is a dull strike on the ball, which can be directly attributed to swingpath.

IF YOU bring the club too much to the inside on the backswing, then return on the same inside angle – in an excessively in-to-out swingpath – the clubhead will be too close to the ground as it approaches the ball. As a result, the clubhead could smack into the turf at any stage before making contact with the ball.

In addition, if you are hitting either fat or thin shots, and find it very difficult to hit the ball correctly when it's not sitting up on the fairway, then you're probably moving the club too much on an in-to-out swingpath

DIVOT PATTERN

The cure is to go back to putting some clubs on the ground and practise the correct swingpath, trying to make the club go more in-to-in. Also, take a look at your divot pattern after every shot you hit. If your divots are pointing slightly to the right, then you know you have a serious problem.

A perfect divot in the golf swing should be pointing slightly to the left. That's because the divot should be struck just after you hit the golf ball, when the club is moving slightly back to the inside during the follow-through. But if the divot is pointing right, that means you are coming too much in-to-out and will almost certainly hit the ball fat. If the ball is sitting down slightly, you will probably top it as well.

SKY SHOTS

If you sky the ball, you are probably lifting the club early on the backswing, raising your arms straight up with poor body rotation. This will produce a chopping motion as you come through. Another fault that leads to skying is the failure to clear the lower body –

An incorrect swingpath is the most common cause of fat or skyed shots.

or turn the left hip – when you swing the club through.

Remember, the lower body must initiate the downswing. But if this doesn't happen and the upper body is allowed to dominate, the club is forced to come outside the correct swingpath. Now you are slashing across the target line, which often results in the club chopping down into the ball and sending it high into the air.

It is important to identify which side of the golf swing is causing you the problem, if not *both*! But this is a situation where you need to have a golf pro, a friend and/or the use of a video camera – you will not be able to identify this fault through feel alone.

LOW AND SLOW

What is the cure? Keep the club low and wide to the ground as you take it away, making sure the left arm and shaft of the clubhead form a complete line, which will promote a wide swing arc. Don't actively lift the club up with your right arm. If you do, you will inevitably chop down on the ball. Find out if you are balanced on the follow-through, and if your weight has moved across onto the left heel? If the answer is no, you may have moved first with your upper body, maybe even with your arms and hands, cutting across the ball.

Practise by trying to ingrain the idea of initiating your throughswing with the lower body, uncoiling from the ground up, first by turning your hips, then naturally letting your upper torso rotate back to the target and through to a full finish.

PRO TIP

The best golfers swing the club in what is known as a 'wide' in-to-in swingpath. At the moment of impact, the clubhead should be moving straight towards the target – the only point in the golf swing when the club *is* moving straight at the target.

When you practise, try to ingrain the feeling of a more neutral swingpath, with the clubhead travelling pretty much in a straight line just before and after you hit the ball. Think about bringing the club back low and straight in the initial part of the backswing, and then straight through the ball in the impact area.

Above: If you sky shots regularly, keep the club low on the takeaway – this will prevent you from lifting the club and chopping into the golf ball.

Above: Teeing the ball high will also help get rid of the sky shot.

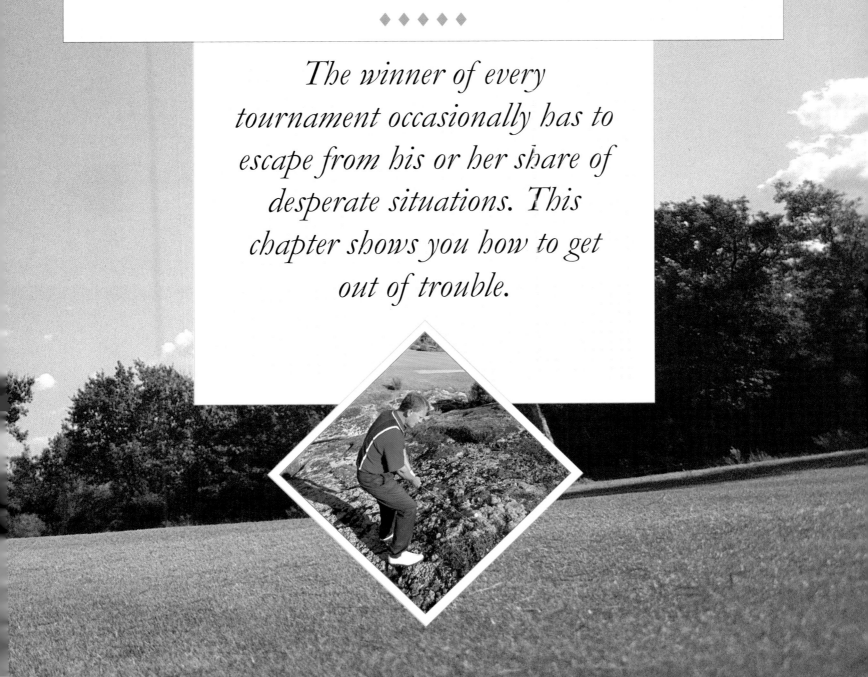

Chapter 11

TROUBLE SHOTS

♦ ♦ ♦ ♦ ♦

The winner of every tournament occasionally has to escape from his or her share of desperate situations. This chapter shows you how to get out of trouble.

TROUBLE SHOTS

◆ ◆ ◆ ◆ ◆

Successfully escaping from trouble is an essential skill in any round of golf. Whether you are a beginner or an experienced professional, you are going to hit your fair share of golf shots into the rough or the occasional fairway bunker.

IN ADDITION, you might have to play an important shot from a divot, a tight lie around the green, a loose lie from the fairway, or off a severe slope. The ball might even come to rest well above or below your feet.

The key to playing trouble shots is to turn failure into success, and thus limit damage to your scorecard. But remember, even the top pros have their own problems escaping from trouble. So be realistic. Play within the limits of the situation and your own ability. This is hardly the time to be over-ambitious. Your goal should always be to recognize a simple idea – get the ball back in play.

MAKING ADJUSTMENTS

How do we escape from trouble? If you are a beginner, I cannot over-emphasize the necessity of practising trouble shots before going out on the course. Most of us, including the most experienced pros, don't do that enough.

But once you are on the course, deciding what shot is possible is the first, and most important, step. Once you have made up your mind, you can select the right club and make any adjustments to your set-up, stance, ball position and swing that are necessary to execute the shot successfully.

Playing back to safety

There are certain situations that you will find yourself in that deserve respect. If you are in trouble, sometimes you have to realize that you're not Tiger and simply get the ball back in play with a sensible shot that you know you can hit.

Then add a final ingredient, which is a psychological one. You must have self-belief. Once you have selected your escape route, play the shot with confidence. If you approach any trouble shot vaguely unsure of how to play it, or without faith in the method you've chosen, your next shot may well end up in an even more difficult spot (as happened to Jean Van de Velde in the British Open in 1999, for example).

The principal goal is not to hit the shot of your life, but simply to get the ball back in play. You'll be surprised how easily you can keep a good round going if you do this, while at the same time building confidence for the next time you play – when you will once again inevitably face some of these same trouble shots.

PLAYING FROM THE ROUGH

When the ball lands in the rough, the average golfer often does not want to take his or her punishment. They forget that the course architect has positioned the rough in certain ways for a reason – to penalize errant shots.

So figuring out what you can or cannot do in this situation is the only way to make a start towards successfully getting out of trouble. You may be forced to accept that you are going to play an extra shot on the hole, and perhaps drop a stroke.

Most golfers try to be too ambitious. They want to carry the ball over a load of trouble, when the best move might be simply to hit the ball out sideways, setting up a decent shot from the fairway.

Remember that in the rough, making solid contact with the ball is generally not going to be very easy, so the amount of flight will be limited. In addition, you must choose a club with enough loft to get the ball up and out of the thick grass.

ASSESS THE LIE

The way the ball lies in the rough will vary considerably – even dramatically. Some lies are so favourable that the golfer can often play virtually a normal shot and get good

Playing out of trouble

contact with the ball. But others are impossible, or in golf parlance 'unplayable'.

The way to judge the lie – and thus what you can realistically do from the rough – is by looking carefully at how much grass there is directly behind the ball. If there are only a few blades of light grass, then that is insignificant – with one word of warning. The grass on links courses can often look harmless. But even a few blades of the stuff can twist a club as if it were wire! So beware.

On the other hand, if there is a lot of grass behind your ball and you cannot see the back of it, then you have a serious problem. The ball might also be sitting down, embedded, or even cradled by what looks like a 'bird's nest'. What can you do?

First of all, you now know that no matter what you do, you will not be able to hit the ball very far. So take the club with the most loft in your bag – the sand wedge. I explain how to play the shot overleaf.

Evaluate your shot carefully before hitting it. There is nothing wrong with being bold when playing from difficult situations, as long as you know you have practised the shot and can play it with confidence.

USING A SAND WEDGE FROM THE ROUGH

♦ ♦ ♦ ♦ ♦

The sand wedge is particularly useful from thick rough because it has a heavy soleplate which helps you swing through grass, weeds, brambles and whatever other nasty stuff is around your ball. A golf club can be stopped cold in the rough, and if that happens, the ball will not move an inch! Or it might just pop out a few feet in front of you.

S O YOU need a heavy club that can lift the ball out. In addition, you have to swing through the grass behind the ball before making contact, which can snag the club and close down the clubface as you make your strike. When that happens, the club is effectively de-lofted, and the ball might not get airborne at all.

In fact, the ball may even be driven further into the grass. I have seen fellow pros hit a ball in the rough that moves only three or four inches (8 to 10cm), sometimes even going downwards into further trouble.

If the grass is deep enough, the ball can even become lost!

OPEN THE CLUBFACE

In heavy rough, even a sand wedge will tend to snag, closing down the face of the club. So open the blade up just a bit to compensate for this, then play the shot the same way you would in a bunker. And remember to open the face first, then take your grip, so that the club is set correctly in your hands, open by 5 to 10 degrees. Finally, take a nice full swing and try to hit right through the ball.

Even if the club eventually does get snagged and stops, focus on trying to go through the ball – that will usually get the ball out.

Play to a point on the fairway that is not too ambitious. Unless you have to, do not try to hit the ball over more rough, because you often will not be successful.

If you find yourself in thick rough, the sand wedge is a good option to get the ball back into play.

Below: No matter how thick the rough is, try to follow through.

MODERATE LIES IN THE ROUGH

◆ ◆ ◆ ◆ ◆

Landing in the rough is not always a disaster. If you can see even a little bit of the back of the ball, you have some hope of hitting a positive shot. But you still need a club with a great deal of loft. An 8-iron is as low as you should go when hitting out of difficult rough. However, if you hit an 8-iron from the rough, bear in mind that you'll probably get a flyer.

A FLYER IS when the grass comes between the ball and the clubface, which prevents you getting any backspin on the ball. The ball might literally shoot off the club, going 30 or 40 per cent farther than it would normally.

Sometimes, that can work to your advantage. If you normally hit an 8-iron 130-150 yards (119 to 137m), a flyer may well send it 170-190 yards (155 to 174m) — especially if the fairway is running a bit. If you have a long approach to the green, that

might be a big help in saving a stroke. But a flyer can also work against you, so take the added length that may result into consideration when hitting from the rough. Knowing the ball will run significantly when it lands at least helps you to plan how to execute the shot.

If you're playing a short approach to the green, remember that you will not be able to stop the ball unless the surface is very soft. Instead, you may have to run the ball up to the green.

Below: Remember when playing from the rough, the ball will run much further than when you are playing from the fairway.

Left and above: If your ball is sitting in the first cut of the rough, a long iron cannot be used. Therefore, depending on the length of the shot and the lie of the ball, consider a lofted iron. For longer shots use a 5- or 7-wood.

USING UTILITY WOODS IN THE ROUGH

◆ ◆ ◆ ◆ ◆

A 7-wood is an innovation that can help tremendously when playing out of the rough. You may also want to try one of the newer 9-woods or even an 11-wood. These days, a lot of women and senior players use such clubs but many low handicap and pro golfers are also increasingly finding them useful.

IN FACT, a 7-wood is probably a better club for the average golfer to carry in his bag than a difficult 3-iron. Utility woods are much easier to use in all sorts of situations around the course, but especially from the rough. However, employing a wood depends on the type of lie in which you find your ball. In order to use a fairway wood from the rough, you must see some of the back of the ball. If you cannot see any ball, then forget about using the wood.

SNAG PROOF

The reason utility woods can work out of the rough is because the clubhead is rounded, and sometimes has a 'V-shaped' sole that will not get snagged in the grass. Also, the clubface is lofted and will elevate the ball very quickly. The quicker the ball gets up, the less it tends to fly sideways.

When using the utility woods in the rough, you should exert slightly more grip pressure than usual. You want to get down

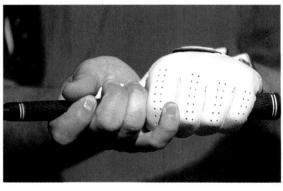

Above: When playing from the rough, you will need to hold the club firmly to avoid the club getting snagged by the grass.

Above: Utility woods are ideal for long shots from semi-rough.

Right: Trying to lead the club with the left hand (like playing a pitch shot) creates more of an out-to-in swing – this helps get a sharper strike in longer grass.

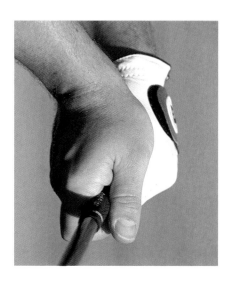

into the ball and through it, leading with your left hand.

SWINGPATH IN THE ROUGH

Whether you use a wood or an iron from the rough, you want to swing more out-to-in, rather than the normal swingpath of in-to-in. You are trying to come at the ball from the outside, so you should take the club back slightly outside the line and pick it up a little more abruptly than with your normal swing – somewhat like a bunker shot.

Then think about trying to angle the club down, imagining you are almost hitting a slice, moving the ball from left to right as much as possible. The more you slice across the target line, the more chance you have of getting a sharp strike on the back of the ball, which will get it up quickly and send it flying forwards, imparting the proper flight to the ball.

Because of this swingpath, you might even get a flyer with a wood. In that case, the ball could travel as far as it would from a normal lie on the fairway. But again, it takes practice to judge these shots properly.

PRO TIP

It's essential to practise hitting balls from the rough. If you don't, once you get into the stuff on a course, you will not know what to do. You'll have no feel for the situation, and you will not be able to assess the shot and choose the right method for escaping from trouble.

Find an empty field in which to practise, or any area where the grass has not been mown. Try a variety of shots and use your sand wedge or utility wood. Another option is to use the rough on your local golf course when playing on a quiet day, or the unkept areas around the practice grounds. Since they are often not maintained, the club probably will not mind you doing this. But it pays to ask first.

When I'm playing from the rough, I take the club back a little outside the line – aim a little left and visualize a fade shot.

At the top of the backswing, maintain your composure – all too often players panic when playing from the rough and rush into the shot.

As you swing through the ball, try to come slightly out-to-in, cutting down and across the ball.

As you swing through the ball, lead with the left hand, as though you're playing a pitch or bunker shot. This will produce a 'cutting' action ensuring a sharper strike on the ball.

Swing through the ball to a positive and athletic finish and watch your ball sail towards the green.

FAIRWAY BUNKERS

◆ ◆ ◆ ◆ ◆

Fairway bunkers vary from the deep pot bunkers you find on Scottish links courses, to the generally shallow ones that dot local public facilities. When you land in a fairway bunker, the first thing you must do is to assess how high the bank is in front of you, and how close you are to it.

THEN YOU can decide how prudent it might be to go for a distance shot, or just take your medicine and simply try to get out – using whatever escape route is open. The first rule with pot bunkers is to avoid them.

ALMOST INVISIBLE

Generally, they are almost invisible, often hidden from view when you are standing on the tee. The land may even slope towards them, drawing the ball in.

So look at a 'course planner' (a booklet providing detailed plans of the individual holes) before you play. Try to establish where the bunkers are and how far away they are placed, taking into consideration the distance you hit a driver or other club off the tee.

For example, if there is a pot bunker some 230 yards (210m) from the tee, it might well be better to use a club that you can only hit about 215 yards (197m) to ensure that you cannot reach the sand.

Then you are safe even if you mis-hit the ball to the left or right of the fairway. For the average golfer, it just does not make sense to take on a fairway bunker like the pros do.

If you end up rolling in, you will face a very tricky second shot.

Where to start

When playing from a fairway bunker, look at the top of the ball. Grip down the club slightly and consider only a club that has enough loft to clear the top of the bunker.

Using a 5-wood

Above: I'm using a 5-iron as I'm a little further back in the bunker, compared to the situation below where I'm closer to the bank and so a 7-iron must be used to clear the front lip.

From many fairway bunkers a shallow lip will allow you to hit the shot with anything up to a 5-wood.

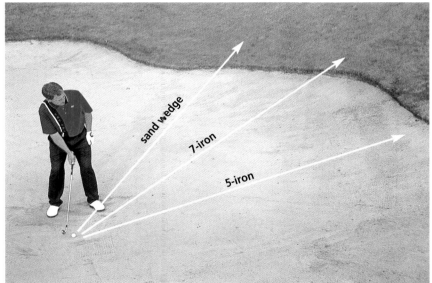

Using a sand wedge

Above: Always play a club that you know will get the ball over the front of the bunker.

Left: Even if you have to use a sand wedge, give careful consideration to where you want to play the ball on the fairway for your next shot – you may still make your par.

USING A LOB WEDGE FROM A GREENSIDE BUNKER

◆ ◆ ◆ ◆ ◆

When you have to get the ball up quickly from a fairway bunker, you might consider using a lob wedge, which many players now carry in their bags. The lob wedge can have 60 to 64 degrees of loft, whereas a sand wedge only has 56 degrees of loft.

BUT FOR most golfers, the best aspect is that you do not have to open the face of a lob wedge, which is the whole reason to own one. A lob wedge can be used with the clubface sitting squarely, which makes it much easier to play through the ball. That can take a lot of pressure off a golfer who already has enough to worry about in a fairway bunker.

MORE LIFT

Of course, you can also open up a lob wedge for even more lift on the ball, but generally I would not recommend doing that. If you try to open up your lob wedge, you run the risk of hitting clean under the ball – with little or no forward momentum and leaving the ball in the bunker.

So take a conventional bunker set-up with the lob wedge, then play the shot with a square clubface, aiming the blade along the line of flight – while making sure you pull the club through the sand, moving forwards rather than down.

LOB WEDGE VERSUS SAND WEDGE

Why use a sand wedge at all if you now own a lob wedge?

A lob wedge generally does not have much of a flange on it – the thicker sole under a sand iron that is angled slightly to give the club bounce and that keeps it from burying itself in the sand.

A lob wedge can have a sharper soleplate, but it certainly will not have the reverse angle of a sand wedge. The sand iron is designed so that the back of the sole sits on the ground, while the front edge of the clubface is actually in the air – by as much as 20 degrees.

BOUNCING EDGE

That is what gives the sand wedge bounce. It is made that way so the back edge will hit the sand and not dig in. In effect, the bounce stops the club from burying itself in the sand, which causes the club to decelerate or even to stop.

So, if you use a lob wedge, keep the differences between the two clubs in mind. With a sand wedge, you can really splash into the bunker knowing that the bounce on the bottom of the club will help it keep moving. But with a lob wedge, the club may stop.

In fact, the lob wedge may just go downwards into the sand and sink in. As a result, make sure you drive through the sand more, moving forwards rather than down. Of course, you should still take some sand. Trying to hit too cleanly opens you up to the risk of thinning or semi-topping the ball.

Trust your lob wedge and swing forwards toward your intended target.

A lob wedge can have up to 64 degrees of loft – it is, therefore, ideal when you have to get the ball up quickly and land it softly.

A sand wedge can be used to play a very high shot but will need to be opened, making the shot more difficult.

Take the club back outside the ball-to-target line.

Make a full backswing.

As you swing through, bring the club across the ball swinging left.

Keep the hands ahead of the clubhead as the club swings through the ball.

Swing all the way through to a complete finish.

GETTING OUT OF
FAIRWAY BUNKERS

◆ ◆ ◆ ◆ ◆

*The standard fairway bunker generally has a much lower lip
than a pot bunker, rising to perhaps only four feet (1.2m) at most.
However, that is intimidating enough if you are the least bit unsure about
how to execute this shot. The problem is that you have to get the ball out
cleanly, and you probably still have a considerable distance to go
before landing it on the green.*

S O TAKE a deep breath and try to
assess what you can and cannot do
given your situation, while conjuring
up a picture of a successful shot flying out of
the bunker.

SIZING UP THE LIP

The first factor to take into consideration is
how close you are to the front part of the
bunker, or the lip. If you are only a few feet
away, that will have a big influence on the
shot, compared to a position at the back,
which can almost take the face of the bunker
out of play.

In the first instance, you may have to
settle for a lofted club to clear the lip, while
in the latter situation, you might even be
able to use a 3-wood to achieve maximum
distance.

ASSESSING THE LIE

The second factor to consider in fairway
bunkers is the lie. This is a shot where you
need to make clean contact with the ball. But
if the ball is plugged in the sand in any way,
that will be impossible. So take a sand
wedge, play the ball out safe, and don't
expect too much.

On the other hand, if you have a decent
lie and some clearance, once again you might
consider using a wood and going for
the green.

Assessing the lie

Assess the lie before choosing your golf club. If the
ball is sitting down in the sand, you will need to use a
lofted club to get the ball out.

Choosing the angle

A trick to help get the ball up quickly,
while still getting distance, is to take a
lower number iron or wood and open
the face. Aim left to compensate,
otherwise the ball will end up in the
rough on the right.

Fairway bunker shot

When I play a fairway bunker shot, I do the following: take aim, (open my clubface if necessary), embed my feet, make a three-quarter swing and look at the top of the ball – and then off you go. Good luck!

CLEARING THE FACE

When the lip of a fairway bunker is a factor, you want to choose a golf club that has sufficient loft on it, both to get the ball out and to cover the appropriate distance – without changing your golf swing. Tinkering with your swing puts you in unfamiliar territory, which is a double-whammy when you are already stranded in a fairway bunker. Performing a normal swing is difficult enough.

SOLVING A DILEMMA

How do you solve this dilemma? Let's say you have a shot that demands the distance of a 7-iron, but the height of a 9. To get the extra distance and height, try aiming left of the target, then open the clubface slightly and play the shot with a slight fade or even a small slice. This will produce a more lofted shot – but using your normal swing.

You should also try to focus on the top of the ball to avoid hitting it fat. And you should make sure that you have a decent footing in the sand so you do not slip. Using a three-quarter to full swing, try to ensure you get clean contact. Hitting the sand first will kill the shot.

But remember – don't be over-ambitious. If you choose a club with which it is almost impossible to get the appropriate lift, the ball will hit the face of the bunker and come back at you. Then you really are in serious trouble.

USING UTILITY WOODS FROM THE BUNKER

◆ ◆ ◆ ◆ ◆

If you are far enough back in a fairway bunker to play a shot without the lip of the bunker being a major consideration, and you have a decent lie, you might consider using a wood for your shot. In this situation, the biggest danger is actually hitting fat, which will kill any chance of either getting out or achieving any distance.

UTILITY WOODS are ideal for this shot, although you can even hit a 3-wood if you feel confident enough with that club. But I would recommend for most golfers to use a 5-, 7- or 9-wood. Any of these clubs will give you the combination of distance and a clean strike that will help get you out of trouble and perhaps even save par.

BIG HELP

Most golfers are surprised when I tell them that any wood is easier to hit in a fairway bunker than an iron. In simple physical terms, when you play a wood, its broad sole is a big help. Even if you do hit the sand behind the ball, the wood cannot dig in – unless you have a major swing fault.

With the proper swing applied, the wood has to keep moving, and it will keep moving forwards across the surface of sand.

GENERAL GUIDELINES

1. The initial weighing-up of the shot is crucial.

2. Knowing which club you are going to use and how much height you can get on the ball is absolutely essential.

3. If you need to do anything different, such as trying to slice the ball slightly, be absolutely sure you know what you are going to do and believe in the shot.

4. Use your common sense with regard to where you are going to land the ball if you cannot reach the green.

5. Try to land the shot in a spot that makes the next shot as easy and straightforward as possible.

6. The worst thing you can do from a fairway bunker is to be over-ambitious and force the shot. That's dicing with death, and a guarantee that you will soon be playing another shot from roughly the same spot.

Play your normal swing from a fairway bunker with a utility wood and you'll be amazed just how successful you will become at playing this shot.

It's easier than you think

Left: Give careful consideration to where you will place your shot – here I'm going to play the ball out to the left and curl the ball with a slight fade back to the middle of the fairway. This will keep me away from the trouble on the right.

The shape of a utility wood (especially the large sole) makes playing a lofted wood easier than a long iron.

Make sure you don't touch the sand at address or on the way back – otherwise you will incur a two-stroke penalty.

As with all fairway bunker shots, to ensure a clear strike look at the top of the ball.

PRO TIP

Do not forget the rules that apply to bunker play:

• Do not ground the club before hitting the ball.

• Do not touch the sand or the back lip of the bunker on the backswing. That goes for practice swings too.

• If you hit the ball and it does not get out of the bunker, do not try to be overly courteous by brushing out your footprints or raking the bunker before hitting your second shot. The ball is still in the bunker, and therefore you cannot disturb the surface of the sand until you have hit it out.

All of the above rules carry a two-shot penalty if they are broken.

PLAYING FROM A DIVOT

◆ ◆ ◆ ◆ ◆

The first problem when playing from a divot is usually a psychological one.
After walking down the fairway, you discover the ball is in a divot hole.
Even worse, unless the ball is sitting up on the front or back edge of the
divot, it will probably be below the level of the fairway.

NOW you're frustrated – especially if you hit a good shot to get there in the first place. But if you start feeling sorry for yourself, you are likely to aggravate the problem even more. Landing in a divot happens, and it happens to everybody, which is something you have to accept and deal with appropriately. In fact, some would contend that hitting into a divot in the final round of 1998 US Open cost Payne Stewart that title. But a year later, Stewart came back and won the 1999 US Open.

So approach this shot positively. Playing from a divot is not impossible by any means. Here's how it's done.

THE APPROACH SHOT

In playing out of a divot, you are essentially trying to get your clubhead down into the divot hole, making as clean a contact with the ball as possible. Therefore, club selection is all-important – although distance is not the only factor.

On a par five or short par four, you are most likely to land in a divot within 100 yards (91m) of the green, which is where almost everyone's approach shot or drive finishes. But if the ball is sitting down in the divot hole – and a sand wedge is the right club for the distance to the green – you have a real problem.

The sand wedge is designed to bounce, rather than go down into a hole. So steer away from the sand wedge, or you will end up thinning the ball.

PLAYING WITH A LOB WEDGE

The lob wedge is a good choice for an approach shot from a divot. Position the ball back in your stance and close the face up a bit. In effect, that will make your lob wedge into a sand wedge, giving you the loft you are looking for without the bounce. And that will help you get the club down into the divot hole.

Keeping your hands fairly forward, favour your front foot with most of your weight, then try to concentrate on driving through the shot.

Use a three-quarter swing for a more

Playing from a divot isn't the easiest shot in golf, but if you use a lofted club, it need not become a disaster.

compact movement, which will help you to drive through the ball and downwards into the shot. I emphasize downwards because if the club brushes or sweeps across the surface of the fairway, you will merely top or thin the shot.

TAKE ANOTHER DIVOT

The key to this shot is to drive down into the ball and take another divot. In other words, if you are playing from a divot, you have to take another divot! However, I must warn you that the ball can shoot out of these lies and take off – or it can fly normally. It's difficult to judge.

MARGIN OF ERROR

So if you have an option in terms of where to land the ball on the green, I would definitely take aim at the broadest open area. You must not take the tightest line, such as over a bunker to a small landing area. You want plenty of space to give yourself a margin of error. Hitting a perfect shot from a divot is extremely ambitious so allow for some degree of error.

Besides the lob wedge, and depending on the situation, you might also consider playing an 8, 9 or pitching wedge. None of these clubs has any bounce on the sole. But stay away from the sand wedge!

Turning a disappointment into a success

GET OUT OF A RUT

Remember that to get out of a divot, you have to take another divot (see below). Many beginners and even some intermediate players often do not take divots after the ball because they lack confidence and have never learned how to hit an iron with a sharp, descending blow. To build that confidence – so you can strike firmly and take another divot when faced with this tricky shot – practise by putting a tee peg an inch or two in front of a ball on the practice range. Then focus on hitting down and through the tee peg.

When I play this shot, I set up with my hands more forward of the clubhead than normally. I keep a little more of weight towards my left foot on the backswing and try to take another divot on my throughswing. This helps me dig down and get under the ball. And finally I drive through the ball towards my target.

PLAYING A LONG APPROACH FROM A DIVOT

◆ ◆ ◆ ◆ ◆

When you are playing from a divot and need distance, do not think of using a 3- or 4-iron. In fact, avoid the long irons like the plague. Once again, the utility woods can come to your rescue, especially if you have the more modern type with a 'V-shaped' sole.

HOWEVER, IF the sole of your favourite wood is flat, that makes things more difficult. Imagine that shape of clubhead going into the divot. With a flat sole, you are going to hit behind the ball.

Modern fairway woods have a low centre of mass, especially the ones with loft. As a result, they can get the ball airborne quickly. You would not hit a 3-wood from a divot, and even a 5- would be ambitious, but the new 7- and 9-woods with 'V' soles are absolutely superb.

REALISTIC GOALS

But let's say you're 175 yards (160m) from the green and you do not have a utility wood. In that case, I would only feel comfortable recommending that you go down to about a 6- or 7-iron. Unfortunately, you will not get any more distance than usual because you will not get a flyer playing out of a divot. So

Digging yourself out of trouble

be realistic about what you can achieve. You may not be able to go for the green.

If there are also hazards around the green, such as bunkers, trees or water, being too ambitious could put you into further misery. The best move in that situation is to take a 9-iron or pitching wedge and just play the ball into position.

And remember, you must take a divot to play out of a divot!

Playing this shot requires commitment and belief. Make a compact backswing and drive through the ball with firm wrists and, most importantly, take another divot.

THE ETIQUETTE OF DIVOTS

The conventional wisdom has always been that players should replace divots. But now some golf clubs discourage this. Check the local rules on the scorecard, or talk to the secretary or pro to find out what their policy is. Golf clubs are finding that divots do not regrow well, and consequently that replacing them causes more of a problem than it solves. Increasingly, greenkeepers prefer to put seed and soil in the divot holes at night. So if you replace the divot, you may be just doubling their work. They will have to search the fairways to take them out, then fill the holes back in.

Aim left of the target as you are going to cut the ball out of this lie. You can do it!

TIGHT LIES AND HARDPAN

◆ ◆ ◆ ◆ ◆

Tight lies are often encountered on links and chalk-based golf courses, or others that do not have fairway irrigation systems – especially when the weather heats up. Because the fairways start to dry out and the grass does not grow lush – or is very fine and mowed closely – the ball will appear to be sitting down. Many golfers find this psychologically difficult. They are sure they will be unable to get under the ball and hit their normal shot.

I N FACT, on courses where the grass is lush, the ball does sit up slightly, with some air underneath. But that does not mean that golfers who are used to those conditions cannot hit off tighter lies.

For instance, the sub-soil under many links courses is often much softer than it appears, and hitting down and through the ball, while taking a perfectly good divot, is fairly easy and straightforward – once the golfer gets used to the idea and is convinced that it is possible.

However, the tight lie that is truly difficult is the shot played off hardpan: dry patches that can bake into almost a rock-like hardness. But even this shot can be hit successfully, and with considerable backspin, if the proper set-up and swing are employed.

OVERCOMING FEARS

The biggest problem with playing from a tight lie is often simply in the player's mind. He or she is petrified of thinning or topping the ball. As a result, this golfer tries far too hard to get under the ball, which can lead to complete disaster.

When one tries to lift the ball on purpose, there is a tendency to stay back on the right foot, then swing upwards. Doing that will ensure topping or skulling the ball. Don't change your stroke for tight lies!

You should still go slightly down into the ball. However, if you are playing on clay or chalky soil – or any other type that has

become compacted in areas prone to wear – then I would add a note of caution. Hitting too hard down into that kind of surface could injure your wrists.

A ball lying on a tight lie or hardpan is most golfers' nightmare. But if you know how to play this shot, it's easier than it looks.

Keeping the weight on the front foot is the key to success in playing from a tight lie.

This is how *not* to play the shot. Trying to scoop the ball up into the air will lead to disaster.

Playing off hardpan

LANDING THE BALL SOFTLY

I always try to analyze my shots. If I have a very tight lie and I'm playing an approach shot from 50 or 60 yards (46 to 55m) to the green – needing to get up and over a bunker and land the ball softly – I want to be careful that I do not get any bounce.

So if I'm using a sand wedge, I set the ball back in my stance, then take that bounce away by closing the club down and putting my hands ahead of the ball. Going through the ball, I try not to dig in too much – which will be impossible anyway – and skim the surface, keeping my hands well ahead of the clubhead and my weight very much on the left foot.

Why? If the weight drifts back to the right foot, I will start to scoop at the ball.

HARDPAN

Hardpan is generally hard, dry, packed mud, and can be encountered anywhere on a golf course. Clay-based courses have the most hardpan, because as soon as it gets dry in the summer, the course starts to bake, the grass dies, and bare patches as hard as rock begin to form.

Hardpan can intimidate the average golfer, but you should keep in mind that you can make a good shot off the stuff. It's not impossible with the appropriate adjustments to your set-up, stance, and ball position.

VIOLENT CHECK

First, put the ball back in your stance – towards the centre or even nearer the right foot – and close the club face down slightly. On short approach shots, use a lofted club and hit down on the ball, trying your best to make a clean contact.

The fact is, you can actually get more backspin on this shot than a conventional one, because – if you think about it – you have nothing between the clubface and the ball.

And once you hit the ball, it will fly in quite low and bounce one, two or three times, then suddenly check quite violently – even spinning backwards from that point.

Here I'm playing a sand wedge off my back foot with a closed face. My hands are forward of the clubface throughout the stroke and my weight is planted firmly on my left foot. As I play the shot, I keep my hands and weight forward at all times.

PRO TIP

If playing off hardpan worries you and you are a short distance from the green, and the ground is very dry and hard, you might use a putter rather than a lofted club – if you can get away with it. Doing this means you do not have to get under the ball and will give you added confidence. Or you might try using a 7-iron with a short putting or chipping stroke in an effort to get the ball running in. Even if you mis-hit this shot, it will not matter that much.

THE LONGER SHOT FROM HARDPAN

If you are playing from further away, do not make too many changes to your normal set-up and swing. I tend to put the ball farther back in my stance than usual and keep my weight fractionally more on my left foot. Reducing my usual weight shift will ensure I do not scoop the ball.

Again, be sure you play through the ball, thinking about making clean contact. You don't want to hit the ground behind the ball.

I recommend that you also look at the top of the ball – as I suggested you do with the fairway bunker shot – to ensure you get clean contact.

Above: Here I'm playing a shot off not only a very hard surface but my stance is also uneven. Therefore I'm limiting my weight transfer and concentrating on keeping my balance.

Above right and far right: I keep my backswing smooth in order to maintain balance and help strike the ball cleanly. A three-quarter backswing is plenty here and, as with my fairway bunker shot, I focus on the top of the golf ball.

Right: As I've swung through the ball, I've nipped it off the surface. This shot was played to a green some 100 yards (91m) away – when the ball landed it spun back some ten yards, which is not uncommon from this type of lie.

LOOSE LIES

◆ ◆ ◆ ◆ ◆

Loose lies are a particular problem on parkland and heathland courses in the autumn, when the ball can land on leaves, twigs or pine needles. But you can also get a loose lie in the rough on links courses and in the sandy areas around greens. Loose stones and soil are also a problem on many courses.

YOU SHOULD assess this shot carefully before hitting the ball, a precaution which many golfers fail to observe. Most players often tend to dismiss this type of lie as not very significant. Plunging in, he or she will give the ball a quick whack and hope for the best.

But if you look carefully at what you are confronted with on a loose lie, you'll see that there are several adjustments that should be made to hit this shot properly.

A clean contact from this lie is essential, so once again focus on the top of the ball.

ASSESS THE DEPTH

With a loose lie, the ball may actually be sitting off the ground, perched on leaves or other debris. If you merely hit downwards with an iron into this kind of lie, you may well leave the ball where it is as the clubhead skims harmlessly underneath, taking nothing but air with it.

So try to assess the depth of the lie, while at the same time remembering that if you disturb the ball, you will incur a penalty stroke. In addition, although you can remove loose debris from around the ball, you cannot rip out any plant, bramble or branch that is rooted in the soil or perhaps connected to a nearby tree or bush.

Another common loose lie is found when the ball lands on a bark pathway. First, you should assess how deep the material is. I would suggest taking up a stance, and, as in a bunker shot, wriggling your feet around to get a sense of how to balance yourself properly.

This is acceptable, as long as you do not start digging into the pathway, and especially

near the ball, since it could move. By the way, always check the scorecard to see if you get a free drop off a bark pathway. That's certainly one way of coping successfully with a loose lie – but here are two other ways of playing a shot off a loose lie.

MAKING CONTACT

Getting clean contact with the ball is difficult off loose lies. I tend to use the same approach as a bunker shot, hitting an inch and a half (4cm) behind the ball to splash it out. Of course, you will not get any backspin, and the ball will run when it lands, so take that into account.

When the ball is sitting on twigs, using the splash shot becomes more problematic. If the debris is hard and brittle, it may well interfere with your strike and make any forward momentum difficult to achieve. Here you need to lift the club more abruptly, again using the out-to-in swing of a bunker shot, trying to pick the ball as cleanly as possible from the surface.

Be careful if removing debris around your ball not to move the ball, otherwise you'll be penalized. Only remove debris if you are certain it will not affect the lie of your ball – and remember that any vegetation moved must not be attached or living material.

Using a utility wood from a loose lie

If you're a long way from the green and distance is a requirement, use your 5- or 7-wood. This will have the added advantage of lifting the ball up over any obstacles in front of you.

Wedge it out

A wedge or 9-iron should easily be able to clip the ball out of a loose lie. Make a three-quarter swing and swing through the ball positively. Don't hit into the leaves and quit, otherwise you'll lose power.

HIT CLEAN

On parkland courses, you might find a loose lie along the tree line, where there are typically leaves, foliage and pine needles on the ground. Taking the distance from the green and the lie into consideration – let's assume you're about 120 to 130 yards (110 to 120m) away – I would suggest playing a 9-iron or wedge. Again, you want to lift the ball and hit it with some height, which means making clean contact, swinging from out-to-in in an attempt to fade the ball.

FOCUS ON TOP

One way to do this is by trying to hit the back of the ball first before the club makes contact with the ground. I focus on the top of the ball to make sure I hit it clean. Of course, you also run the risk of thinning or topping the ball, but I would prefer to do that rather than hit fat, or strike the ground before the ball, which deadens the shot and loses distance.

You might also consider using a utility wood if you can make any contact from a loose lie. The wood will help get the ball airborne, and the big soleplate will help glide the club across the surface, so it will not be as adversely affected by the lie.

With an iron, if anything gets between the clubface and the ball when playing off a loose lie, power will be reduced.

UPHILL LIES

◆ ◆ ◆ ◆ ◆

Playing off an uphill lie will make the ball fly higher, and thus travel a shorter distance, so you should always take at least one more club than normal (i.e. a 5-iron rather than a 6-iron). The other major effect this lie produces is a right-to-left movement of the ball, similar in effect to a draw.

PLAY THE ball further forward in your stance and position yourself in alignment with the slope, in this case allowing the right shoulder to drop down a bit more to mirror the rise in the land.

Weight distribution will also be affected. Don't fight the slope. Simply allow more weight to settle on to your back foot.

Now aim more to the right of the target because you are going to pull the ball slightly, and don't worry about your weight transfer, which will stay a little towards the back foot.

KEEPING BALANCE

One of the most important things to remember about any sloping lie is that you have to keep your balance throughout the swing. Take a few practice swings to determine how far back and through you want to bring the club in order to maintain good balance.

You might have to shorten your swing, thinking more in terms of an arms-and-hands shot, because you will not get as much body rotation and weight transfer as you would normally. If you did, you would simply fall over!

KEEPING FAITH

Because you will probably use more of a hands-and-arms swing for this shot — especially on the follow-through — the clubhead will tend to close. Aiming more to the right counteracts that.

Execute the shot with that in mind. You have to believe that the compensations that you have made will be enough to allow you to hit a reasonably good shot. Keeping faith with the shot is important.

You should also make sure that your rhythm is very smooth. Trying to force the shot is the worst sin you can commit. If you are afraid that you don't have enough club, take one more. And if you cannot do that, tell yourself that you must live with the consequences and keep it easy.

KNOW YOUR GAME

When playing from sloping lies, you have to think in the context of your own game, and apply that knowledge. For instance, if you tend to hit a slice or fade, you are not suddenly going to start to hit a draw from an uphill lie.

Instead, the slicer will hit a smaller slice, and a fader will hit the ball straight. But if you normally hit straight, you will hit with a draw. And if you hit it with a draw, you'll hit a hook.

It's all relative. So if you usually hit a fade, do not aim for a big draw, you will just hit it straight or fade it a bit.

Opposite: **When you are confronted with an uphill lie, allow for the ball to move left with a draw (right-to-left) flight. So aim to the right, position the ball slightly further forward in your stance and angle your shoulders so that they follow the slope that your are playing from. Your weight will settle a little more towards your right foot.**

DOWNHILL LIES

◆ ◆ ◆ ◆ ◆

The downhill lie is generally a more awkward shot than the uphill lie for most players. It is always a little scary to have your back foot above your front foot, especially at the top of the backswing, where you may tend to lose balance.

HOW DO you compensate for the slope? The first thing to remember is that the lie will deloft the clubhead, which will mean that you will hit the ball lower and further than normal. So take at least one less club.

Then think about the effect on the spin imparted to the ball. From a downhill lie, you will generally hit the ball with a fade, or left-to-right. So aim more to the left and allow the ball to fade. Do not try to fight it.

FOLLOW THE SLOPE

In lining up, let your shoulders follow the line of the slope. Take an open stance, playing the ball further back because the club will come into contact with the ground sooner than on a level surface.

When you visualize the shot, remember that it will fly lower and have less backspin, so the ball will run further on its approach. Think about how it will land, kick and run on, and remember that it will work from left to right and kick in.

Picturing the shot always helps when playing from awkward lies. If you see a positive outcome and believe in the shot,

that will go a long way towards helping you to hit it properly. But many players allow themselves to be put off by the situation, and that is the beginning of the end. They will certainly not play the shot well because they will lack the mental confidence to do so.

FOCUS BACK

The downhill lie also poses more problems in terms of keeping your balance. You are definitely looking more at a three-quarter swing, with the weight tending to stay on your front foot when you take your backswing. You should accept that you will not get much weight transfer, which will shorten your swing anyway.

The follow-through will be fairly straightforward, but you must make sure you do not move ahead of the ball. It's easy to allow your head to drift too far forward when playing from this type of lie.

I try to ensure that I stay behind the golf ball by watching the back of the ball. Focus on the back of the ball. Otherwise, you'll top it. In addition, your rhythm needs to be very smooth. If you hurry the stroke, you will lose your balance.

The downhill lie is the most difficult for most players.

Place your ball further back in your stance.

PRO TIP

If you normally hit the ball with a draw, you will not suddenly hit a slice off a downhill lie – you might hit it straight. On the other hand, if you do slice or hit a fade, you might hit a massive slice from this type of lie. So take that into account.

Left: Angle your shoulders to match the slope.

Opposite: A three-quarter backswing with your weight staying more on your left foot is inevitable.

BALL ABOVE THE FEET

◆ ◆ ◆ ◆ ◆

Hitting a shot when the ball is above your feet is fairly straightforward, if you are aware of a few things. The ball will definitely move from right to left, or draw. You really cannot prevent that.

THE MORE acute the slope, the more the ball will move to the left from this type of lie. In fact, if you are playing from a really steep sidehill lie – with the ball perched right in front of your face – the ball will just go straight left.

AIM RIGHT

So you really have to aim right, and a long way off line, to hit the ball at your target, especially with a severe lie.

Grip down on the golf club. Depending on how far above your feet the ball is, you might have to grip a really long way down to reduce the club's length. With the worst of these lies, play a very lofted club, such as a

sand wedge or a wedge, because the ball will go sideways, and the flight path could be very dramatic.

MORE CLUB

From a more conventional sidehill lie, with the ball maybe six inches (15cm) above your feet or less, the ball will still move to the left. So again, depending on the way you normally hit the ball, allow for that by aiming more to the right. Then grip down the golf club, which reduces its length and takes distance off the shot.

For example, if you have to grip three inches (8cm) down, that means hitting two or three more clubs than you would normally.

With the ball above your feet, aim more to the right of the target.

A more compact swing will ensure a good strike on the ball.

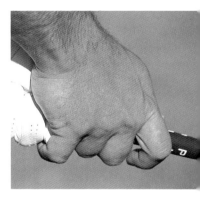

Above: Grip down the club in order to compensate for the slope and the fact that the ball is above your feet.

How to play the ball above your feet

A three-quarter back- and throughswing will help you to control this shot and hit the green with a controlled draw.

You judge that depending on the severity of the slope. If you don't grip down, you'll hit straight into the ground behind the ball.

TIGHT ACTION

If the ball is only slightly above your feet, don't change your normal golf swing. Just keep your tempo smooth and make a clean hit. You also do not need to change your ball position. Just allow for the ball to go further left than usual and play your normal shot.

But if the ball is six or eight inches (15 to 20cm) above your feet, then you have to go for a very precise strike. In this case, use a three-quarter swing, keeping your action nicely tight and compact, making sure you get clean contact with the ball.

Again, allow for the ball to go less distance because you have gripped down on the club. Don't try to overdo it, or get too much out of the shot.

The ball will draw more because you are standing more upright, which produces a flatter swing plane and causes the ball to move more right-to-left.

BALANCE IS THE KEY

When hitting off any sidehill lie, balance is the key component to your swing. So this is one instance where taking several practice swings – while observing proper etiquette and not holding anyone up – is essential. Step back from the shot and find a position along the slope that is comparable to the place where your ball lies. Then take several practice swings, trying to keep your weight forward to compensate for the flat swing arc this lie forces you to use. Remember, if you lose your balance on this shot, you'll be defeated from the very start because you will fall backwards as you take the club away on the backswing. And if you do that, making any adjustment during the swing that allows a decent hit on the ball will be virtually impossible.

BALL BELOW THE FEET

◆ ◆ ◆ ◆ ◆

Playing a shot when the ball is below your feet is probably the most difficult shot for most golfers. With the ball so far down, we instinctively know that it's easy to lose our balance. So the first thing I think about when addressing the ball is keeping my weight back — or more towards my heels — and making sure it stays there.

OF COURSE, that does not mean that you do not get over the ball. When you take up your posture, you still must bend over sufficiently. But many players do not do this. They try to use their conventional posture. Standing up far too straight, they are surprised when they top the ball.

So, provide a counterbalance with your bottom. Stick it out. Sit back. Imagine you are almost sitting into the bank.

TAKE MORE CLUB

What effect will this lie have on the flight of the ball? It will definitely go left-to-right with a fade, and that could be significant. It could even produce a slice. Of course, that means a loss of distance, so you need to take more club to compensate. But taking more club will also help, since added length will lessen the effect of having the ball below your feet.

When you set-up, plant your weight firmly back on your heels, assume your posture close to the ball, then take a few practice swings. You have to feel comfortable with this shot, even though it's not a familiar one that you play everyday.

Sense what kind of swing will work, and how much weight transfer you will realistically get — until you almost fall over. Then try to get an idea of how to play well within that range.

STAY WITH THE SHOT

Do not use anything more than a three-quarter swing off a downhill lie, even if it isn't very severe — simply to ensure that you keep your balance. At the same time, make sure that you aim far enough to the left, and don't underdo it, because the ball will spin and definitely slice.

The ball below the feet is a difficult shot for any golfer. This key to success here is being realistic in deciding on the shot you are trying to play.

The key to success is to stay with this shot. That's the biggest failing of most players. You have to stay over the ball. If you come up even a fraction, it will be a disaster. You will top it.

Stay relaxed, stay over the ball, use a compact swing, and believe in what you are about to do, trusting that the ball will move from left-to-right. And remember to stay down as long as you can.

The ball below the feet

Left: At set-up concentrate on keeping your weight back towards your heels in order to maintain balance. Aim to the left as the ball will always fade or slice from this lie.

Left: At the top of the backswing there is just one thing that matters – balance.

Below left: At impact concentrate on watching the club strike the ball. It's essential that you stay down with this shot, otherwise you will top the ball.

PRO TIP

If you have problems that cause you either to top or to thin the ball, it's good practice to hit off downhill lies. With such a shot, you have to force yourself to stay with the ball. Most players do not find that very easy, so the more you practise this way, the more you will feel relaxed when you face one of these difficult shots on the course. Take some lessons on sidehill lies as well. Also, most driving ranges these days have mats with varying slopes. They allow you to play the full spectrum of shots whenever you practise.

Below: When you complete the swing, keep your balance and watch the ball fly left initially and then move right towards the target.

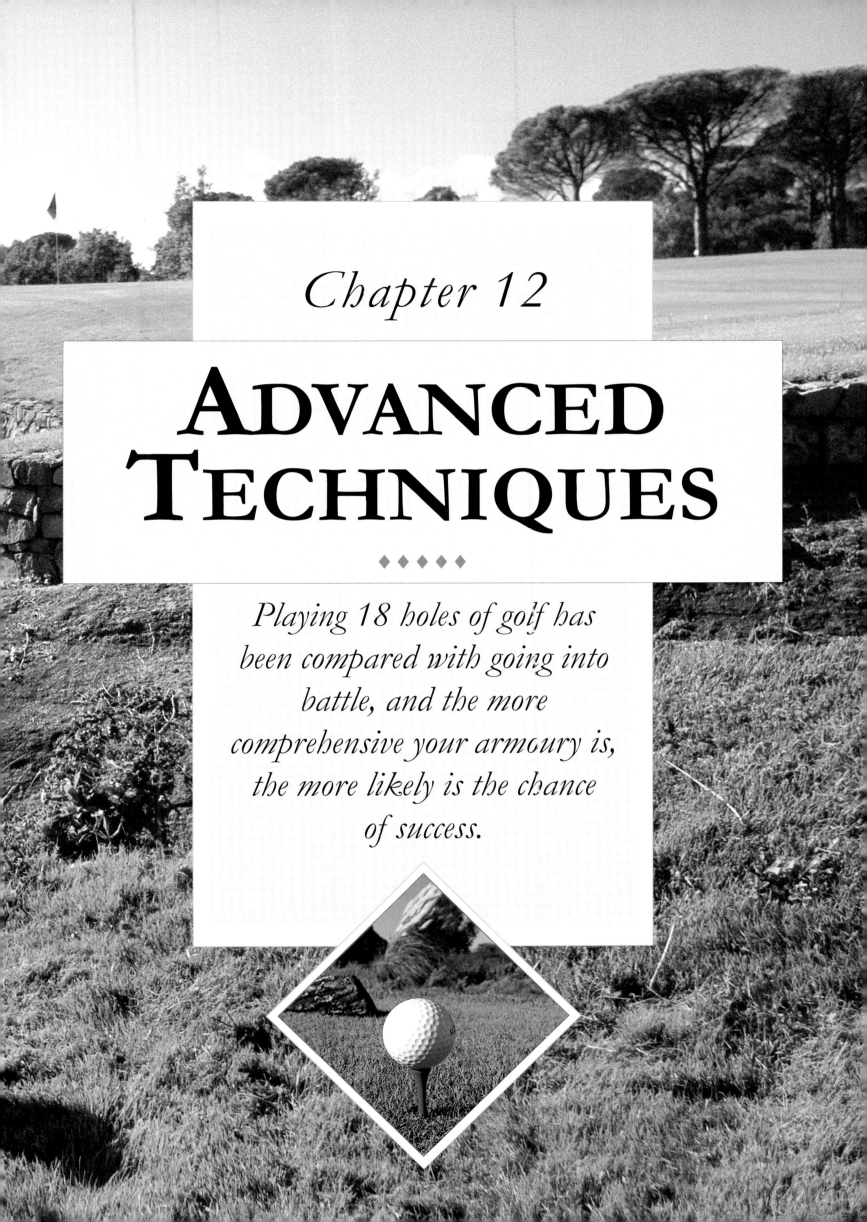

Chapter 12

ADVANCED TECHNIQUES

◆ ◆ ◆ ◆ ◆

*Playing 18 holes of golf has
been compared with going into
battle, and the more
comprehensive your armoury is,
the more likely is the chance
of success.*

ADVANCED TECHNIQUES

◆ ◆ ◆ ◆ ◆

Welcome to the master class. The term advanced techniques implies just what it says, and, at the risk of sounding rude or insulting, I have to caution you — beginners need not apply just yet. This section is aimed at players who have mastered the basics of the game.

BY DEFINITION, advanced techniques are difficult to learn and even harder to execute on the course. As a result, trying to learn these shots before you are ready could do some serious damage to your current game. In turn, that may remove both your ability to score and all the fun from playing — a risk hardly worth taking for the beginner or even an intermediate player.

COMFORTABLE AND COMPETENT

So before trying anything in this section, make sure you are already competent and comfortable with your overall golf game. In fact, I urge you to check the following list first to determine if you are ready to learn the advanced techniques of golf:

• Have you have mastered the fundamentals of stance, alignment, posture and ball position, so that you can set up to the ball instinctively?

• Do you have a swing that is both reliable and repeatable — even under pressure and in high winds?

• Do you possess a solid short game — one that ensures you always get out of a bunker on the first attempt, that you can chip and pitch well enough usually to threaten par, and that you can consistently sink those two-foot putts that make all the difference in your score?

If you didn't answer a firm 'yes' to all three items, beware of taking on any advanced technique. Doing so would be overly ambitious.

Once you have mastered the basics of the game, we can begin to broaden your repertoire of shots by playing intentional slices, hook shots, hitting the ball high and low, and much more

It is a great advantage when you need to create extra backspin, for instance, to have the shot in the bag. These pages contain the information to play a wide variety of golf shots you may not have considered before.

Golf courses are designed in many shapes and forms with a variety of hazards. To play consistently to a low handicap you need not only to master the fundamentals of the golf swing and short game, but also to know how to cope when conditions call for something special.

On the other hand, if you think you're ready, then this section is not only essential to the development of your game, but is the final path to both consistent play and the possibility of that dream round.

STAYING OUT OF TROUBLE

Why do you need these shots? Golf courses are designed (some would say by sadists!) to present a different series of challenges and to test a wide variety of shot-making ability.

Even on the first tee, the golfer is often confronted with a situation that calls for an advanced shot. The most common challenge, of course, is a dogleg-shaped hole, which demands a ball flight that will move from left to right or vice versa.

At the same time, the golfer may also need to shape a shot that avoids trees, bunkers, water and/or rough.

Once on the fairway, the golfer may then have to play any number of shots that both avoid trouble and call for creative skills in order to reach the green and score well. The weather may also combine with the architecture of the course to present a host of problems and demand a series of choices.

In a previous section, I discussed 'trouble shots' – ways of getting out of difficult situations. It should be noted that advanced techniques are not the same thing, because if you play these shots well, you will stay *out* of trouble. What I want to do in this section is show you how to play shots that are slightly different from your conventional golf swing, and yet which are often demanded by golf courses and/or adverse weather conditions.

For example, if you need to play a low shot into the wind, and do not know how to play it correctly, you will probably hit the ball too high, more than likely sending it spinning off into the rough, water or sand. Then you will be in trouble and need to employ a trouble shot to salvage a bogey or worse.

In this section, I'll show you how to hit a draw or fade, apply backspin to the ball, execute the bump-and-run or lob shot, and deal with a variety of wind conditions. Knowing how to play in the wind is a key to great golf. You can use the wind to your advantage at times, but you must also know how to limit the damage when that's not possible.

So playing golf well is not only a case of having a repeatable, textbook swing. Every golfer needs variety of shots in his or her repertoire that will allow them to adapt when the situation demands – and they are called upon to raise their game.

Learning these advanced techniques is the only way to succeed in these circumstances.

Playing a dogleg or bending the ball around a tree require some adjustments to your normal swing. These will need to be practised if you are to have the confidence to play the shot when it is needed.

THE DRAW SHOT

◆ ◆ ◆ ◆ ◆

A draw is a shot that propels the ball from right to left and it can increase distance, because the ball will generally run well when it lands. So it's a handy shot if you are looking to increase your length with the driver, fairway woods and long irons. The shape of the shot also helps you to avoid trouble off the tee, or play around hazards from the fairway.

I N ADDITION, a draw has a lower flight path, so it's an essential shot to have in your bag for windy days.

In order to hit the draw correctly, you must swing more in-to-out than normally, and develop some feel for how to shape the shot.

UNIQUE SWINGPATH

How do you produce the unique swingpath of a draw? Start with your alignment, pointing your feet, hips and shoulders slightly right of the target – or in what is often referred to as a 'closed' stance. But don't overdo it. Unless you are trying to bend the ball dramatically around an obstacle, the standard draw requires that you aim right by only about five degrees.

Next, set the ball back in your stance by about an inch to an inch and a half (3 to 4cm) from where you would normally place it for the club you are about to hit. This will encourage you to hit the ball from the inside.

Finally, adjust your grip by turning your hands to the right, or more underneath the club – this is often called a 'strong' grip. But be careful because overdoing this can easily turn a draw into a hook!

In fact, it's vital to experiment with various grip positions when you practise hitting a draw. If you hit the ball with a natural fade, or tend to slice it, drawing the ball will be difficult for you.

But mastering this shot can be fun. If you slice, trying to draw the ball is both challenging and rewarding, as you learn how

To play the draw shot, allow your hands to move slightly to the right on the grip.

The draw shot

to produce the opposite effect, which can also lead to hitting a straighter ball.

HOW TO HIT THE DRAW

In order to encourage an in-to-out swingpath, I tell golfers to imagine they are standing on a clockface with 12 o'clock being on the target-line straight ahead. Aiming the club at 1 o'clock, you want to take your swing back to 7 o'clock, then fire through to 1.

But why are you aiming at 1 o'clock rather than closing the face or squaring it to the target, which is the traditional way of teaching the draw?

I believe that if you see the clubface sitting closed to your swingpath, then you'll tend to swing to the left. But if you open the clubface a bit and aim at the 1 o'clock position, then you are already thinking in-to-out.

I also do not think that a golfer should do anything extraordinary on the backswing when learning a draw. I make a conventional backswing, then think about swinging the club from the inside on the throughswing, trying to let it drop in relatively close to my body. I promote this feeling by keeping the right elbow fairly close to the side of my torso as I start through, while visualizing how the club should swing out to the right.

IMPART SIDESPIN

I think it also helps to imagine you are playing this shot with a table tennis bat, attempting to impart sidespin – which in this case will be anti-clockwise. We are trying to get draw spin here, swinging the club from the inside to the outside, coming from fairly close to the body to away.

So a little extra right hand does not hurt as you come through the ball. Conjure up the idea of the right hand at the bottom of the swing arc and focus on the impression of using a table tennis bat. Looking at it another way, it's much like putting forehand topspin on a tennis ball.

Obviously, it is important that your hands are very free. A bit more release in the right hand than usual will not do any harm in developing the feel of a draw. But if you lock up in the hands, you'll lose confidence as you come through and block the ball miles to the right.

Remembering this is especially important if you tend to slice.

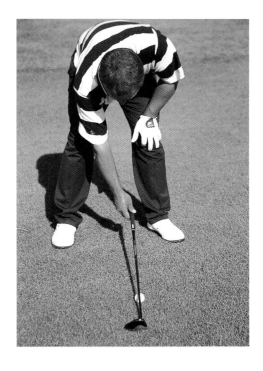

Below: Place the ball slightly (around an inch) further back in your stance.

Below: Aim slightly right of your target and hit from 7 o'clock to 1 o'clock. Swinging out to the right will help impart draw spin and move the ball from right to left.

KEYS TO LEARNING THE DRAW

◆ ◆ ◆ ◆ ◆

Try putting an umbrella into the ground just in front of your left foot to encourage the idea of swinging in-to-out. Now you must swing out from the right of the umbrella to avoid hitting it, and not allow the club to come back inside.

LAYING CLUBS on the ground is another way to groove an inside-to-out swingpath. Put one club near your feet, aiming slightly to the right of the target. Then put another club on the other side of the golf ball, pointing farther right of the target. Now swing along the lines of the club that is next to the ball to get the feel for the correct swingpath.

VISUALIZING THE SHOT

It's important to visualize any shot, but particularly so for the draw. You have to see this shot in order to feel it, imagining how it will bend from right to left. But unless that flight path is very clear in your mind, you should not even attempt to play a draw.

Think of it this way. Your brain can trigger a reflex in your body, which helps develop feel for the shot. And if you can feel the proper action for making the shot, then you can impart that to your arms and hands, which will work the club across the ball –

like that table tennis shot hitting the ball with sidespin.

But you also have to know where you want the ball to start. You must feel it starting out to the right, then working its way back around to the target. I cannot emphasize that enough. You must really feel that in order to execute this shot properly, producing a movement that allows you to swing down the right path.

REMAINING CONFIDENT

Golfers often lose confidence in their ability to hit a draw just when they get to the top of the backswing. If that happens, they pull right across the ball and hit it way left.

Again, it's because they do not want to swing the club out to the right, which goes against their natural instincts. You must have confidence to hit the ball out to the right and then let it come back again. And only with confidence will you allow yourself to swing with a free movement.

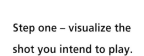

Step one – visualize the shot you intend to play.

Step two – once you've decided on the shot, commit yourself to a successful outcome. Here I'm trying to play the shot around a tree and bend the ball back to the left to hit the green.

Moving the ball right-to-left around an obstacle

Practising hitting shots with your right hand only is a great way to learn and understand the draw. Imagine you are playing a topspin table tennis shot as you make your swing and watch the ball move right to left.

PRACTISING THE DRAW

In order to learn this shot properly, you should practise first with only a 5- or 6-iron. You don't want to use a club with any more loft than that, because the more lofted a club is, the less potential you have to put spin on the ball.

That is why golfers generally hit their short irons straighter and more accurately. When the ball is going up, there's usually less sideways spin on it.

By contrast, the easiest clubs to draw (or fade) are the driver and long irons, because you can really get the ball spinning using less loft. However, you can also impart very violent spin with these clubs, so be careful.

HIT HALFSWINGS

Hit the 5- or 6-iron with little halfswings, concentrating on the swingpath to get a concept of how to impart spin – and gain an appreciation of how spin works. Again, this drill is about building a mental impression that you can transfer into the proper body movements.

Focus on your right hand, and how it has to work through the ball to create anti-clockwise spin.

Do this for some time and don't rush it, until, very gradually, you start to see the ball

moving from right to left. When that happens, you can start increasing the length of your swing, working slowly up to a full swing.

When playing a draw from the tee, position the ball on the far left of the tee box. You can then swing to the right which will encourage the draw shot.

PRO TIP

In order to promote the idea of hitting a draw when you are teeing off, tee the ball really high. That will automatically force you to sweep through the ball and encourage a feeling of hitting around it.

THE FADE SHOT

◆ ◆ ◆ ◆ ◆

Most players already naturally hit a fade, or its ugly sibling, the slice.
Lee Trevino, the master of hitting the ball left-to-right, once said that you
can talk to a fade but you can't talk to a hook. He's got a point.

LIKE A slice, a hook will make the ball run into all sorts of trouble. But when you hit the ball with a soft fade, at least you know the ball is going to stop nicely.

That's the beauty of this shot. The fade is ideal when you are faced with a left-to-right dogleg from the tee, when you have to bend the ball the same way around a hazard, or when you need to get more height to clear a tree and land the ball softly.

HIGH SHOT

Unlike the draw, the fade is a high shot that will not run very much when the ball reaches the ground. That makes it a great shot for long approaches to the green, but much trickier to use in the wind.

That's the good news. The bad news is that the average golfer will not get as much distance with a fade. And since most golfers lack some penetration with their shots anyway, always playing a fade is not desirable. In fact, most golfers would be better off trying to generate a draw in their swing, and using that particular option as their normal shot.

Having said that, knowing how to fade the ball is necessary for a variety of situations and absolutely essential if you truly want to improve your game.

HOW TO HIT A FADE

To hit a fade, I first open my stance by moving my front foot back of the target line. Aiming left, I align my feet, hips and shoulders in an open stance that points to 11 o'clock on the imaginary clockface.

In terms of swingpath, you want to think about moving out-to-in, pulling the club across the ball from 5 to 11 o'clock. That will impart clockwise spin.

If you tee the ball on the right-hand side of the teeing ground, it will encourage you to aim left and hit the fade shot.

How to play the fade

When you play the fade shot, aim slightly left of the target, move your grip fractionally to the left (a weaker grip), play the ball slightly further forward in your stance and picture the ball moving left-to-right.

ADJUSTED GRIP

The next thing you should do is to adjust your grip. If you naturally draw the ball, you will have to turn your hands round to the left – or 'weaken' your grip. This may be an advantage for some, but if you already hit the ball from left to right – or with a fade – it's important not to overdo this adjustment.

Opening your hands – or moving them more to the left – could produce a massive slice.

Remember that every change we make to create a golf shot has to be relative to *your*

game. So for the natural slicer, simply opening the stance a bit and aiming slightly left might be enough to produce the correct swingpath.

BALL POSITION

But let's assume you hit the ball straight and go from there. To hit a fade, especially if you want more height, means playing the ball a touch more forward in your stance than you would normally. Depending on where you start from, putting it about an inch (2.5cm) further forward should be enough. In simple terms, that means playing it off your left heel.

However, if you already play the ball from inside your left heel, you do not need to move it further forward for a fade. Playing any shot with the ball too far up in your stance will cause you to pull it – or hit straight left.

Left: To encourage the fade you can play the ball slightly further forwards – but don't overdo it!

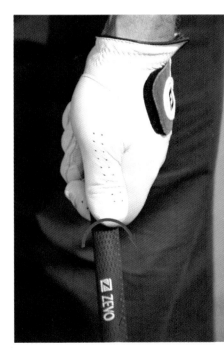

Above: Weaken the grip by turning the hands fractionally to the left.

KEYS TO THE FADE SWING

◆ ◆ ◆ ◆ ◆

I like to play a fade a little bit more from my left side.
After taking an open set-up, I swing back along the line of my stance,
without modifying anything in my backswing. Since I am aiming left,
I have already swung naturally outside the target line.

B UT WHEN I come through the ball, I want to cut across the same line and move the club inside by delaying the release of the clubhead just a fraction.

RELAXED HAND

How do I accomplish that? I first relax my right hand at address, and then grip the club a little bit tighter with the last three fingers of my left hand – the little, ring and middle fingers. In other words, the right hand stays very light, while the leading hand grips just a bit firmer.

When I come through the ball, I then try to feel as though I'm delaying the release of the clubhead just a bit, or simply preventing the club from coming through as early as normal. That should be enough to hit slightly across the ball.

However, this does not mean that I do not release the clubhead! What it means is the release comes just slightly later than it would for a regular shot. Apart from that, I just swing normally.

AVOIDING TROUBLE

Professional golfers routinely move the ball in varying directions to avoid trouble on one side of a golf course or the other. If the trouble is on the right, they'll hit a draw. If it's on the left-hand side, they'll play a fade. The key is actually to start the ball towards the trouble spot, then move it away.

The 18th hole on the championship West Course at Wentworth is a good example. This is a classic set-up for a fade because the hole doglegs left to right, with a big bunker on the left. Most pros will hit the ball at the bunker and then let it slide.

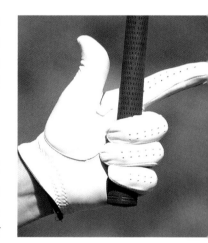

To encourage the fade, grip the club slightly firmer with the top three fingers of the left hand. Keep the right hand relaxed.

When you are trying to fade the ball off the tee with a wood, tee the ball down (above). This is especially useful when you're under pressure and there's trouble on the left. By teeing the ball down you are almost certain to fade the ball with a driver.

To play the fade shot, imagine you are swinging from 5 to 11 o'clock, moving the club across the ball on an out-to-in path. Feel more left-side control as you swing forwards with the left hand leading the clubhead through the ball.

So if you ever play Wentworth, I would suggest you tee the ball low on the 18th, get out your driver, and hit it straight at the bunker, gripping a little bit tighter with those last three fingers of the left hand.

You will pull the club through the ball as you do normally. But because you're hitting with the leading hand gripping just slightly tighter than the other hand, the clubface will come through a split second later. That will impart the necessary spin to curve the ball away from the bunker and into the middle of the fairway.

USE LESS LOFT

If you're hitting a wood and want almost to ensure you fade the ball, the less loft the better. In other words, if you normally hit a 3-wood off the tee, take a driver. And if you usually employ a 5-wood off the fairway, you might want to drop down to a 3.

The 3-wood is easier to fade because it makes the ball spin more than the loft on a 5-wood. In addition, you might even try hitting a driver off the fairway. To hit a draw in that situation is virtually impossible, but you have a chance if you try to fade the ball.

PRO TIP

If you are on the tee and want to make sure you do not hook the ball because there is real trouble down the left-hand side, tee the ball low and take out your driver. Now think about hitting a fade. With the ball so low to the ground, and the driver in your hand, it's almost impossible to hook. Instead, your natural instinct will produce a fade, because you'll be thinking you virtually have to swing from out-to-in on the ball to make it get airborne.

BE PROPERLY EQUIPPED TO CREATE BACKSPIN

◆ ◆ ◆ ◆ ◆

The better the player you become, the more you will find yourself in certain situations where you want to apply backspin to the ball to save par, or to give yourself chances for birdies and even an eagle.
The correct equipment helps.

YOU MIGHT want to land the ball on a green with a hard surface, and a tough pin placement. You might be aiming at a green that's surrounded by bunkers and long rough – with no way to run the ball up to it. Or you might even be going over water to an island green and need to stop the ball within only a few feet of landing.

The better the player, the more greens they will hit in regulation, using short clubs such as the pitching, sand or lob wedge. In these situations, knowing how to apply backspin to the ball is as much a luxury as a necessity.

GREAT PRECISION

So it goes without saying that if you are going to start working on putting backspin on the ball, you must first be a very competent player. That's because the only way to create backspin is by having the ability to strike the ball with great precision. Conversely, if you strike the ball poorly, you'll never create any backspin. This is truly an advanced technique.

Many average golfers start experimenting with shots like this and hurt their overall game as a consequence. Often, they are influenced by watching too many golf tournaments on television. When they see pros like Greg Norman hit the ball into a hard green, and then watch as the ball spins back six feet as if yanked by an invisible string, they cannot wait to try emulating their favourite pro.

But Norman can create tremendous backspin because he has a great golf swing. Only when you can say that your swing is at least reliable and solid is this technique worth learning.

THE RIGHT BALL AND EQUIPMENT

Having a great swing is the first, but not the only, requirement for applying backspin to the ball with a wedge or other short iron. In this case, both the ball and the right equipment are major contributing factors.

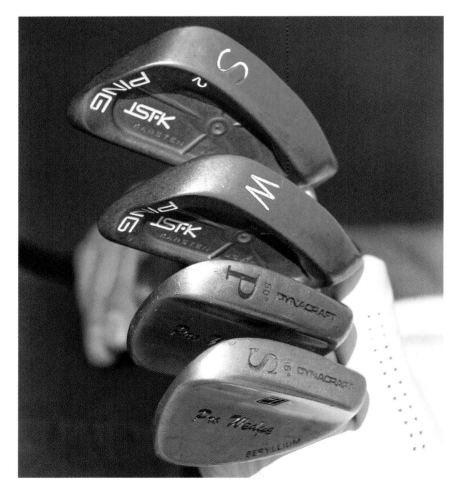

Different metals used in the manufacture of clubheads make a significant difference with regard to how much backspin you can create.

Most golfers do not even realize the variety of different golf balls available on today's market. But there's only one particular type of ball that will allow you to create effective backspin – the balata.

By contrast, most amateur golfers use a two-piece, surlyn-covered ball because it's cheaper than balata, wears considerably longer, and goes greater distances when struck well.

Balata-covered balls are expensive, cut easily and mean a sacrifice in distance. But they do allow you to apply backspin, because the soft balata cover, in conjunction with the liquid centre and wound construction inside the ball, compresses more than conventional golf balls when struck precisely. As a result, the balata ball actually stays on the clubface longer, rotating up the blade and gathering anti-clockwise spin – which helps generate backspin and stops the ball on landing.

MILD STEEL AND SOFT INSERTS

Another factor in creating backspin is the material used in your clubs. Your wedges should be made from softer metal than the hard steel used in a 2-iron, and many of the best wedges available these days feature clubfaces of mild steel with chrome plating. Some also have a copper insert. These materials help the ball stay on the clubface longer and, once again, will create more backspin and help ball control.

So remember, if you want to maximize the backspin you create, you must have:

• A good technique.
• A balata ball.
• The right equipment.

Left: Never try to lift the ball upwards – simply swing forward to your target.

Left: If you hit the ball consistently and want more control around the greens, use a balata-covered golf ball.

Far left: A wet clubface is a slippery clubface – if you want backspin keep the club dry.

Left: Keep your grooves free of grass and dirt. Use a tee or a special groove cleaner to keep your club in pristine condition.

SWING KEYS TO APPLYING BACKSPIN

◆ ◆ ◆ ◆ ◆

The key to applying backspin is how you develop a very precise strike on the ball. You have to make sure you hit the ball before you hit anything else. If you hit the ground just slightly before you hit the ball, you will fail to create backspin.

ONE WAY I encourage a precise strike is by looking more closely at the top of the ball, much as I do for a fairway bunker shot. Focusing in this way will help to ensure that you make clean contact.

I also play a more out-to-in type of swing, almost trying intentionally to fade the ball. That makes me think about hitting down and across the ball. Coming at the ball from out-to-in gives me a better chance of hitting the ball crisply and sharply.

TAKE A DIVOT

I also try to take a divot. With the shorter irons, I'm already hitting on a slightly downward path, and this helps me create backspin as it will make the ball spin up the clubface. But I would add a note of caution here. Hitting down on the ball too much runs the risk of chopping the clubface into the ground – either before or after impact with the ball.

Both mistakes will affect the strike considerably, and you will not get a positive result. Remember that you want to take a divot, but you do not want simply to hit down, so ensure that you hit down and *forward* towards your target. As with any golf shot, you always want to be going forwards and through the ball.

In addition, because you are using a short, lofted club, you will be bent over more. So be careful not to exaggerate your action too much. The divot does not need to be half the size of the state of Ohio – or even Surrey!

To apply increased backspin, you need to open your stance, with your weight slightly favouring your left side. Take the club away with your arms and break your wrists early to produce a sharp downward strike into the ball. You should use a three-quarter swing, keep your hands ahead of the clubface, and keep your weight transfer down to a minimum.

To help create backspin I open my stance, keep my weight forward and break my wrists quite early in my backswing. This results in a sharp downward strike on the ball.

The priority here is not distance but a clean strike. A more compact swing helps you to make a precise strike, because, with your weight favouring the left side and your hands ahead of the club, you will naturally hit the ball with a descending blow.

Alternatively, if you try to lift the ball with your club, your weight will probably stay on the back foot, which will cause you to hit the ground first with the clubhead or top the ball.

Trying to scoop the ball upwards is the major fault of most golfers in this situation. They forget the great paradox of golf – that you must strike down to hit the ball up, letting the loft of the clubface produce a high-flying shot.

KEEP IT CLEAN

A clean ball and clubface is also essential to applying backspin. Make sure you check your ball whenever you can during a round, and see that the grooves in your clubface are free of dirt and grass. I am in the habit of tidying up my wedges after every strike with a groove cleaner or a tee peg, while also making sure the clubface in general is clean.

Always remember to carry a towel on your bag for this purpose as well. Even in dry conditions, it is important to clean the ball and your clubs regularly.

THE BUMP AND RUN

◆ ◆ ◆ ◆ ◆

The bump and run is an effective shot when you are trying to keep the ball low under the wind, playing off hard ground, or simply trying to run the ball up to a green. The shot is much easier to judge and control than a high pitch, and is ideal when you do not have to fly bunkers, water or rough to reach the green.

MOST GOLFERS associate this shot with links courses, where it is often employed to avoid tricky winds. Playing target golf on such courses can be a disaster. When the ball gets airborne, it can be blown off line, especially with a wedge.

But the bump and run can be used on any course under the right conditions – or the wrong ones for that matter.

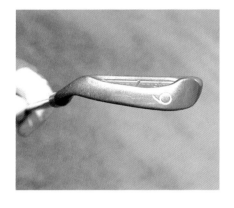

THIN HOPES

In the summer, when the fairways tend to dry out, the bump and run is also useful because it allows for a wide margin of error. Even if you thin the ball, it will still run forwards along your intended line, perhaps accomplishing pretty much what you had hoped for anyway.

Using the bump and run to an uphill green is also a great idea, since it's easy to misjudge the distance and park a lofted shot

on the bank and short – or fly the green completely.

You can use a variety of clubs for the bump and run, and hit the shot anywhere from 60 to 160 yards (55 to 145m).

THE APPROACH SHOT

As with any golf shot, club selection is the first important decision you must make. You can play a bump and run with anything from a sand wedge to a 6-iron, depending on what you want to do.

These are two clubs you may consider when playing the bump and run shot.

Here I'm playing a shot from around 65 yards (60m) from the hole.

Bump and run

Try practising a variety of bump and run shots at the range to learn the best choices for you in different situations.

Selecting the right club will have a lot to do with how far you want the ball to fly before it starts running, or what you want it to clear initially. If you are playing a links course and have a lot of humps and bumps ahead, you may want to take many of them out by flying the ball further. That may demand a wedge.

But if you really want to keep the ball flat to the ground, or low and running most of the way, then you might choose a 6-iron.

CONTROL AND FEEL

I'll use a 60-yard (55m) shot to the green as a typical example.

In that case, you might want the ball to fly 40 yards (37m) and roll 20 yards (18m). Take out the wedge and choke halfway down the grip for better control and feel. Then open your stance, with the hips and feet pointing slightly left of the target, but the shoulders remaining parallel to the target line.

The shoulders should be positioned as they would be for a conventional shot because the last thing I want to do is to hit the ball with an out-to-in swingpath.

Ideally, I want the club actually to come from a slightly in-to-out direction, which will help get the ball running.

GOING LOW

Now I set the ball back in my stance, from the centre to slightly behind that, which helps make the ball fly lower. In turn, my hands are set ahead of the clubhead, which helps deloft the club and also helps make the ball run low.

Finally, I set my weight towards the left side and keep it there. I don't want much weight transfer when making this shot.

BUMP AND RUN WITH A PUTTER

A shot that often can be very successful is a bump and run with a putter. I have used my putter from up to 50 yards (45m) from the green if there are no hazards, conditions are dry and the grass is short.

The length of the back- and throughswings should control the distance you will hit the ball.

Playing the ball along the ground with a putter from up to 50 yards (45m) can be very successful. Ensure that the ground is dry and that there are no obstacles (such as sprinkler heads) in between you and the hole. And remember, never up – never in!

SWING KEYS TO THE BUMP AND RUN

◆ ◆ ◆ ◆ ◆

Once I am set up properly for the bump and run, I plan to take a half- to three-quarter swing – depending on the length of my approach – trying to keep even and balanced throughout.

THE BEST way to do that is to think about matching the length of the throughswing to the backswing. I also want to take the body out of this movement and just swing with the arms and hands.

SMOOTHLY DONE

A smooth, unhurried tempo is essential. It's very easy to rush these shots, especially with a little wind around. The tendency is to get forwards too quickly.

At the same time, you want to ensure you accelerate through the ball, with the feeling that you are almost squeezing it between the clubface and turf.

Remember, you want to create overspin on the ball to get it running, and from your set-up, you will naturally be bringing the clubface from in-to-out – helping you nip the ball off the ground.

POINTS SKYWARD

Think of this shot as dominated by the left side. What you do not want to do is to lift the ball by using too much right hand. So keep both hands ahead of the clubface, but lead the shot with the back of your left hand.

You don't want to break your wrists too much on the backswing, and you don't want to release the right arm on the throughswing. So visualize that, at the end of your swing, the back of your left hand will be facing up at the sky.

Letting the wrists break would lead to a chopping action on the ball, rather than promoting the idea of squeezing it off the turf to get a nice, flat trajectory.

THE LONGER APPROACH

You can use the bump and run from 100 yards (91m) out to even 160 (145m), employing a sand wedge down to a 6-iron although with the former you will need to substantially deloft the face. The approach on this shot is similar to when using a wedge from only 60 yards (55m).

Again, you want to take an open stance, but with the shoulders still parallel to the target line. Then use a three-quarter swing, with your weight and hands forward. Try to squeeze the ball off the turf by hitting down with a firm left wrist, making sure the swingpath is slightly in-to-out. Finish with your left wrist pointing at the sky.

VISUALIZING THE SHOT

Once again visualization plays its part. This is especially important on a links-type course

Below left: When playing the bump and run, keep your hands well ahead of the clubhead as you make your throughswing.

Below: Remember to allow for contours in the ground as they will affect the run of your ball.

The bump and run requires you to make a low takeaway. Keep the weight principally on your left foot and then pull the club forwards with the hands staying well ahead of the clubhead through impact, as shown here.

with a lot of humps and bumps. If you were to hit a lofted club in this situation, and the ball came down on the wrong hump, it could fly off sideways or even worse. Running it in is a better option, because the ball can roll along with the contours of the land.

So pick a spot where you want the ball initially to come down, and try to imagine how it will react. Then focus on that spot – much as you would for a chip – and hit your shot.

HELP FOR THE WEEKEND GOLFER

The bump and run is a great shot if you only play golf once a week. Trying to play target golf without hours of practice is difficult. But if you hit more low runners than high-flying pitches during a round, you have the advantage of probably succeeding even if you mis-hit the ball.

With the bump and run, a semi-thinned shot will still produce a half-decent result – you are already anticipating running the ball.

When the ground is hard and dry, it's much safer and more predictable to keep the ball low. With the grass reasonably fine, the ball will trundle along nicely, reacting almost as it would on the green.

THE LOB SHOT

◆ ◆ ◆ ◆ ◆

The lob is one of the toughest shots in golf. But with the proper technique and lots of practice, many golfers can learn how to execute it consistently. You need this shot when you have to play over a hazard and then stop the ball quickly in a small landing area around the pin — sometimes as close as just a few feet away.

S O THE lob is a shot that you are sometimes *forced* to play, rather than one you might occasionally choose. I play this shot from only five to 15 yards (4.5 to 13.5m) away — maybe 20 yards (18m) at the most. Trying to hit a lob shot from much farther than that is getting into very dangerous territory.

SPECIALIST CLUB

The advent of the lob wedge has helped every golfer play this shot better. Of course, the pros can still open up their sand wedges and play the lob shot with great precision. But the average golfer risks thinning the ball if he tries a similar technique.

A sand wedge has a high degree of bounce, so opening the blade and trying to play this shot from low-cut grass, a tight lie or hardpan can be extremely problematic. However, if the lie is good and there is a lot of grass under the ball, then a sand wedge might work for you.

HITTING THE LOB

Open your stance, with your feet, hips and shoulders pointing left by 15 to 20 degrees. You must aim that far left to compensate for how far you are going to open the face of the sand wedge. Now open up your wedge by as much as 8 degrees, depending on how high you want to lift the ball — really laying the clubface open.

Play the ball off the inside of your left heel or front foot, angling the club for an out-to-in swingpath with your weight favouring the left foot in a ratio of about 60/40.

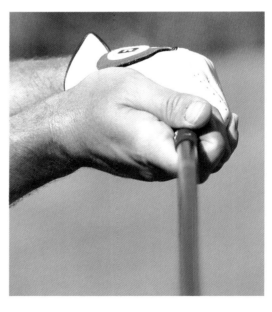

Below: This shot requires the left hand to be in control through the ball.

Below left: Almost all professionals carry a lob wedge these days.

Left: Only try the lob shot if you have grass beneath the ball. Don't even consider it if you're sitting on hard ground.

The left side in control

When I play the lob shot, I try to imagine my left arm pulling the club through the ball, with the back of the left hand slicing across the ball. The back of the left hand should be pointing towards the sky at the end of the swing.

Below: With the lob wedge I generally don't need to open the face as the club is very lofted anyway.

REALLY STABLE

You want real stability with this shot. Try to keep as centred as possible and keep your head still and your weight towards your left foot.

Take a three-quarter backswing with a sharp pickup of the wrists. Then really try to feel the butt of the club coming through ahead of the clubhead, so that you pull across the ball.

I try to imagine almost slicing under the ball with the back of my left hand. That will help me shoot the ball quickly up in the air with lots of backspin, then let it drop down very softly.

MORE HEIGHT

I can get even more height with a lob wedge because the club has so much more loft. I also don't need to open the face quite so much – if at all. The rest of the technique employed to hit the lob shot stays pretty much the same. But, like any shot, make sure you practise it regularly to build confidence.

THE LOB FROM GREENSIDE ROUGH

◆ ◆ ◆ ◆ ◆

Leftie Phil Mickelson excels at hitting soft lobs around the green, even from the sort of horrific rough typically found at the US Open. And although Mickelson takes a longer backswing than I recommend for most players – because he has the clubface so far open – emulating his method will help you escape from greenside rough.

MICKELSON TRIES to get the ball as high as possible, to compensate for the lack of backspin caused by the high grass. Even with a lob in this situation, you have to accept that the ball will run a bit on landing. But if you were to play a more conventional chip from such rough, the ball would run forever.

LESS QUIT

Another reason to play a lob shot from greenside rough is because if you can really swing through it, you stand less chance of quitting on the ball. That's a big danger when playing out of this type of rough. The natural inclination is to let the club stay in the grass because your swing is inhibited.

If you hit the lob correctly, you will get some momentum on the clubhead as you come through, which produces the height as the loft on your wedge sends the ball up in the air.

Remember, it's easy for the clubface to snag and close in the rough. But with the clubface so open initially – or naturally lofted in the case of the lob wedge – that will help prevent turning the club over.

Using a lob wedge from greenside rough allows you to accelerate through the shot, reducing the possibility of your club getting caught up in the long grass.

Lob shot from rough

The only precaution when playing the lob wedge from the rough is that you have to take care not to pass clean under the ball without moving it forwards – most embarrassing!

Below: A perfect use of the lob wedge.

PRO TIP

Even though you play a lob shot from greenside rough in a similar way to a bunker shot, be careful about hitting too far behind the ball. When I say you should play a splash shot, I am trying to emphasize technique, rather than the idea of hitting a few inches behind the ball. If the rough is deep enough, plenty of grass will inevitably come between the clubface and the ball, making contact slippery. Try to hit the ball as precisely as possible.

Lob from downhill rough lie

PLAYING IN THE WIND

Great golfers learn how to use the wind to their advantage, and minimize the damage when that is not possible. So do not let the wind play on your mind, or you'll lose confidence – which leads to tension and ultimately a breakdown in your swing. Playing in the wind can be both challenging and fun, if you know what you are doing.

A TAILWIND CAN help you to increase your distance dramatically and actually help you to strengthen the fundamentals of your swing. On the other hand, hitting into the wind can reduce your distance, but aid you in stopping the ball quickly on the green and even impart some backspin.

Crosswinds are trickier. But once you learn how to hit into the windstream correctly and then let it carry your ball, you will be on the way to lowering your scores – even when the wind blows a gale.

USING A TAILWIND

Most golfers automatically feel more comfortable with the wind at their backs because they know it will help them hit the ball further. However, unless they understand and employ certain advanced techniques for hitting in the wind, they'll never fully capitalize on that obvious advantage.

Let's say you are on the tee of a long par four where you would normally play a driver. Now, of course, every golfer knows that hitting a 3-wood off the tee generally guarantees more accuracy and control when it is struck properly, though distance is sacrificed.

But in this situation hitting a 3-wood rather than the driver is the best play, because the added loft will get the ball up higher and into the prevailing wind. In addition, even if you do not get a perfect strike on the ball, less sidespin will be imparted, and the ball will go straighter and further.

Decisions, decisions – choosing the right club is crucial in windy conditions.

Far left: The wind in your face is a real test of how much you believe in your golf swing.

Left: Looking at the tops of the trees will tell you more about the wind than conditions at ground level do. Use the knowledge to your advantage.

Far left: Wearing a hat can stop you hair blowing around – not that I have to worry too much about that!

Left: A stable base to your golf swing is very important. If it's windy, I increase the width of my stance.

PRO TIP

Not enough players practise in the wind. If you are on the course on a windy day and it's quiet, drop some balls and experiment with a few clubs to see what effect the wind has on how each performs, and how the wind affects your natural ball flight.

The same principle applies once you are on the fairway. Where you would normally use a 3-wood, you can now try the 5- or even 7-wood and get just as much distance – if not more because they are easier to hit – with the added benefit of more control.

STRAIGHTER FLIGHT

A tailwind will also straighten out your natural ball flight – whether you hit with a bit of fade or draw – because the wind lessens the amount of spin. That makes for a more penetrating hit and allows you to place the ball more accurately for your next shot.

Make sure you aim for the side of the fairway that will allow you to run the ball up to the green – using perhaps a long bump and run shot. Remember that you will never stop the ball on the putting surface with a high wedge shot in a tailwind.

You should also know that the ball will kick and run on from your tee shot, so mentally you have to allow for that. As for approach shots, a strong tailwind will produce enough boost to move a 7- or even 8-iron shot 150 to 200 yards (137 to 183m).

Golfers often cannot convince themselves of that fact. They may take the correct club, but when they get to the top of their backswing, they suddenly panic and think they have not got enough club, thus forcing the shot.

Assess the effect of the wind, select a club and then keep faith with the shot you have decided to hit.

Keep the swing compact and this will help you to maintain control while others around you are flailing away.

PLAYING INTO A HEADWIND

◆ ◆ ◆ ◆ ◆

Hitting into a headwind will increase the spin on the ball, which is an excellent incentive for firing confidently at the pin, and trusting the ball to stop quickly on the green. But if you are on the tee or facing a long shot from the fairway, you have to remember that this aspect of hitting into the wind will exaggerate any problems you have with the long woods and irons.

I F YOU hit a driver with a bit of draw, playing with the wind in your face could change that shot into a hook. Alternatively, if you hit the ball with a nice little fade, that could become an ugly slice. You have to make allowances for these tendencies, or you will pay a significant price.

PLAY IT SAFE AND SMOOTH

Take the safest route up the fairway that you can, choosing one side or the other while accepting the fact that you will lose considerable distance – perhaps as much as 50 to 75 yards (45 to 69m) on a drive. But less length is better than parking the ball in the rough or something worse.

Try teeing the ball higher than normal, then think about picking it clean off the top in an attempt to hit a penetrating shot that flies low into the wind.

Tempo is also a key here. You have to maintain your composure, and keep a smooth, even rhythm to your swing. Losing it in the wind can destroy your game very, very quickly.

THREE-CLUB WIND

Once you are down on the fairway, play very conservatively and remember that you might have to hit one, two or three more clubs than you usually would to achieve certain distances. How often have you heard people say that a 30mph (50km/h) wind is 'a three-club wind?' If you've ever played in such winds, you know the truth of that phrase all too well.

Tee the ball high and aim to sweep the ball clean off the tee.

A combination of stability and compactness are the keys to playing in the wind.

Good balance in windy conditions

wind direction

Hitting a golf ball into a headwind is one situation where playing the long irons, rather than utility woods, is a good idea. Using a 5- or 7-wood in strong winds is not advisable because the ball will just shoot into the air.

But the 3- and 4-irons can really play their parts superbly in these situations, because they will help you keep the ball flat.

Even a driver off the fairway is worth trying, if you have practised the shot on the range. In an emergency, with the wind against you, hit a little three-quarter swing with the big club, trying to keep your movement as smooth as possible.

Don't worry about mis-hitting the ball, because you might get a better result than using something like a 5-wood, since the ball will stay flat. But even if you top it, that's better than hitting the ball up in the air, where it can go just about any place.

STAYING SAFE

Whatever club you use on the fairway, be certain to look for the safest route to approach the green – and don't try anything too ambitious. If the hole is a par four, expect that it might well take you three shots, or perhaps even four, just to reach the green.

Consider this: if you two-putt from there, it's a six, rather than the eight or nine you're more likely to record if you fly out of bounds or into significant trouble.

Remember, you are going to have a hole somewhere else on the golf course where the wind is with you, and you will have a chance to repair the damage to your score.

It's tough – but always visualize a positive outcome to your shot, even when the wind is howling around your ears and burning your face.

DRIVER OFF THE DECK

I would never recommend hitting a driver off the fairway in normal circumstances – especially for the beginner or high handicap player who should also avoid using a 3-wood anywhere except from the tee. But if you are an experienced golfer, possess a solid, repeatable swing, and have the confidence to attempt this shot, I recommend it for playing in the wind. The first thing to consider is the lie. Hitting a driver off the fairway demands an excellent lie, so always avoid a tight lie or any situation where the ball is sitting even slightly down. Put the ball about an inch (2.5cm) farther back in your stance than you would off the tee and try to keep your hands slightly ahead of the ball at impact. If you make solid contact, the ball should take off with a low, penetrating line of flight.

KNOWING HOW TO USE A HEADWIND

◆ ◆ ◆ ◆ ◆

Hitting into a headwind will give you considerably more backspin than normal, which can be a great advantage when planning your approach shots. I have even achieved backspin with a driver from the fairway!

I CAN STILL picture the shot. I was playing into a 35mph (56km/h) wind at Royal Portcawl in Wales, on the 350-yard (320m) 1st hole. But I had to hit driver, then another driver. Believe it or not, my second shot hit ten feet (3m) behind the hole and spun back to about a foot. You can achieve the same thing with less club and more confidence.

MAINTAINING YOUR COMPOSURE

A strong headwind is indeed very difficult to play in, but you cannot afford to allow that to wreck your game. Many golfers completely deteriorate in the wind, especially a headwind. The natural tendency is to try hitting the ball harder than normal. That's a recipe for disaster.

Tom Watson always said that he tried to hit the ball softer into a headwind. I believe that's the best way to express what a golfer

must do in this situation. Your instincts are all screaming at you to take a good smash at the ball. Instead, you simply must control yourself and hit softer. Hitting softer balances you. If you just go with that, you will in fact hit the ball harder.

DON'T HOLD ANYTHING BACK

A proper weight transfer is essential to hitting any shot in golf, but even more vital when playing in the wind. As I have said so often in this book, many golfers try to help the ball into the air by either thrashing at it, or trying to lift it up – or both! But the result of such futile effort is that weight is inevitably left back on the right side. The result can be a fat or topped shot, when what you need most is a low, penetrating flight to cheat the wind, which will inevitably knock the ball down and reduce distance no matter how well it is hit. So concentrate on swinging with a smooth, even tempo, while transferring all your body weight to the left side – in effect, firing through the ball.

The happy hacker here is trying much too hard – it's a guaranteed disaster.

How not to do it!

USING A CROSSWIND TO AID YOUR BALL FLIGHT

✦ ✦ ✦ ✦ ✦

When the wind is coming from left to right across the tee, you want to hit the ball into the wind and let the jetstream take it. But, at all costs, avoid doing the opposite – sliding the ball with the wind and letting it go.

IN THAT case, if you go with the wind, and you naturally hit the ball straight or slightly to the right, the ball will move violently to the right and you will get into serious trouble.

The first thing you want to do in a left-to-right wind is to tee the ball up on the right side of the tee box, because the best policy is to hit across to the left, or into the wind.

CARRY FARTHER

It's like flying an aircraft. You want to go straight into the flow of the wind. Even if you hit into the wind with a little bit of fade, you can use the wind to carry the ball further. With a soft fade, the ball will get picked up by the wind pattern and taken forwards another 20 yards (18m) or so.

In his heyday, Seve Ballesteros was a great exponent of how to use the wind particularly well, which is why he won the British Open three times. The Spanish wizard was a brilliant exploiter of the wind.

THE DRAW IN A CROSSWIND

On the other hand, if you draw the ball, it will pretty much go straight in a left-to-right wind. In that case, the wind will hold the ball up, because you are hitting directly against it. So even with a draw, you will get less distance in this scenario and should always allow for that when planning your shot.

Of course, the opposite applies in a right-to-left wind. Then you want to hit it right to left. You always want to hit at the wind. So tee it up on the left side of the tee and hit it at the wind again, letting it come around. That's the ideal circumstance in which to play a draw.

Sometimes a crosswind can help you – in this case grip down the club to reduce distance.

Below: Always use the wind creatively – if you do, you'll enjoy playing in windy conditions.

Hitting into crosswind

wind direction

Chapter 13

FIT TO COMPETE

◆ ◆ ◆ ◆ ◆

*Flexibility, strength and
stamina are all golf essentials.
Learn how to stretch and build
your golfing potential to
its maximum.*

FIT TO COMPETE

◆ ◆ ◆ ◆ ◆

Golf is not just a leisurely stroll in the park, best suited to weekend athletes or older men and women who have never before competed in any sport. In fact, golf is increasingly an athletic game that demands suppleness, strength and stamina.

THAT MAY seem like an obvious statement these days, when everyone seems to be working out – or at least contemplating starting their own personal fitness programme. And while the media constantly bombard us with the message that exercise is essential to our overall health and longevity, we can hardly miss the point.

In recent years, we have also learned that the increased fitness level of some professional golfers, such as Nick Faldo, compares well even with Olympic athletes.

THE MISSING INGREDIENT

But how often does the average golfer really approach a round the way such finely tuned athletes prepare for a track meet or any other sporting event? Simply put, I believe that you can arrive at your favourite course with a good strategy for the day's play, a sound swing and even a red-hot putter – and yet still not score well.

The missing ingredient is often the result of not having spent any time building up your golf muscles, and failing to warm up and stretch before you hit that first shot.

Even worse, you might arrive frazzled mentally and in too much of a hurry. How many times have you sat in the traffic, growing increasingly tense as you check your watch, only to arrive with just minutes left before your tee time?

You know what happens after that. You race to the first tee, do a few quick practice swings, and then slice the first shot into the rough or a hazard. Now you are already staring at bogey and feeling frustrated, possibly setting the tone for the rest of the day.

Try and swing everyday with a couple of clubs. It will keep you supple and remind your body of the correct swing action.

I exercise every day – even running up and down steps is good cardiovascular exercise.

FITNESS IS KEY

Fitness separates the hacker from the successful golfer. You have to find time during the week and before a round of golf to stretch and exercise if you want to improve your game. And if you are overweight, you will also probably suffer from bad posture and a loss of balance in your swing. But even if you are wire-thin, a lack of fitness will mean less distance.

I cannot emphasize enough both the necessity and the benefit of being fit for golf. I guarantee that building up your golf muscles when you are not playing, and stretching just before you tee off – or even during the round – will help to lower your scores and, perhaps even more importantly, prevent an injury.

DRAMATIC CUTS

Adopting a sound exercise routine will help every aspect of your game. Your set-up will be better in terms of posture, balance and the ability to keep a wide stance. Your body rotation and backswing dynamics will improve, increasing clubhead speed and ensuring that you will hit the ball farther and with less effort.

In addition, you will have the strength to get out of the rough, the added stamina to feel fresh on the 18th tee, and the concentration needed consistently to make those short putts.

But perhaps best of all, increased fitness will even improve your feel and touch, which is especially important for getting up and down in your short game – and dramatically cutting your score.

Strengthening exercises, like those shown above, can pack power into weaker muscles like those in the left forearm.

Observing your reflection is great practice.

STRETCHING GOLF MUSCLES

◆ ◆ ◆ ◆ ◆

The key to getting fit starts with the warm-up. As the name implies, a warm-up session is a gradual, safe way of increasing the temperature of the body by speeding up your heart rate and getting blood pumping into your muscles. This will prevent you straining muscles, in addition to damaging tendons, joints and ligaments. It will also help to sharpen both your physical and mental state.

A GOOD WARM-UP session is a great way to make the transition from the daily stress of life to the joy of playing a winning round of golf. Do an abbreviated version of your warm-up routine before you reach the first tee.

RELEASE TENSION

Each warm-up session should consist of a series of stretches, which may be followed by a vigorous workout if you have the time. Or you might want simply to confine yourself to warming up with a few stretching exercises whenever you feel tense or stiff.

You might start the morning this way, use your lunchbreak at work, or even as a way to release tension before you go to bed. But remember, whenever you stretch a muscle, make sure you are reasonably relaxed and that you take it very easy until the body is ready. Breathe slowly and deeply and don't force anything. Go at your own

Golf's not just a game of strength: it is also about flexibility.

Develop an exercise routine and stick to it every day. Make the time to do this – you only have one body.

pace and try not to be competitive if you are doing this in the presence of others.

Ideally, a warm-up should last at least ten minutes, but it can go on for over a half hour. You might include riding a stationary bike or a real one, jogging on the spot or running outdoors, taking a brisk walk, or just doing some of the simple stretching exercises pictured on these pages.

Full rotation of the arms should be included in your routine.

Can you touch your toes?

GAINING FLEXIBILITY

The term stretching implies exactly the effect you want. When you do not exercise for long periods of time, muscles tend to shorten and get tight. Stretching helps warm the muscles up with increased blood flow, then allows them to loosen and become more supple.

In other words, by stretching, you gain flexibility that translates into a better golf swing. Just think of Tiger Woods and you'll get the general idea. Most of us — at least without a proper warm-up — would pull a muscle or even throw our back out if we tried to hit a ball the same way Woods does with such seeming ease.

We can all strive to gain greater flexibility by gentle stretching. The secret is to do each stretch to the point of slight discomfort — your body will tell you when to stop. The general rule is to hold the position and then count to five if you're a beginner, working up to ten and 15 seconds as you become more experienced.

ADVICE BEFORE STARTING

• Always consult your doctor before starting any exercise programme. He may suggest a stress test if you are over 40, and will be glad to give you guidelines on maximum heart rates for your size, build and age group should you also be doing any type of vigorous aerobic training.

• You might want consult a physical therapist or fitness trainer who can design a programme suited to your specific fitness level and goals. Most health clubs provide such help, and in the early stages of such a programme, it's always good to have someone observe what you are doing and try to catch any mistakes that could lead to strains or even injury.

• Never do even mild stretching or muscle-building exercises when injured or suffering from a viral infection. And never do exercises if they cause real pain. Forget about the 'no pain/no gain' maxim. That does not mean you work through pain.

• Never lock up any muscles or joints when you exercise. For instance, your knees should always be slightly flexed and your neck relaxed or even supported when doing stretching that involve the shoulders or back – particularly press-ups and crunches.

BUILDING GOLF MUSCLES

◆ ◆ ◆ ◆ ◆

Most golfers would never qualify for, let alone win, a 'Mr or Ms Universe' contest – and rightfully so. Although a finely sculpted physique and excellent muscle tone can benefit even the average golfer considerably, most of the body-building techniques of an Olympic weightlifter would interfere with, rather than promote, a good golf swing.

BUT THERE are any number of exercises that will help the golfer hit the ball further and play better around the greens. The key is to combine strength and flexibility, while avoiding bulk. Being fit is also a magic circle – the better you feel, the more confidence you are likely to bring to the golf course.

The forearms, wrists and hands are a particular area on which golfers should concentrate their training regimen. Strengthening muscles here will help you fire the golf club through impact at higher speeds, and thus with extra power.

ADDED FEEL

The extra bonus is added feel, even if that sounds paradoxical. The fact is, stronger hands and wrists allow the golfer to control the clubhead with less effort during those nerve-wracking little pitch and chip shots around the short grass.

Strengthening the torso, hips and legs is also important, since the legs provide the foundation for the swing and resistance to the turning of the upper body in the backswing. The legs and hips also help the golfer unleash his full power in the throughswing.

In addition, building golf muscles helps provide stamina, which is important in any round. But on warm days, or when the golfer is under pressure to score, having that extra reservoir of strength to draw upon can make the difference between winning and losing.

Below left: Hold your stretching positions for at least ten seconds – this will develop your elasticity.

Below: Sit-ups done correctly are great for your game. Gary Player still does 1000 every morning before breakfast and he's almost 70 years old – so no excuses!

Press-ups are especially good for the arms, and if this seems too easy try finger-tip press-ups.

Training can involve free-standing exercise such as running, press-ups and crunches, the use of your own golf clubs – with or without small weights added – and extensive repetitions with both small and large-sized free weights.

BUILDING THE LEFT SIDE

Most golfers play the game right-handed, and therefore have to counteract the tendency of the right side to dominate the swing. This means using a series of exercises specifically designed to build up the left side of the body. Swinging a golf club with only the left hand is a good way to start, and once you build up confidence, try to hit some balls in this fashion.

Squeezing a hand grip is another way to work on the left hand, wrist and forearm. Keep a pair of grips handy at the office or in your car and use them in both hands, while concentrating slightly more on the left.

Another excellent exercise is to grip a golf club in the left hand with the palm upwards and the arm extended from your body. Now turn your hand over to make the club rotate in an arc like a windscreen wiper.

USING WEIGHTS

The major muscle groups we use to swing and control the golf club can all be toned and conditioned by lifting weights. Special attention should be paid to the the hands, wrists and arms, which can be strengthened with a series of exercises involving weights

measuring only five to 15 pounds (2.3 to 6.8kg).

Remember, it's the skill with which one does the exercise and the progressive number of repetitions that count towards building the right muscles for golf. Do them routinely, and you will soon notice an increase in power on the course.

No, I haven't gone to sleep – this is part of my warm-up routine before playing.

BUILDING GOLF MUSCLES

• Always do your warm-up routine and stretching exercises before moving on to more vigorous work that can involve major muscle groups and the use of weights.

• Strength training is progressive, which means you should gradually increase the number of repetitions you do, or the amount of weight you lift – within a safe limit of comfort. Remember, pain is your body's early warning system.

• Skip a day between workouts. Three sessions per week is ideal for building new muscles, but your body needs time to recover in between.

Chapter 14

THE RULES OF GOLF

◆ ◆ ◆ ◆ ◆

*Knowing the rules of the game
will not only prevent the
occasional embarrassing
moment, but might also save
you strokes and make the
difference in a winning round.*

THE RULES OF GOLF

◆ ◆ ◆ ◆ ◆

Golf is a pretty simple game. We hit the ball with a club, trying to sink it in 18 different holes around the course, counting the number of attempts, or strokes, it takes to achieve this result – which gives us our overall score.

HOWEVER, DURING any round of golf, a number of situations can arise that are governed by a complex set of official rules, both universal to the game and local to the course that you are playing.

As a result, knowing the rules of golf is essential, because the penalties for ignorance and mistakes are severe. A rule infraction can cost strokes, make the difference between winning and losing a round – or even result in immediate disqualification.

In addition to the rules, the game also has a code of etiquette which should be observed by all golfers – and, in particular, be studied by beginners.

GOVERNING BODIES

The rules of golf are administered and interpreted by two major world bodies, the Royal and Ancient Golf Club of St. Andrews (R&A) in Scotland and the United States Golf Association (USGA). The USGA has the final word in North America, while the R&A covers the remainder of the golfing universe, which encompasses over 60 affiliated countries from Europe to Asia.

A booklet entitled *The Rules of Golf* is published annually by both the USGA and R&A, and can be obtained from most golf clubs at no charge. Small and thin, this manual is designed to fit comfortably into a golf bag or your rear trouser pocket. I recommend you obtain a copy and carry it when you play.

KNOW THE RULES

Knowing the rules is the responsibility of each person who plays the game, and no golfer can ignore or waive a rule of golf – even

Above: Young trees may be staked. Most courses will allow a free drop from this position.

Above: Dropping – you must keep your arm fully extended and allow the ball to drop directly beneath your hand.

Left: Paths are areas where a free drop may be allowed. Your scorecard will state which paths allow you to take a drop without penalty.

Always carry a rule book and pay attention to the local rules printed on the scorecard.

with the mutual consent of playing partners. Should you later be challenged, everyone could pay the price for a rules infraction.

So remember, even if someone else makes a mistake about the rules – you can end up the loser. That also applies to your caddie. If he or she breaks a rule – and you do not correct him or her if possible – you receive the penalty.

This applies equally to both amateurs and professionals, although the pros have the added advantage of being able to call upon officials to aid them in interpreting questionable situations. Despite that, the pros are sometimes tripped up by the sheer complexity of the rules – or, by contrast, can sometimes forget even the most basic laws of the game momentarily.

PROFESSIONAL ERRORS

In recent years, I know of at least one American pro who lost a tournament – and a very big pay cheque – because he was not familiar with the rules governing the grips allowed on putters. Another pro, while in a sandtrap, shifted his feet in such a way that, it was ruled, improved his stance.

Most people have also heard about the most unfortunate infraction of the rules in the history of the game. In 1968, the Argentinian golfer Roberto de Vicenzo scored a birdie at the 17th hole in the final round of the US Masters, although his playing partner marked it down as a par 'four'.

De Vicenzo then signed the erring card and had to live with the mistake. The rules clearly state that a signed card is the final

word, and that it's the responsibility of the player to note any discrepancies and correct them. De Vicenzo lost one of the world's most prestigious and coveted tournaments by one stroke! Don't let that happen to you!

LOCAL RULES

In addition to the universal rules of golf, each course also has a number of 'local rules'. These are usually printed on the back of its scorecards and should be read and studied thoroughly before play.

For instance, many courses have specific rules about whether the golfer can take relief – dropping the ball in another spot without penalty – from such obstacles as staked trees, cart paths, sprinkler heads and 'ground under repair' areas.

Special attention should also be paid regarding how the course defines 'out of bounds', and where markers are placed, information which is also included in the local rules section on every scorecard. Again, failure to do this can be extremely costly.

The definition of 'movable obstructions' is another key local rule to know. Some courses allow golfers to remove stones and other debris from bunkers if they interfere with play – and some do not.

Above: An example of an immovable man-made object. This was not designed to be a hazard or obstruction. A free drop will be permitted – two club lengths away, but not closer to the hole.

Left: Once the dropping point is established, mark it with a tee to ensure no breach of the rule is committed.

Below: A damaged ball may be replaced once it has been agreed with your playing partner.

ETIQUETTE AND SLOW PLAY

◆ ◆ ◆ ◆ ◆

Golf etiquette is based on common sense and consideration for other players. However, in recent years, with the explosion of golf as a popular sport, many beginners have neglected this aspect of the game, which has led to slower play and even occasionally a dangerous situation.

SLOW PLAY is one of the true curses of the modern game. While rounds once were completed in well under three and a half hours on even the most demanding of courses, I now hear tales of golfers spending four, five and even six hours trying to get around!

That's frustrating and can lead to poor play. At best, you will probably lose any winning momentum or rhythm that you have built up. At worst, you could be risking divorce and/or alienation from your children!

In addition, when golfers are not patient enough to wait for the group ahead to move out of range – or simply don't know any better because they have not spent enough practice time on the range – they risk causing serious injury to others by hitting their shots too soon.

LINGERING ON GREENS

One of the most common breaches of etiquette I see is the failure of golfers to exit a green crisply after everyone has putted. Instead, they linger on the short stuff, marking scorecards and discussing how to award any possible points in matchplay.

Always mark your card *after* leaving the green!

You also shouldn't leave your bag or trolley in front of the green. This slows play considerably, because you must walk all the way back to the front edge to retrieve your clubs. Instead, always leave your bag near the pathway to the next tee before moving onto the green to putt.

Think of it this way: if someone wastes just a minute of your time on each green, they have added almost twenty minutes to your round. Of course, you can always ask to play through. But often golfers who are ignorant of such simple courtesies will also be unaware that they are obliged to allow you to pass.

Never mark your scorecard while still on the green. It holds play up and is very frustrating for players following behind.

Above and right: Mark your scores on the next tee or, even better, when walking to the next tee.

ETIQUETTE GUIDELINES

- Don't talk, move, make a noise, or stand too close – or directly behind – the ball of a player who is addressing the ball, taking their swing, or stroking a putt.
- No player should hit a ball until the group in front is well out of range.
- A player is allowed five minutes to search for a lost ball. But if it's apparent that the ball will not be found quickly, the group behind should be allowed to play through.
- Before leaving a bunker, a player should carefully rake or smooth over any footprints, hole marks or any other disturbance in the sand.
- Two-ball matches have precedence over three- and four-ball matches and should be allowed to pass through without delay. A single player has no standing on the course and should give way to any group.
- Divots on the fairway should be replaced immediately and pressed down into the turf – unless the course has a local rule specifically asking that you do not do this. Pitch marks on the green should be repaired with a suitable tool as soon as possible. Spike marks should be patted down after putting.
- If a group falls more than one hole behind the match in front, they should allow the players behind to pass them. Some competitions will penalize such players two strokes, and some courses have rangers who will even ask the group to leave.

- A player should avoid causing any damage to the course – especially in the teeing area – when taking practice swings. It's also a good idea to avoid taking too many practice swings, since this invariably slows play.
- Players should make sure no damage is done to the green or the hole by their bags, clubs or the handling of the flagstick. When removing the ball from the hole, the player should not lean on his putter for support – even though you see the pros doing it every Sunday on television!

If you're playing a friendly game, why not agree with your partner to concede all putts within 8in (20cm) of the hole? It really will speed up your play.

Far left: When arriving on the green, place your bags near the next tee. It will speed up your exit.

Left: Always rake the bunker after hitting out.

AVOIDING GAMESMANSHIP

Golf is one of the few sports that hasn't been invaded by the aggressive mentality we sometimes see elsewhere. But good old-fashioned 'gamesmanship' can still creep into the game of some players. For example, saying things to your opponent or playing partner such as 'I know you can make this putt' can put your fellow golfer off his or her game, whether you are genuinely trying to be encouraging – or quite the opposite! Conversely, complimenting your opponent on a good shot is considered a common courtesy.

Above: Searching for a ball – you are allowed five minutes.

SEEKING RELIEF FROM BAD WEATHER

◆ ◆ ◆ ◆ ◆

The term 'winter rules' does not necessarily govern play only during that season of the year. Whenever the course is in poor shape because of bad weather, winter rules – or what are also sometimes called 'preferred lies' – may be in effect.

THE BASIC idea behind this temporary local rule is to protect the course from further damage and to promote fairness, since it allows the golfer relief from conditions that can adversely affect the lie of the ball and its flight. Under winter rules, you can remove mud from the ball, then hopefully hit off a decent lie and avoid any sloppy footing. But because such rules are temporary, they will not be included on scorecards. Check to see if a notice announcing that winter rules are in effect is posted in the clubhouse or on a signboard near the first tee.

Knowing this – and how such rules might work to your advantage – can potentially save you countless strokes during a round.

Under winter rules you are allowed to mark your ball, lift and clean it, then replace it within six inches (15cm) – but no nearer the hole. However, this provision only applies to balls clearly on the fairway or the apron in front of the green – what is called 'close mown areas through the green' in the Rules of Golf.

CASUAL WATER

Another bad weather rule that a knowledgeable golfer can sometimes use to his or her benefit is the one governing 'casual water'. Of course, no one should have to play a golf ball out of a puddle caused by a long, or sudden, rainstorm – especially if the ball has landed on the fairway.

Far left: The rules can often come to your rescue. Here the ball has come to rest in ground under repair (GUR) and the player will get a free drop.

Left: Often bad weather conditions or poor maintenance will result in situations where relief can be granted without penalty – carry a rule book and use it.

The same applies to taking your stance in any accumulated water. In both instances, you can pick up the ball and drop it without penalty.

If you have a clear patch of fairway behind the wet spot where your ball landed, you can mark the 'nearest point of relief' with a tee peg and pick up the ball and clean it. Then drop it within the length of one club of this point, making sure it lands no nearer to the hole. In this case, 'nearest point of relief' – a term used in the 'Rules of Golf' – simply means the closest dry spot behind the water puddle.

This also applies to casual water in the rough. But the catch here is that you must drop the ball at what is called the 'nearest point of relief' that is not nearer the hole. In other words, if that means dropping back into the rough, you may not improve your lie much. And if it means you will end up dropping into a hazard, back into the water or onto a green, you are out of luck.

The best option in that case may be to play the ball as it lies, or to go back as far as you can from the point where the ball last crossed the casual water to seek relief, keeping that point between you and the hole. Then you can drop anywhere along that line without penalty.

CASUAL WATER IN A BUNKER

What if the ball goes into a bunker filled with water? This one is more problematic. You can play the ball as it lies – which in this case may actually be the best option – if it is possible. Or you may drop it as near as possible to where the ball landed in the water – the spot where you get the maximum relief – as long as that landing zone is still in the bunker.

Lastly, you can drop outside the hazard, going as far back as you wish along the line from the hole to where the ball came to rest. But, in that case, you have to take a penalty stroke.

A free drop is always welcome.

DANGEROUS WEATHER CONDITIONS

Under the rules of golf, bad weather is not necessarily a reason for suspending play during any amateur or professional competition – although lightning is the exception. If a golfer believes he or she is in danger, the golfer may immediately leave the course and be protected from disqualification from any official body governing the tournament. On the other hand, if a player ignores an order to vacate the course by an official or a warning siren – which many clubs sound in the event of lightning – he or she can be disqualified for putting both themselves or others in danger. In the case of lightning, avoid: 1) Open areas. 2) Water. 3) Wire fences, overhead wires and power lines. 4) Isolated trees. 5) Elevated ground. 6) Maintenance machinery. 7) Motorized golf buggies. What the golfer should immediately seek is: a) Any lightning shelters that might be on the course. b) Any on-course buildings, such as a maintenance shed. c) The clubhouse. d) An automobile. Failing the above, a golfer might try to shelter in dense woods or a low-lying area. Remember also that raising a golf club or umbrella above the head increases the risk of being struck by lightning. On the other hand, contrary to some popular beliefs, metal spikes do not increase risk.

RULES OFTEN MISUNDERSTOOD AND ABUSED

◆ ◆ ◆ ◆ ◆

The old axiom that 'rules were made to be broken' certainly does not apply to golf, though one might get a different impression from watching some of the people who play the game. Many golfers simply do not fully understand certain rules, and as a result, continually break them.

TAKE THE teeing ground. Most golfers know that the width of the area is defined by the markers, and that the depth is two clublengths. You can tee the ball up anywhere in that imaginary rectangle, and even take your stance outside it. But you cannot stand inside the rectangle and tee up the ball outside it.

If your ball falls off the tee or you knock it off while taking your address, you can re-tee it without a penalty – since the ball is not yet in play. But if you swing and miss the ball, then accidentally knock if off the tee, you have taken one stroke. And even if the ball doesn't move, your airshot counts.

PLAYING A PROVISIONAL

If you think your ball might be lost, you can play a 'provisional'. But you must declare this clearly to your playing partners. If you do not, the second ball you hit will automatically become the one in play and the first will be presumed lost. In that case, you have now played your third shot, because the penalty for a lost ball is stroke plus distance.

If after the allotted five minutes you cannot find your ball, carry on playing the provisional, taking the one-stroke penalty. However, if you do find the original ball, the provisional is discarded and you have not suffered a lost stroke.

PRO TIP

Although dropping the ball is one of the simplest procedures in golf, many people do it incorrectly. The only acceptable way is to stand upright with your arm outstretched – or at right angles to your body – dropping the ball vertically from shoulder height.

Right: Drop the ball correctly or you could be penalized.

Use the rules to your advantage

Below: Be careful when identifying your ball in the rough – you are allowed to ensure the ball is yours but not to unduly improve your lie in the process.

Above: A plug ball may be lifted and dropped anywhere on the golf course – except on the green where it has to be marked and replaced after repairing the pitch mark.

There can also be a third scenario. If you find the first ball, but it's unplayable, you have three options. You can take a drop within two clublengths, but not nearer the hole, and take a one-shot penalty. You can choose a spot on the ball-to-target line anywhere from where you first hit to where the ball landed, and again add a stroke to your score. Or you may go all the way back to where you hit the last shot and play from there again, adding a two-stroke penalty.

Why can't you just play the provisional? Because when the original ball is found, the provisional becomes a dead ball.

WATER HAZARDS

When a ball lands in or touches a water hazard (marked by yellow stakes), or is lost in one, you have three options. The first is to play the ball as it lies, if possible. The second is to replay your strike from the original spot, while adding a penalty stroke. The third is to go as far back as you like before dropping, keeping the point where the ball last crossed the margin of the hazard between you and the hole – adding a penalty stroke.

Golfers often misunderstand that last one. Remember, it's not the line of flight into the hazard that is important – it is the point where the ball last crossed the margin of the hazard that matters under the rules.

LATERAL HAZARDS

The same options apply if your ball goes into a lateral hazard (marked by red stakes), but there are two more to be taken into consideration.

The first choice might be to drop within two clublengths of where the ball last crossed the margin of the hazard, but no nearer the hole. The second, and more misunderstood, option is to drop within two clublengths of a point on the other side of the hazard, equidistant from the hole.

Many people go to a point on the opposite side of the hazard. But if the hazard runs along the side of the fairway, it will be at an angle to the green. In that case, a spot equidistant from the hole will not necessarily be directly opposite the original point of entry.

Water hazards

Far left: Removing loose impediments: you are not allowed to remove loose impediments if playing from a hazard.

Left: Don't ground the club. You cannot ground the club in any hazard.

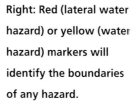

Right: Red (lateral water hazard) or yellow (water hazard) markers will identify the boundaries of any hazard.

Left: Recognize the kind of hazard you are in. Are you in a lateral water hazard, or a water hazard? Look for yellow or red stakes.

RULES GOVERNING GOLF CLUBS

◆ ◆ ◆ ◆ ◆

The R&A and USGA are continually testing new golf clubs to make sure they conform to agreed standards and do not give golfers an extra advantage in competitive play. The average player is not likely to encounter clubs that have been declared illegal by either body — though they may be available on the black market — and most golfers do not know how to alter golf clubs in a way that breaks the rules.

HOWEVER, SOME non-professionals do experiment with modifying their clubs, such as by adding lead tape to change swingweight and balance. That's fine, as long as you do not do it during a round.

By the same token, if in a fit of pique you break your 7-iron or putter over your knee, you cannot replace it while playing if you began the round with the regulation number of clubs.

CLUB ALLOTMENT

The maximum number of clubs allowed on the course is 14. If you start with fewer clubs, you can add some to get up to that amount. But never exceed 14, which is easy to do these days as golfers increasingly add extra clubs — such as lob wedges and utility woods — to their arsenal.

The penalties are severe for playing with too many clubs. In matchplay, you lose one hole for each infraction of the rule, up to two holes. In strokeplay, you must add two strokes for any hole where the breach of the rules has taken place, up to four holes!

Once you discover that you are over the limit, declare any extra club out of play and make sure you do not use it during the round. Failure to remember that rule can get you disqualified.

The controversy over Callaway ERC golf clubs resulted in the USGA banning a club that the R&A allowed. So know the rules by which you are governed.

PRO TIP

Many golfers now carry a variety of utility woods and extra wedges. But remember, if you add any clubs to your bag, you may have to subtract others to ensure you don't exceed the regulation 14 clubs. This rule is easy to forget, but potentially costly.

RULES GOVERNING GOLF BALLS

◆ ◆ ◆ ◆ ◆

The responsibility for playing the correct ball is yours alone. Always inform your playing partners of the make and number of your golf ball before the round starts. However, because others may use the same brand, put your own identification mark on the ball with a permanent marker.

IF YOU LOCATE a ball on the course but are not sure it is yours, be careful to follow the right procedure. You can ease back grass to identify the ball, but make sure you do not improve the lie. And if that does not do the job, you can lift the ball to check it anywhere on the course except in a hazard.

Before you do this, declare your intentions to fellow players, then mark the spot before picking up the ball. You may clean the ball just enough to find the identification mark, before replacing it where it lay. If the ball is in a bunker, you can brush aside enough sand and/or debris to check it.

CHANGING BALLS

You can change the ball you are playing at any time between holes. But if your ball is damaged and you want to replace it during play, you must announce this to your fellow players, then allow them to inspect its condition. The ball must have a visible defect to be declared unfit. If your partners agree it's damaged, place a new one on the same spot from which you removed the former one.

You can always clean your golf ball on the green after marking its position, and you can clean the ball when you are taking relief from an unplayable lie.

Below left: Always inform your playing partner of the make and number of your ball.

Below: Putting your own mark on your ball will avoid you making the mistake of playing another player's ball.

PRO TIP

If you cannot identify a golf ball as yours in a bunker – even after brushing aside any sand or leaves covering it – you can hit it without penalty. If you then discover that it was not your ball after all, the player to whom it does belong may place his ball where it originally lay in the bunker.

GLOSSARY

◆ ◆ ◆ ◆ ◆

ACE: A hole played in one stroke; a hole-in-one.

ADDRESS: The position a golfer assumes over the ball before making his or her strike.

ALBATROSS: A score of three under par on a hole; also known as a 'double eagle' in America.

ALIGNMENT: The way a golfer positions his or her body in relation to an imagined ball-to-target line. In the case of most shots, the shoulders, hips and feet are aligned parallel to the target line.

APPROACH: A shot played to the green from either the fairway or rough; also the area in front of the green.

APRON: The area immediately bordering the green, which is usually mowed at a height between that on the fairway and green.

AWAY: The golfer whose ball is farthest from the hole, whether on the fairway, green, or any other part of the course. This player generally hits first.

BACK NINE: The second set of nine holes on an 18-hole golf course. On a scorecard, these holes are designated as 'in'.

BACKSPIN: The backward or anticlockwise spin imparted to the ball, usually to make it check up on the green.

BACKSWING: The initial part of the swing, starting from address, when the golfer brings the club away from the ball to a position just before shifting back into the down or throughswing.

BAFFY: An obsolete club that was similar to the modern 3- or 4-wood and had a lofted clubface for hitting shots off the fairway.

BALATA: A natural or synthetic compound used in the cover of the highest-priced golf balls. Soft and pliable, balata is generally favoured by touring pros and low handicap players because it helps produce more backspin on the ball and provides greater feel.

BANANA BALL: A shot that starts left and fades violently to the right; a slice.

BENT GRASS: A type of fine grass that is often considered ideal for use on greens, though it's difficult to maintain in hot climates.

BEST BALL: A competitive format where the best individual score among team members counts toward the final total; also known as 'better ball'.

BIRDIE: A score of one under par on a hole.

BITE: How well a ball hit with backspin stops when it lands on the green.

BLIND SHOT OR HOLE: A situation where the golfer cannot see his or her target, whether aiming into fairway or green.

BOGEY: A score of one over par on a hole.

BORROW: On the putting green, the amount of deviation from a direct line to the hole that a golfer allows for because of any slope. In America, the term used more often is 'break'.

BRASSIE: A club used in the late 19th and early 20th Century that most resembled the modern 2-wood.

BUMP AND RUN SHOT: A low approach shot that is often used on links courses when there are no hazards between the golfer and the green and the player wants to keep the ball under the wind. The shot is designed to land short of the green and then roll up to the flagstick.

BUNKER: A natural or man-made depression on a fairway or around the green which is usually filled with sand, but sometimes simply earth or grass.

BURIED LIE: When a ball is partially or completely covered by the sand in a trap.

CADDIE: A non-player who carriers the golfer's bag and is allowed to give advice on club selection and strategy within the prescribed rules of golf.

CARRY: The distance from where the ball is struck to the spot where it first strikes the ground – especially when a ball is hit over water or a bunker. In such a case, it is said to 'carry' the hazard.

CASUAL WATER: A temporary accumulation of water on the course from which a player can take relief under the rules.

CAVITY-BACKED IRONS: Modern irons where the weight has been removed from the back of the clubhead and distributed around the perimeter of the clubface; also known as perimeter-weighted irons.

CHIP AND RUN: A short approach shot, usually from just off the green, that is hit low onto the putting surface so it will roll most of the distance to the hole – much like a putted ball. Also known simply as a chip.

CLEEK: An obsolete club that most resembled today's 2-iron, although several variations were also made – including shorter 'cleeks' with iron clubfaces and extra loft that were the forerunner of today's wedges.

CLOSED STANCE: An alignment generally used to hit a draw, with the front foot closer to the target line than the back and the arms, shoulders and hips parallel to that angle.

CLUBFACE: The grooved area of the clubhead, or blade, that is used to strike the ball.

CLUBHEAD: The lower part of the club, which is attached to the end of the shaft and used to hit the ball.

COLLAR: The short-cut grass surrounding the green.

CROSS BUNKER: A bunker that lies across the line of a fairway.

CROSS-HANDED: An unconventional putting grip where the left hand is put below the right. Often used by golfers who have lost confidence in their putting stroke and are looking to eliminate tension and stabilize their movement.

CUT: A score designated by tournament officials after the first 36 holes of a 72-hole event to reduce the field of players. Failure to score under that total leads to disqualification, whereas those who score the same or better 'make the cut' and qualify to play the final 36 holes.

CUT SHOT: Slicing the ball with an out-to-in swingpath that produce a bending, left-to-right shot. A cut shot can either be a mistake, or done purposefully in order to avoid trees, water and hazards, shape the ball around a dogleg, impart height and some backspin – or all of the same.

DIVOT: A slice or piece of turf cut away by the clubhead or blade when a shot is played, usually on the fairway.

DOGLEG: A hole where the fairway bends sharply from left-to-right or right-to-left, the angle generally starting in the area where a tee shot would land. Sometimes, a hazard or obstacle such as a tree is also positioned at the angle to make cutting across it difficult.

DORMIE: When a player or side in matchplay are up as many holes as remain to be played and therefore can not lose – though the possibility of a tie remains.

DOUBLE BOGEY: A score of two strokes over par.

DOWN: In competitive terms, the opposite of being ahead, indicated by the number of strokes or holes in various types of play. A golfer is said to be down, or trailing, when he has shot more strokes than his individual competitors, or has lost more holes.

DOWNSWING: The shift from the backswing to the initial attack on the ball, then through to impact; also known as the throughswing. Often, the backswing is initiated by a gradual turn of the hips toward the target, followed by the shoulders, arms and hands.

DRAW: A low, penetrating shot where the ball starts slightly to the right of the target, then curves back to the centre, usually landing with a great deal of forward roll.

DRIVE: A shot that is played from a tee, usually with a driver or long iron.

DRIVER: Generally the longest club in the bag and one with the least loft; used for hitting the ball the maximum distance off the tee and sometimes the fairway.

DUFFER: A high handicap or unskilled player; also a hacker.

DUCK HOOK: An errant shot where the ball veers from right-to-left and drops sharply or never gains much height.

EAGLE: A score of two strokes under par.

EMBEDDED LIE: A ball that when landing embeds itself in the rough, sand or wet and muddy turf.

EXPLOSION SHOT: A shot used in a bunker where the clubface is brought under the ball and through the sand, resulting in the ball being lifted out on a spray of sand.

FADE: A shot where the ball starts slightly left of the target, then curves back toward the centre, usually landing softly and with little roll.

FAIRWAY: The closely mown area between the tee and green.

FAT: Hitting the turf behind the ball first, then the ball, which drastically reduces distance.

FEATHERY: One of the earliest golf balls, which was made from a leather pouch filled with boiled feathers. Easily damaged, it went out of use in the mid-1880s, replaced by the 'guttie'.

FESCUE: A fine grass with deep roots common on seaside links and heathland courses and ideal for putting surfaces because it thrives with little water.

FLAGSTICK: Also known as the pin, the flagstick sits in the hole and marks the golfer's target, usually with the number of the hole printed on a pennant that flies from the top.

FLAT SWING: A backswing where the club is more horizontal than vertical.

In some golfers, this is considered a fault, although such great players as Ben Hogan, and now Justin Leonard, have used generally flat swings.

FLYER: Any shot hit out of the rough that travels farther than normal, usually because grass has come between the clubface and ball, reducing control and backspin.

FOLLOW-THROUGH: The final part of the swing after the ball has been struck, in which the arms and hands come up over the shoulders to a finished position.

FORE: A shouted warning to anyone in danger of being struck by a ball hit off-line or simply in their direction.

FOURBALL: A competition in which two players use only the better of their scores on each hole; also known as 'Best Ball'.

FOURSOME: A competition in which teams of two golfers play against each other in an alternate-shot format. Also, a term for four golfers simply playing together, as in 'threesome' and 'twosome'. A twosome always has precedence on the course over the other combinations, and all three groups can play through a single.

FREE DROP: A ball that is dropped without penalty away from an obstruction in accordance with the local rules of a club and the general rules governing golf throughout the world.

FRONT NINE: The first nine holes on an 18-hole golf course, referred to on the scorecard as 'out'.

FULL SET: The 14 clubs allowed for play, usually including three or four woods, six, seven or eight irons, two or three wedges and a putter.

GRAIN: The lie, or how the grass is growing and leaning, on a green.

GRAPHITE: A carbon-based substance now commonly used in golf shafts to make them strong, yet extremely light, enabling high handicappers, women and seniors to increase clubhead speed and thus hit the ball farther and straighter. Graphite is now also being employed in clubheads and finding a more general audience among golfers at every level of the game.

GREEN: The putting area of short, tightly-mowed grass around the hole.

GRIP: The upper part of the club, made of leather or rubber, that the golfer holds; also, the term for how the golfer holds the club itself and how he or she arranges the hands and fingers.

GROSS SCORE: A golfer's score before any handicap strokes have been deducted.

GUTTIE: An obsolete ball first used in the mid-1880s which replaced the 'feathery' and was made of gutta percha, a rubber-like substance from an Asian tree.

HALF: In matchplay, a score equal to an opponent's on an individual hole.

HALF SET: A set usually consisting only of the even or odd irons, two woods and a putter; often used by beginners, juniors, women golfers – or anyone just trying to carry a lighter bag.

HANDICAP: An official number issued by a club or society to a golfer in accordance with the rules of the governing bodies of golf around the world. A handicap designates how many strokes a golfer usually plays over par and offers him or her the opportunity in competitive play to deduct those strokes from a gross score. Handicaps are designed to measure a golfer's true ability and offer him or her a chance to play even up against any other player.

HANGING LIE: A lie in which the ball rests on a downward slope.

HAZARD: A bunker, stream, ditch or lake positioned on the course to catch errant shots and penalize the golfer. Playing out of a hazard is difficult, challenging and governed by several different procedures outlined in the official rules of golf.

HOLE: A general term for the entire area between tee and green; or literally, the actual hole into which the golfer finally putts the ball – also known as the cup.

HOLE-HIGH: A shot that comes to rest even with the hole; also known as 'pin-high'.

HOLE-IN-ONE: A tee shot that finishes in the hole; an ace.

HONOUR: The right to drive or play first, as determined by the lowest score on the previous hole.

HOOD: Holding the club so the toe of the clubface is ahead of the heel, decreasing the loft on the club.

HOOK: A shot that starts right or straight at the target, then bends sharply to the left.

HOSEL: The socket that connects the clubhead to the shaft.

IMPACT: The exact moment when the clubface or blade meets the ball during the full swing.

INTERLOCKING GRIP: A grip style generally favoured by players with small hands or short fingers in which the little finger of the right hand intertwines with the forefinger of the left hand. Jack Nicklaus is the most famous golfer to use this grip.

IRON: The metal, steel, titanium or graphite-headed clubs used for most shots between tee and green, including wedges.

LATERAL HAZARDS: Usually a water hazard that cuts across the fairway or borders a green, as defined by stakes or lines painted on the ground. Several specific rules govern play in and around all such hazards.

LAY-UP SHOT: When a golfer chooses to play short of the green or any intermediate target on a hole to avoid trouble, such as a bunker or water hazard.

LIE: How the ball rests in relation to the ground, grass, sand or other matter around it which determines what kind of shot can be played next; also the term for the angle between the clubhead and shaft.

LINE: The direction along which a golfer aims to hit the ball, either from the tee, fairway, rough, a hazard or on the green.

LINKS: A golf course usually found along the sea or other large body of water and traditionally situated in the fallow land between the beach, sand dunes and more fertile inland soil.

LIP: The edge of the hole or the front rim of a bunker.

LIP-OUT: A putt that rolls around the rim or edge of the hole and then does not fall inside the hole.

LOB SHOT: A short, high-trajectory shot played into the green to avoid a hazard and stop the ball short with increased backspin.

LOCAL RULES Rules unique to a particular golf course – and printed on the scorecard – that often govern out-of-bounds areas, hazards, paths, staked trees and course conditions.

LOFT: The angle of the clubface, which determines how high and far a ball travels; also a term for the height a golfer puts on a shot.

LOOSE IMPEDIMENTS: Natural objects such as stones, leaves, twigs and so forth that can be removed – sometimes even in bunkers in accordance with local rules – from around the ball, provided that does not cause the ball to move, which would incur a one-shot penalty for the golfer.

MASHIE: An obsolete club that most resembled today's 5-iron.

MATCHPLAY: Competition between two players or sides which is determined by the number of holes won or lost – as opposed to strokeplay, where the number of shots taken determines the outcome.

MEDAL PLAY: Another term for strokeplay.

MULLIGAN: A second ball that is sometimes allowed a player after a poor shot – though this is forbidden in competitive play under the official rules of golf.

NET: A golfer's score after any handicap strokes received have been deducted.

NIBLICK: An obsolete club that most resembled the modern 9-iron or pitching wedge; a niblick was an early lofted club that was used for hitting off bad lies or over hazards.

OPEN STANCE: An alignment generally used to hit a fade, with the front foot farther from the target line than the back and the arms, shoulders and hips parallel to that angle.

OUT-OF-BOUNDS: An area where the golfer is prohibited from hitting his ball, which is usually outside the boundaries of the course and designated by white stakes.

OVER-CLUBBING: Selecting a club that sends the ball a greater distance than intended, thus missing the target.

PAR: The standard score for any given hole that a zero handicap player is expected to make, usually based on the length of the hole. Holes up to 250 yards are often par 3s, up to 475 yards par 4s, and anything longer a par 5.

PENALTY STROKE: An extra stroke, or strokes, that must be added to a score after hitting out of bounds, losing a ball or any number of violations of the rules committed by a golfer.

PGA: Acronym for the Professional Golfers' Association.

PITCH: A short approach shot usually from 100 yards (91m) or less into the green that has a high trajectory and lands softly with little roll.

PITCHING WEDGE: A short iron with a high degree of loft, usually used to hit approach shots into the green or for chipping.

PITCHMARK: A small depression or divot-like slash left by a shot hit into the green. The etiquette of golf requires that all players repair their pitchmarks before leaving the green.

PLAY OFF: One or more extra holes played after two or more golfers have ended the regulation number in a tie.

PLAY THROUGH: Under the rules of golf, when any group slows down and holds up play, it is expected to allow faster groups behind it to play past, or 'though' them.

PLUGGED BALL: A ball embedded in the ground or sand.

POSTURE: A golfer's body position – especially the angle of his spine or back – at address and through the swing.

POT BUNKERS: A small, round and deep bunker commonly found on links courses.

PREFERRED LIE: Usually a local rule that allows golfers to move their ball several inches to an improved position on the fairway in order to avoid wet and/or muddy lies.

PRE-SHOT ROUTINE: A consistent procedure a golfer goes through as he or she prepares to strike the ball or stroke a putt.

PROVISIONAL BALL: A second ball that is hit when the golfer believes his or her first shot may be out-of-bounds or lost. Then, if the original ball is indeed out-of-bounds or not found, the provisional becomes the ball in play and a one-stroke penalty is added to the final score. However, if the original ball is found, the provisional is discarded.

PULL: An errant shot that flies straight left, with no curve.

PULL-HOOK: A errant shot where the ball starts left and then spins left.

PUNCH SHOT: A low shot usually hit to approach a green and keep the ball under the wind; also known as a knock-down shot.

PUSH: An errant shot where the ball travels straight right, with no curve.

PUSH-SLICE: An errant shot where the ball starts slightly right of the target, then curves to the right.

PUTTER: The shortest club in the bag – with the exception of the broomstick-long varieties now in vogue with some golfers – that has a blade with no loft. Primarily used to roll the ball along the putting surface to the hole, but sometimes employed to hit from the apron, fringe or rough near the green – and even out of a semi-level sandtrap.

R & A: Acronym for the Royal and Ancient Golf Club of St. Andrews, which, along with the USGA, administers and interprets the official 'Rules of Golf'.

READING THE GREEN: When a golfer examines the slope and contours of a putting surface to judge the probable line and speed of a putt.

RECOVERY SHOT: A sometimes risky shot executed from the rough, trees or other trouble in an attempt to land in a more favourable position for the next shot from either the fairway or green.

ROUGH: The grass or other vegetation outside the fairway which can vary considerably in height and is meant to penalize the golfer who shoots off-line by making the next shot more difficult to hit.

RUBBER-CORE BALL: Invented in 1898, this ball revolutionized the game and replaced the guttie. The ball was composed of a solid rubber centre around which was wound yards of tight thread and covered by gutta percha.

RULES OF GOLF: The official rules of the game, which are administered and interpreted by two major bodies, the Royal and Ancient Golf Club of St. Andrews (R & A) and the United States Golf Association (USGA). Both publish widely available booklets summarizing the rules and etiquette of the game for play throughout the world.

RUN: How far the ball travels once it hits the ground.

SAND WEDGE: Until the recent advent of the lob wedge, the shortest

and most lofted iron, generally used for playing out of bunkers and for some chipping and pitching.

SCORECARD: A card that lists the local rules for a course, the par for each hole (with its handicap or degree of difficulty), and contains space for the golfer to record his or her score and that of playing partners or competitors.

SCRATCH PLAYER: A player with a handicap of zero.

SHAFT: The long extension of the club from grip to clubhead, formerly made of wood and now steel, metal or graphite.

SHANK: An errant hit off the neck or hosel of the club that flies violently right.

SHORT GAME: All shots from around 100 yards (91m) in to the green, including pitching, chipping, bunker play and putting.

SKULL: An errant hit on the top half of the ball.

SKY: An errant shot that flies high into the air with little distance.

SLICE: A shot that starts left or straight at the target and then curves violently to the right with clockwise spin.

SNAP-HOOK: An errant shot that curves sharply from right-to-left.

SOLE: The bottom part of the clubhead; or letting the bottom of the clubhead or blade touch turf, sand or rough at address.

SPOON: Archaic term for an obsolete lofted fairway wood that most resembled today's 3-wood.

SQUARE: The position of the clubface and/or feet in the stance, when placed at right angles to the imaginary ball-to-target line.

STABLEFORD: A system of scoring where points are awarded for each hole after handicap strokes are subtracted from each gross score. For example: a net par = 2 points, net birdie = 3 points, net eagle = 4 points and net bogey = 1 point.

STANCE: The position of the feet before striking the ball in relation to the imaginary ball-to-target line, whether square, closed or open.

STANDARD SCRATCH SCORE (SSS): The score a scratch player would be expected to shoot on any given course, usually posted near the first tee and/or on the scorecard. The SSS can vary slightly from par because of weather and course conditions.

STROKE: The action of swinging a club or putter at the ball and the method of keeping score, as in each time a stroke is executed it must be recorded against par.

STROKEPLAY: Competition in which each player's score for a total round – or rounds – is compared with

other players to determine the winner by fewest strokes; also known as medal play.

SUDDEN DEATH: An extra hole or holes played after a competition ends in a tie, with the overall win going to the golfer who records the first better score than his opponent on any subsequent hole.

SURLYN: The trademark name of a thermo-plastic resin that is used in the covers of most modern golf balls because it is durable and highly resistant to cuts and dents imparted by mis-hit shots. Surlyn also provides the average golfer with the most distance. However, unlike balata, it has less feel and makes it harder to apply backspin.

SWEETSPOT: The most effective hitting area on the clubface or putter blade, usually at or near the centre.

SWING PLANE: An imaginary plane connecting the shoulders and ball that the golfer strives to swing the club along – or within close proximity.

SWINGWEIGHT: The weight and balance of a golf club, which should be constant throughout a set.

TAKEAWAY: The start of the backswing; the initial movement away from the ball.

TARGET LINE: An imaginary line from the ball to target that the golfer visualizes to help aim his shot.

TEE: The area between the tee markers, including an imaginary square two club-lengths behind, that is used for the first shot on every hole.

TEE PEG: A small wooden or plastic shaft used to hold the ball off the ground when hitting a tee shot.

TENDING THE FLAG: Holding the flagstick while it is still in the hole to help someone else's aim while they are putting from a distance or across a severe break – then removing it after the ball is struck and rolling toward the hole. Failure to remove the flagstick, or pin, can result in a penalty stroke.

TEMPO: The timing and rhythm of a golfer's swing, which at best should remain even and smooth throughout.

TEXAS WEDGE: Using a putter from off the green or out of a sandtrap.

THINNING THE BALL: Hitting the top half of the ball with the leading edge of the clubhead or blade, producing a shot that generally flies low and will roll a long way, but with little accuracy.

THROUGH THE GREEN: Term often used in the 'Rules of Golf' for the entire area of the course except the tee and green of the hole being played and all hazards.

TOE: The tip or end of the clubhead or blade, opposite where the clubshaft and head or blade join.

TOPPING THE BALL: Hitting the top half of the ball with the bottom edge of the clubhead or blade, which causes the ball to drive into the ground momentarily, then pop out and fly forward – with a considerable loss of distance.

TRIPLE BOGEY: A score of three over par.

UNDERCLUB: Using a club that the golfer can't hit as far as necessary to his or her target.

UNPLAYABLE LIE: A ball that a player cannot take a swing at, usually because of a nearby obstruction such as a tree or bush. The golfer should declare the ball 'unplayable' to his playing partners, then move it clear and drop it elsewhere at the expense of one penalty stroke.

USGA: Acronym for the United States Golf Association, which along with the R & A administers and interprets the official rules of golf.

USPGA: Acronym for the United States Professional Golfers' Association.

VARDON GRIP: The most common grip in golf in which the little finger of the right hand overlaps the forefinger of the left. Popularized by the legendary Harry Vardon.

WAGGLE: One or more short swings of the clubhead just before striking the ball off the tee. Used to reduce tension and/or as an aiming device.

WATER HAZARD: Any lake, river, stream, ditch or other body of water such as a swamp defined by stakes or lines painted on the ground. Specific rules govern play in or around all hazards.

WHIFF: When a player's stroke misses the ball completely. Under the rules of golf, a whiff counts as a stroke if the address position has been taken, the ball falls off the tee, or both.

WOOD: A club usually used for longer shots off the tee or fairway. Once made of wood, most such clubs now have shafts and clubheads constructed with steel, titanium or graphite.

YIPS: A vague anxiety condition in which the golfer becomes so tense while putting that he or she has trouble stroking the putter comfortably, usually resulting in a jerky stab at the ball.

INDEX

◆ ◆ ◆ ◆ ◆